# ORCHID™

## VOLUME 3

SCRIPT
### TOM MORELLO

ART
### SCOTT HEPBURN

COLORS
### DAN JACKSON

LETTERS
**NATE PIEKOS OF BLAMBOT®**

COVER ART
**MASSIMO CARNEVALE**

DARK HORSE BOOKS

PRESIDENT & PUBLISHER
**MIKE RICHARDSON**

EDITOR
**JIM GIBBONS**

CONSULTING EDITOR
**SIERRA HAHN**

COLLECTION DESIGNER
**JUSTIN COUCH**

SPECIAL THANKS TO DAVE LAND AND MICHELE FISHER.

Neil Hankerson Executive Vice President • Tom Weddle Chief Financial Officer • Randy Stradley Vice President of Publishing • Michael Martens Vice President of Book Trade Sales • Anita Nelson Vice President of Business Affairs • Scott Allie Editor in Chief • Matt Parkinson Vice President of Marketing • David Scroggy Vice President of Product Development • Dale LaFountain Vice President of Information Technology • Darlene Vogel Senior Director of Print, Design, and Production • Ken Lizzi General Counsel • Davey Estrada Editorial Director • Chris Warner Senior Books Editor • Diana Schutz Executive Editor • Cary Grazzini Director of Print and Development • Lia Ribacchi Art Director • Cara Niece Director of Scheduling • Tim Wiesch Director of International Licensing • Mark Bernardi Director of Digital Publishing

Published by Dark Horse Books
A division of Dark Horse Comics, Inc.
10956 SE Main Street
Milwaukie, OR 97222

DarkHorse.com
NightwatchmanMusic.com

To find a comics shop in your area, call the Comic Shop Locator Service
toll-free at (888) 266-4226.

First edition: July 2013
ISBN 978-1-59582-967-2

10 9 8 7 6 5 4 3 2 1
Printed in China

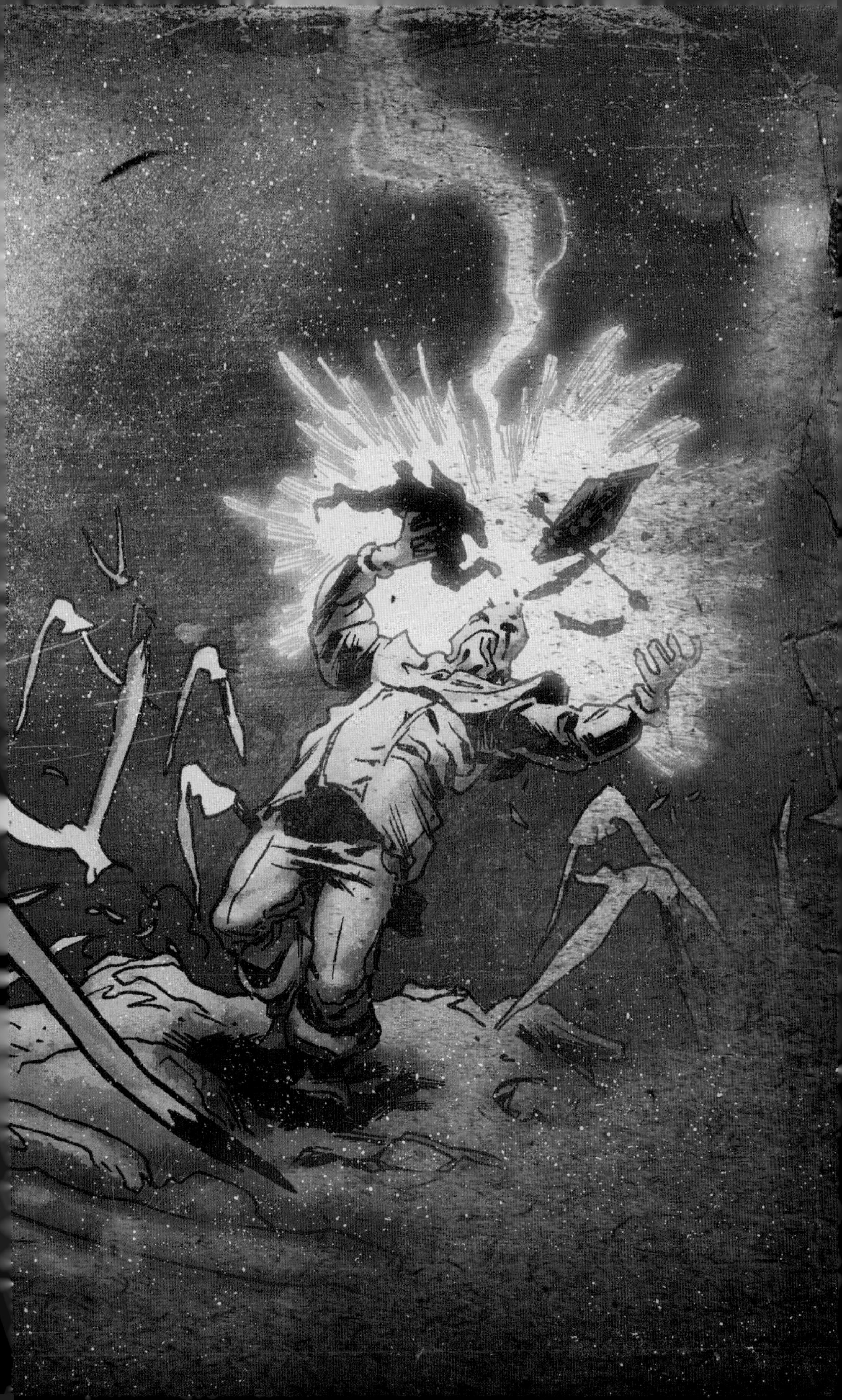

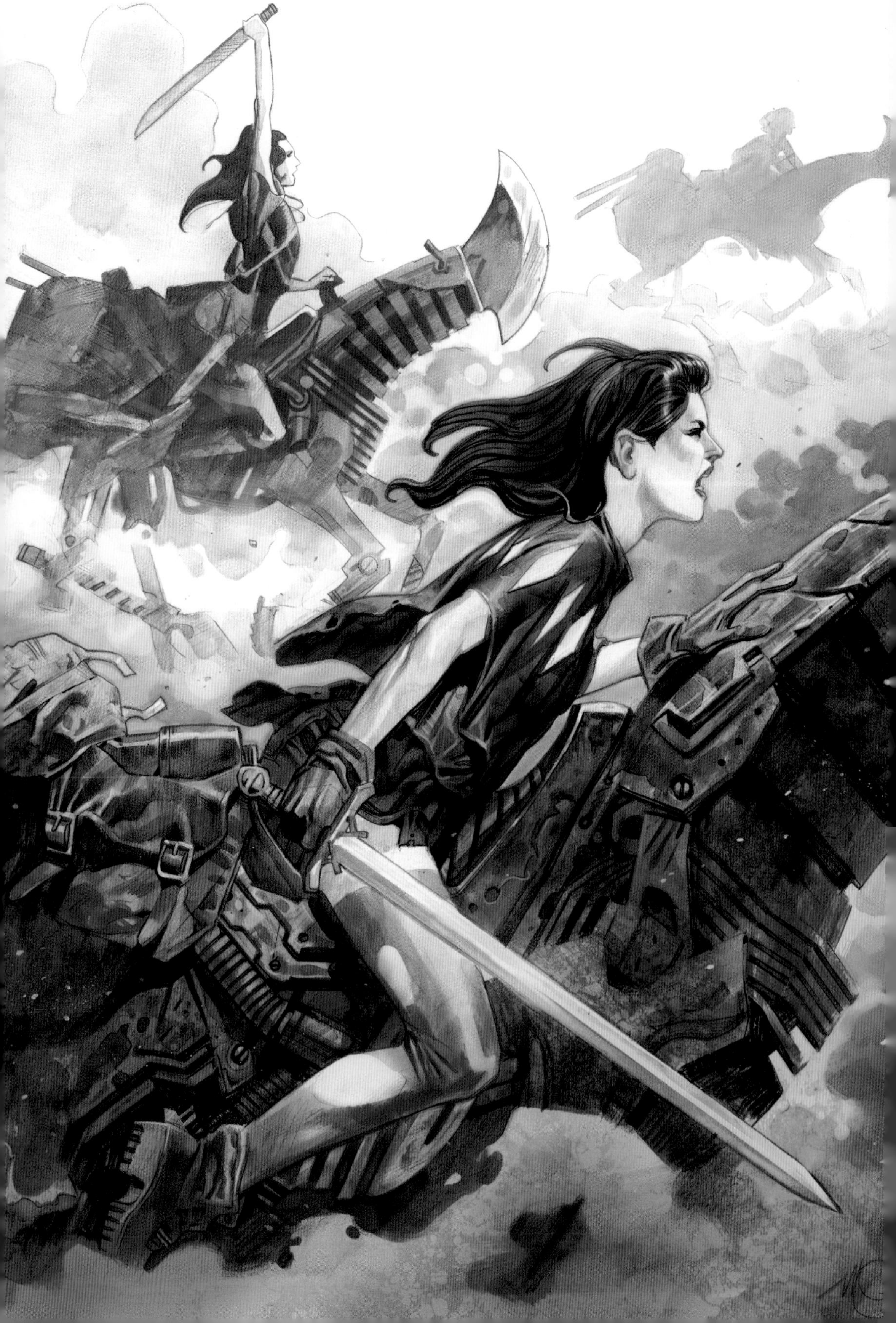

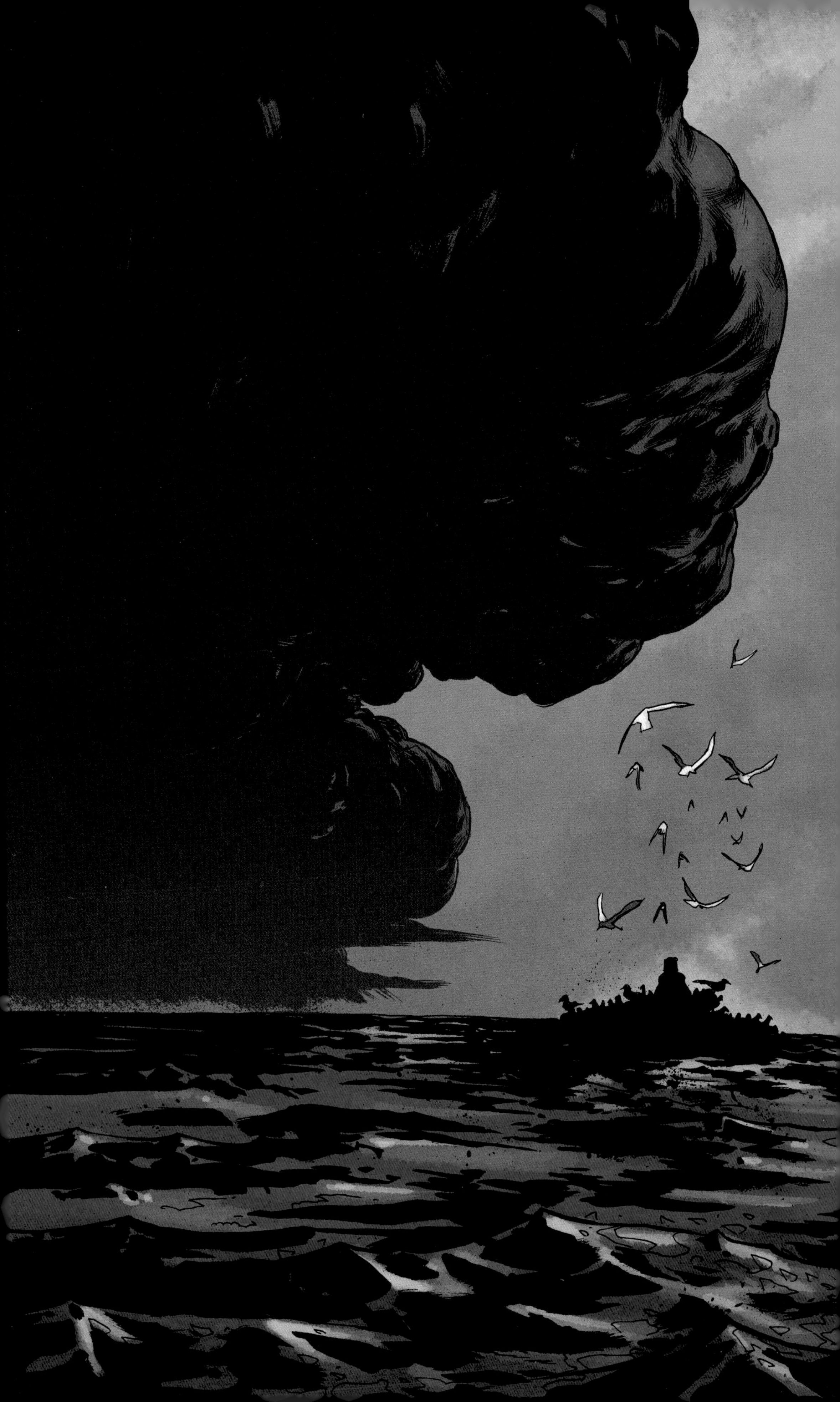

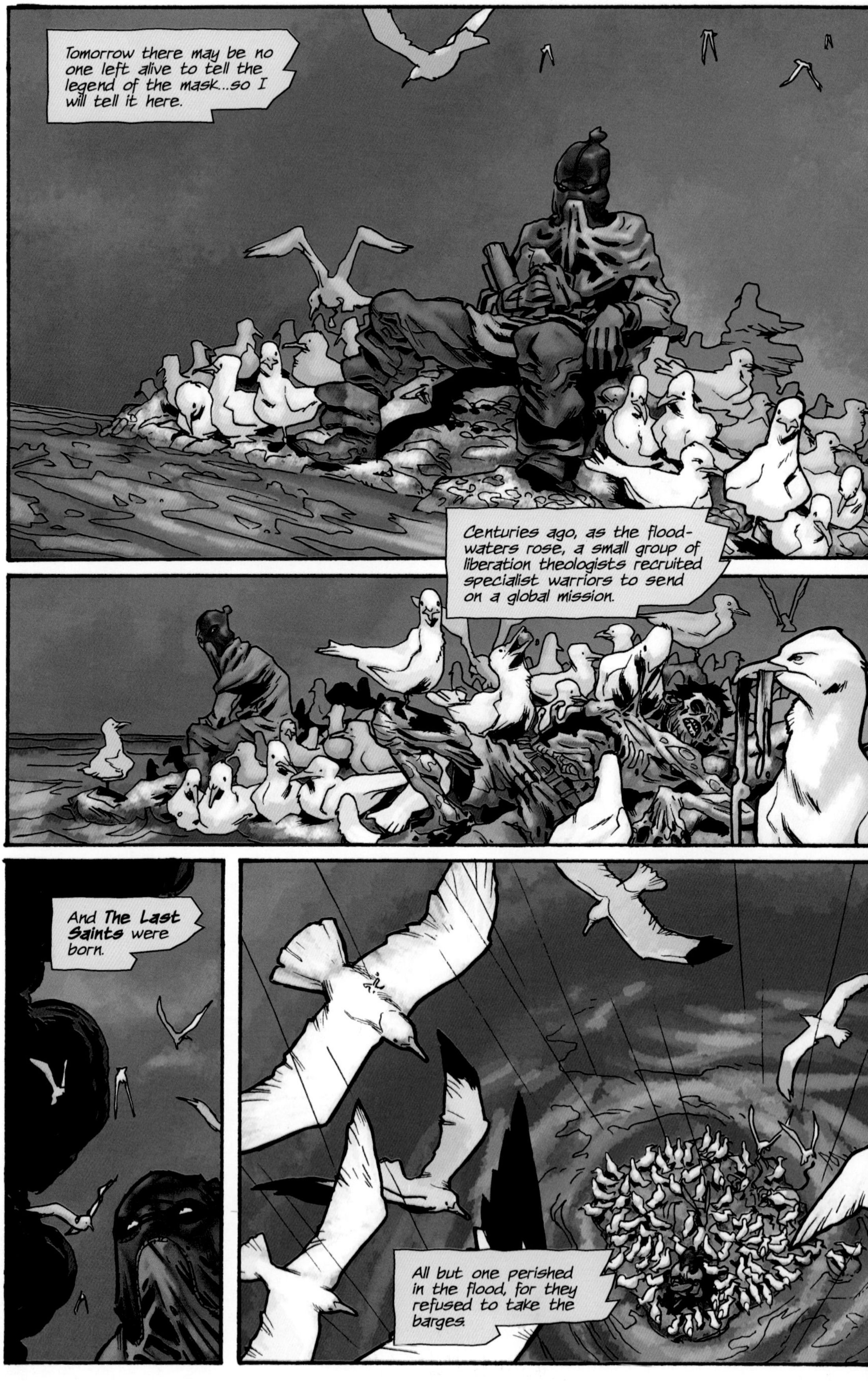
Tomorrow there may be no one left alive to tell the legend of the mask...so I will tell it here.
Centuries ago, as the flood-waters rose, a small group of liberation theologists recruited specialist warriors to send on a global mission.
And **The Last Saints** were born.
All but one perished in the flood, for they refused to take the barges.

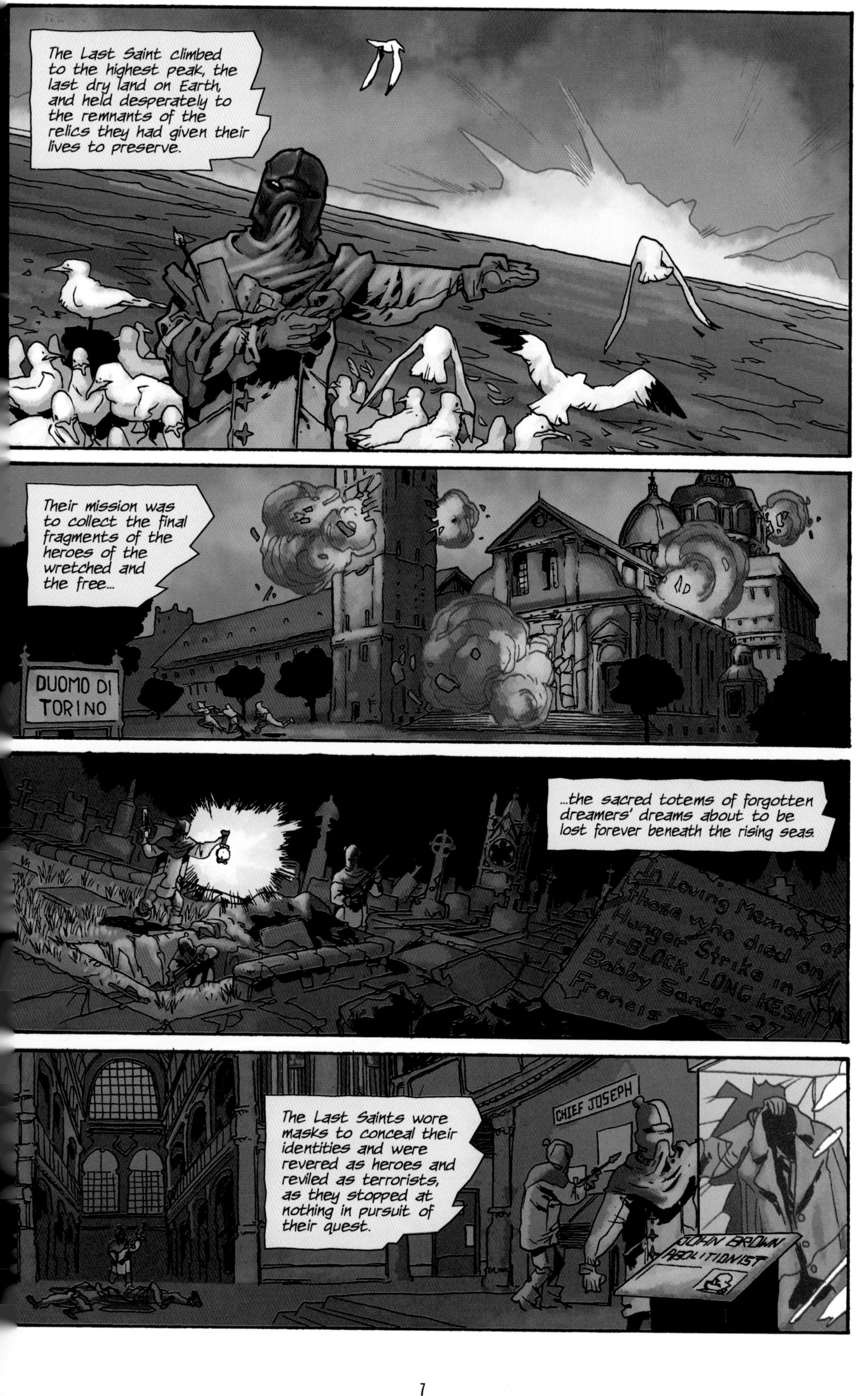
The Last Saint climbed to the highest peak, the last dry land on Earth, and held desperately to the remnants of the relics they had given their lives to preserve.
Their mission was to collect the final fragments of the heroes of the wretched and the free...
DUOMO DI TORINO
...the sacred totems of forgotten dreamers' dreams about to be lost forever beneath the rising seas.
In Loving Memory of those who died on Hunger Strike in H-BLOCK, LONG KESH
Bobby Sands - 27
Francis
The Last Saints wore masks to conceal their identities and were revered as heroes and reviled as terrorists, as they stopped at nothing in pursuit of their quest.
CHIEF JOSEPH
JOHN BROWN ABOLITIONIST

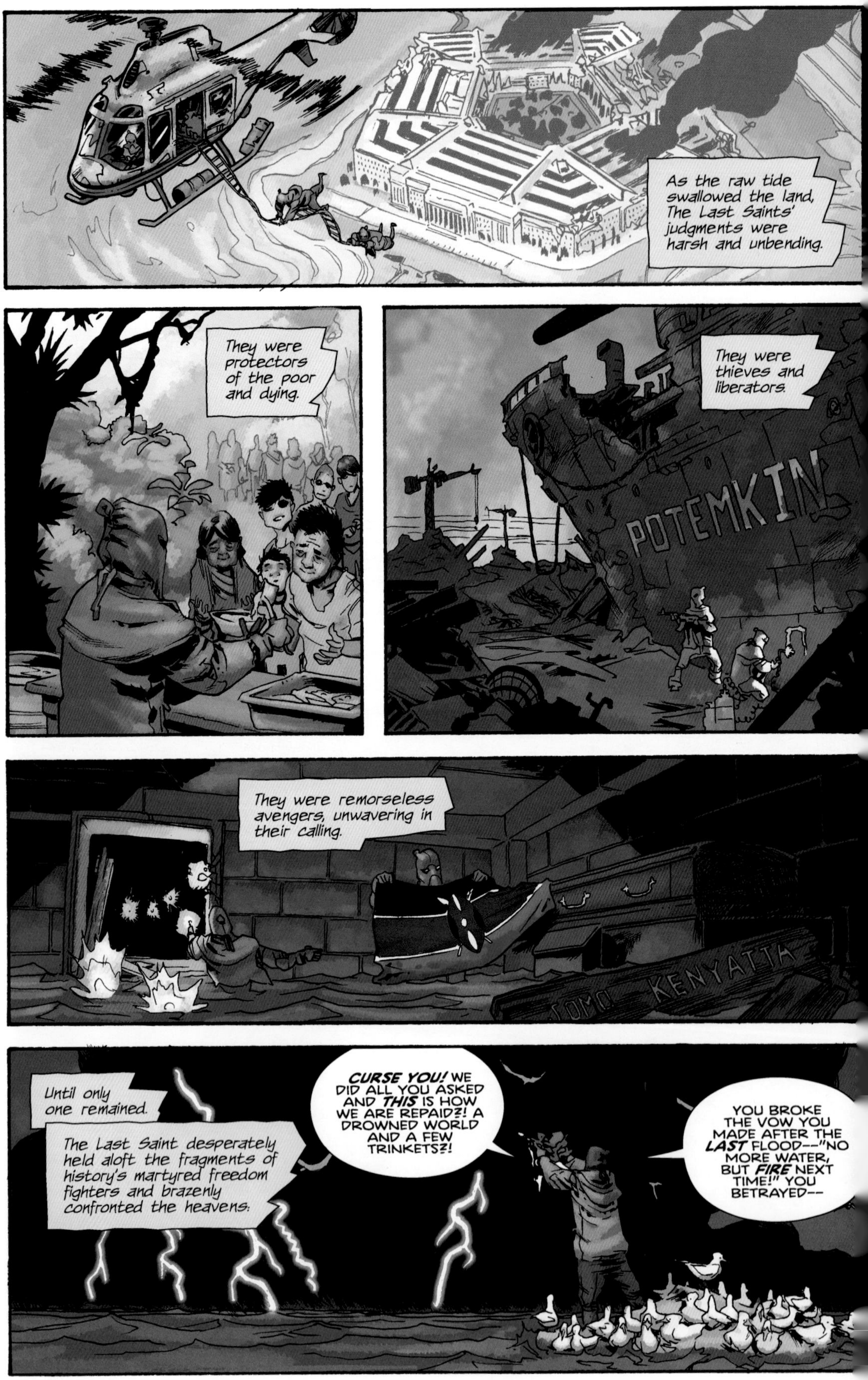

As the raw tide swallowed the land, The Last Saints' judgments were harsh and unbending.
They were protectors of the poor and dying.
They were thieves and liberators.
POTEMKIN
They were remorseless avengers, unwavering in their calling.
KENYATTA
Until only one remained.
The Last Saint desperately held aloft the fragments of history's martyred freedom fighters and brazenly confronted the heavens.
CURSE YOU! WE DID ALL YOU ASKED AND THIS IS HOW WE ARE REPAID?! A DROWNED WORLD AND A FEW TRINKETS?!
YOU BROKE THE VOW YOU MADE AFTER THE LAST FLOOD--"NO MORE WATER, BUT FIRE NEXT TIME!" YOU BETRAYED--

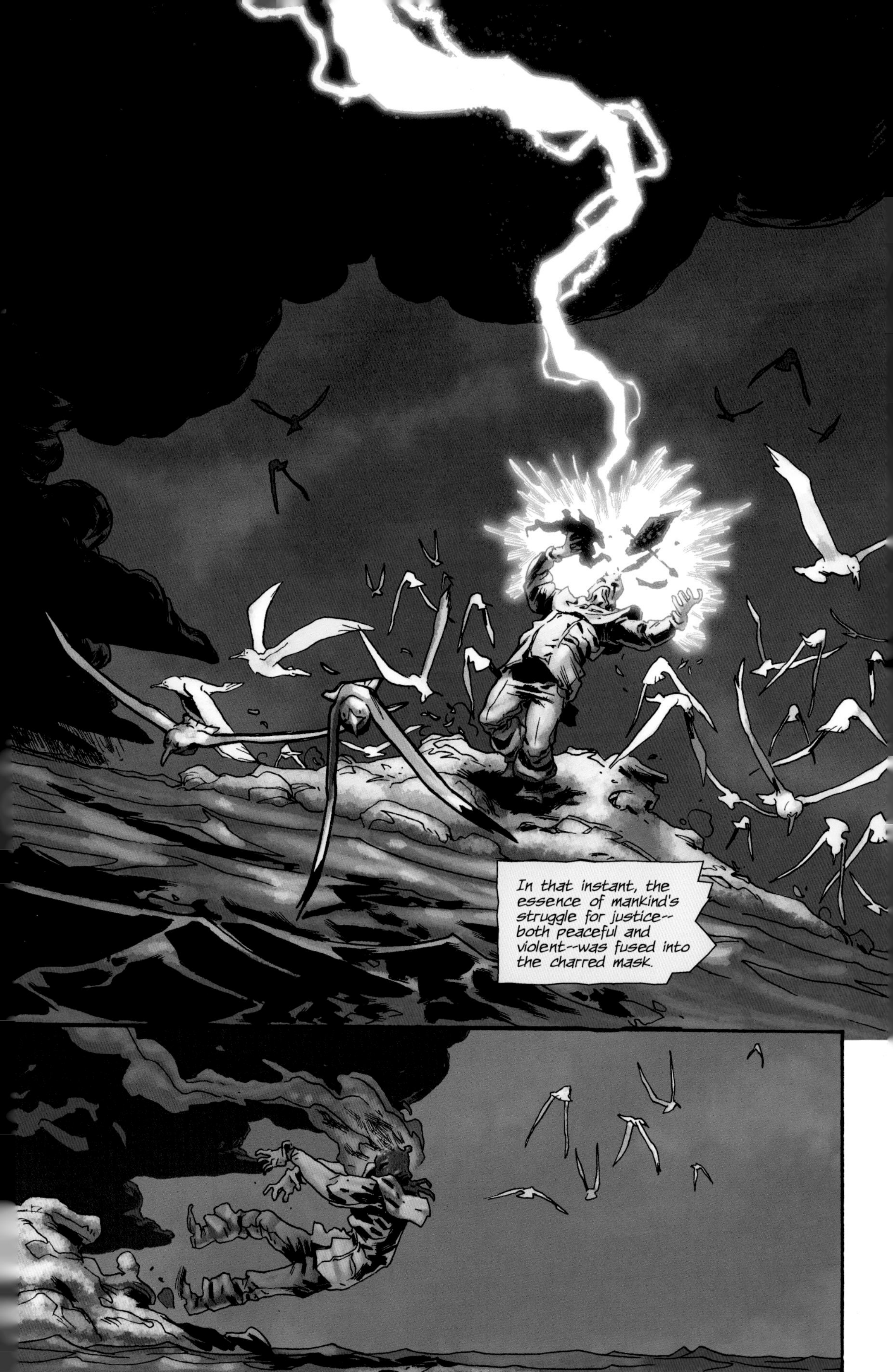
In that instant, the essence of mankind's struggle for justice--both peaceful and violent--was fused into the charred mask.

And with the sacrifice of the Last Saint...

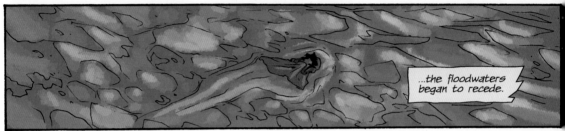

...the floodwaters began to recede.

There is a pent-up rage in the suffering masses that has no expression except inward. The mask gives that anger a voice. A face. A fist.

The mask drifted at sea, eventually found by scavengers. It kills any who wear it, except, it is rumored...

...a Saint.

IT'S TIME, SIMON. I JUST WANTED TO SAY GOODBYE. GOODBYE AND THANK YOU—

Oh, YOU'RE CERTAINLY NOT GOING ANYWHERE WITHOUT ME. WHO WOULD GET YOU OUT OF TROUBLE?

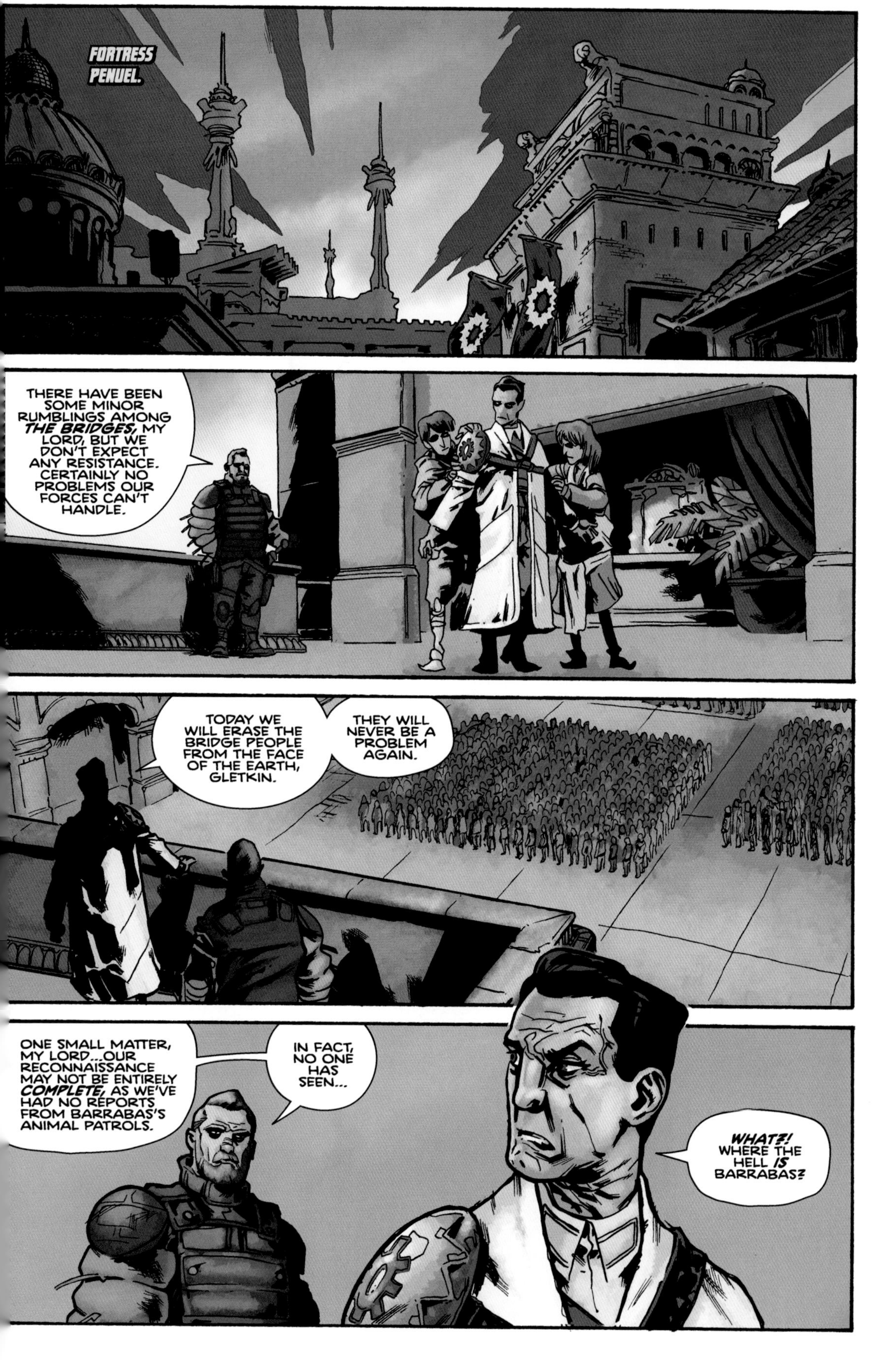
FORTRESS PENUEL.
THERE HAVE BEEN SOME MINOR RUMBLINGS AMONG *THE BRIDGES,* MY LORD, BUT WE DON'T EXPECT ANY RESISTANCE. CERTAINLY NO PROBLEMS OUR FORCES CAN'T HANDLE.
TODAY WE WILL ERASE THE BRIDGE PEOPLE FROM THE FACE OF THE EARTH, GLETKIN.
THEY WILL NEVER BE A PROBLEM AGAIN.
ONE SMALL MATTER, MY LORD...OUR RECONNAISSANCE MAY NOT BE ENTIRELY *COMPLETE,* AS WE'VE HAD NO REPORTS FROM BARRABAS'S ANIMAL PATROLS.
IN FACT, NO ONE HAS SEEN...
*WHAT?!* WHERE THE HELL *IS* BARRABAS?

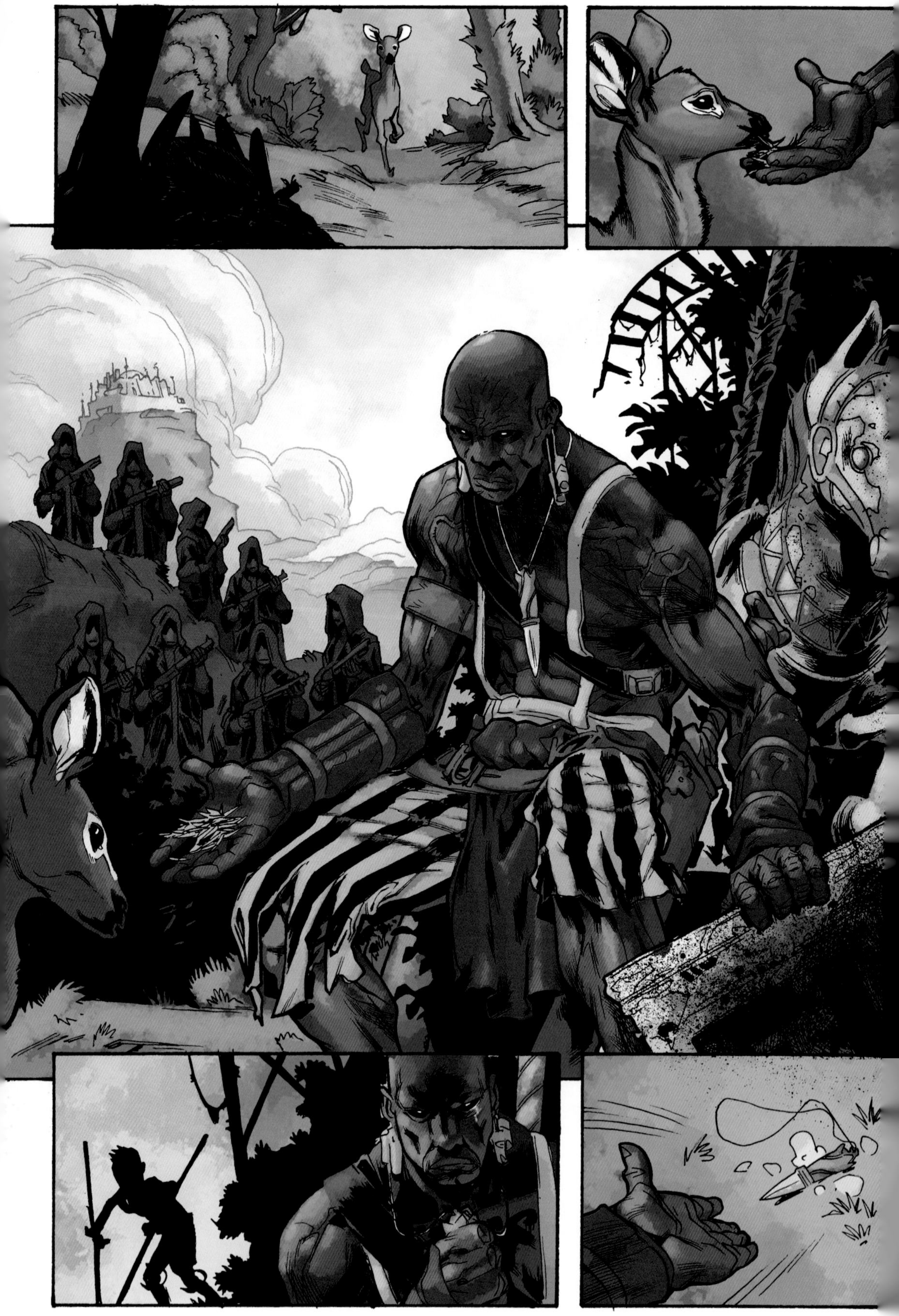

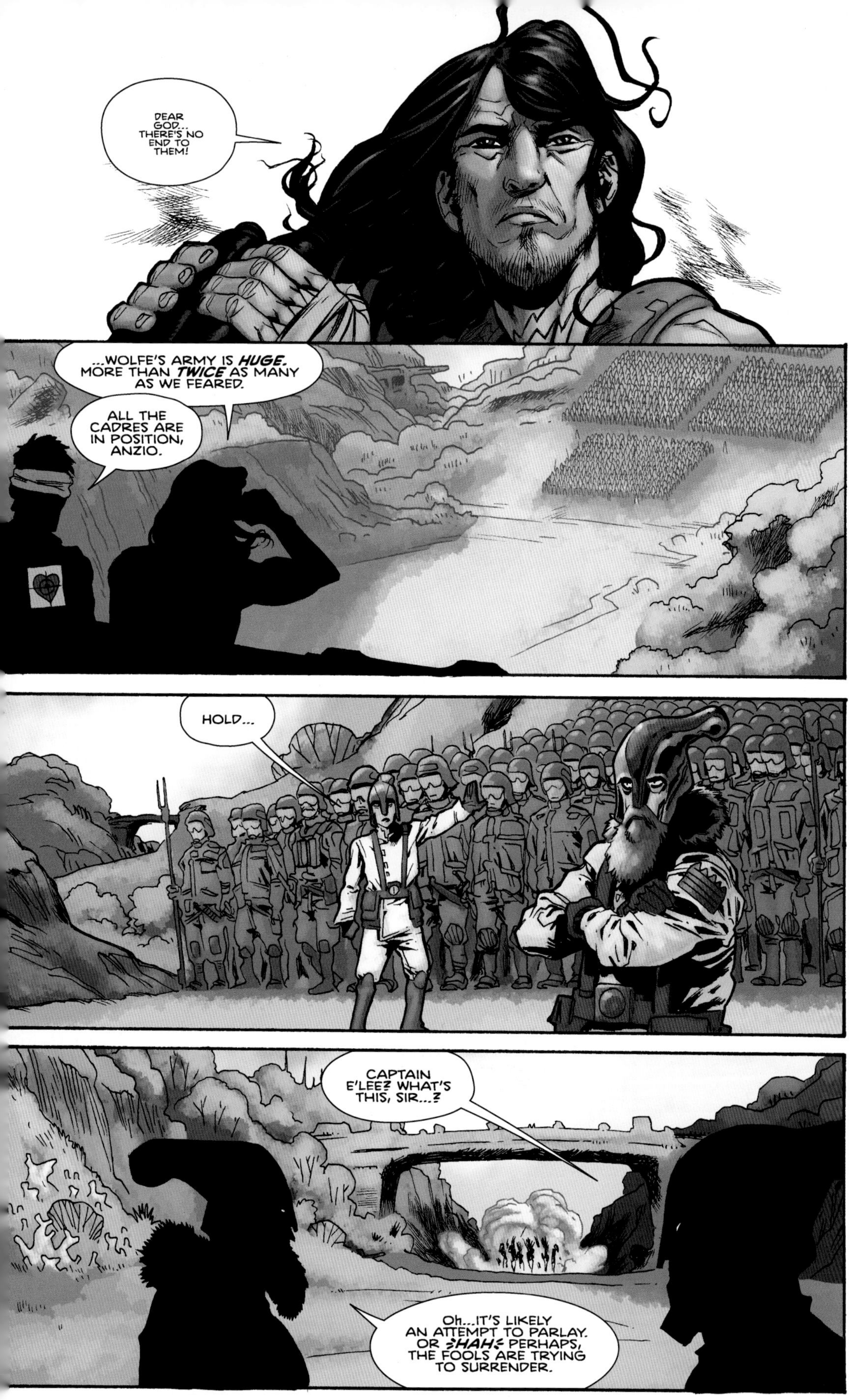
DEAR GOD... THERE'S NO END TO THEM!
...WOLFE'S ARMY IS HUGE. MORE THAN TWICE AS MANY AS WE FEARED.
ALL THE CADRES ARE IN POSITION, ANZIO.
HOLD...
CAPTAIN E'LEE? WHAT'S THIS, SIR...?
Oh...IT'S LIKELY AN ATTEMPT TO PARLAY. OR HAH PERHAPS, THE FOOLS ARE TRYING TO SURRENDER.

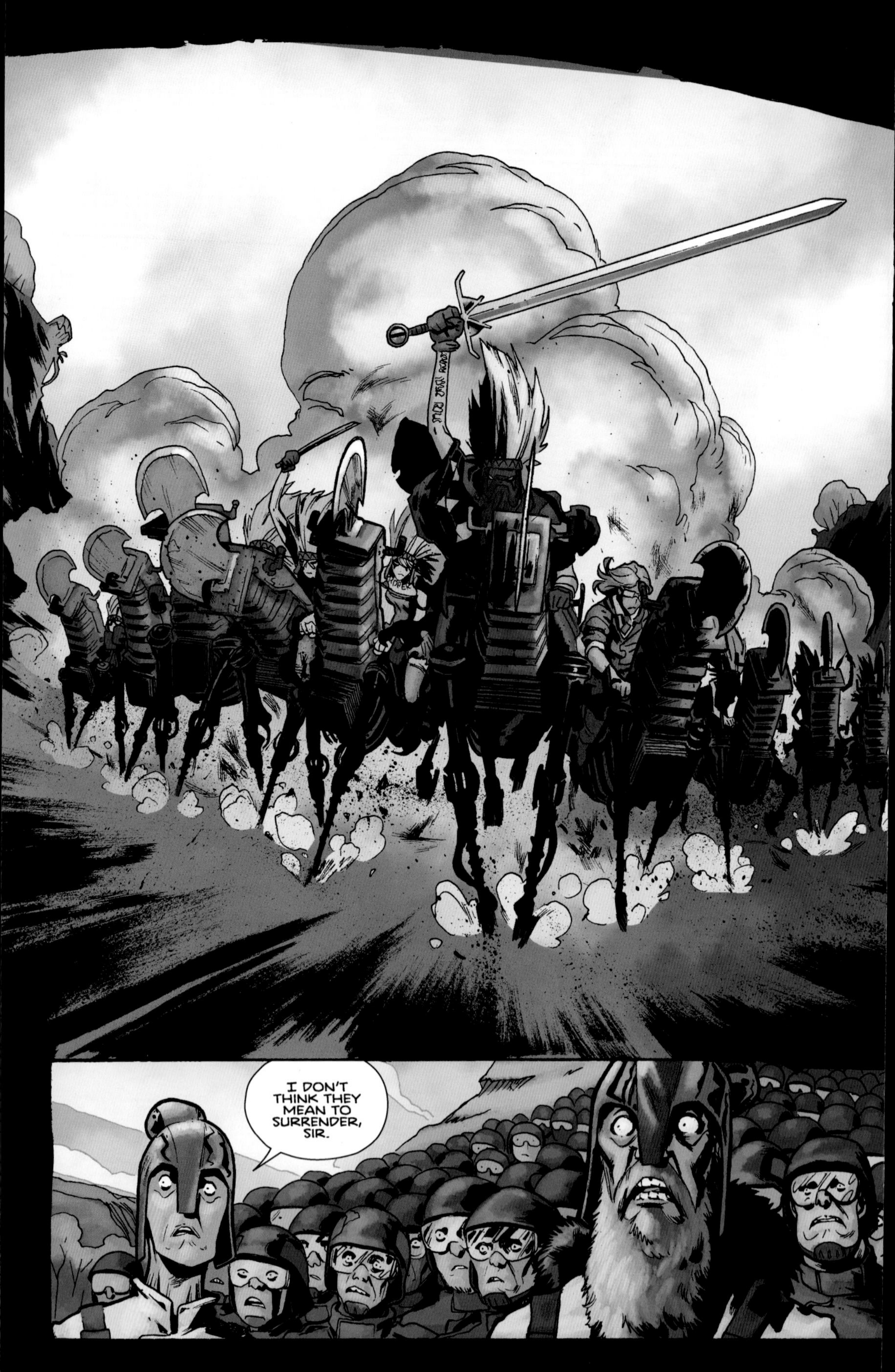
I DON'T THINK THEY MEAN TO SURRENDER, SIR.

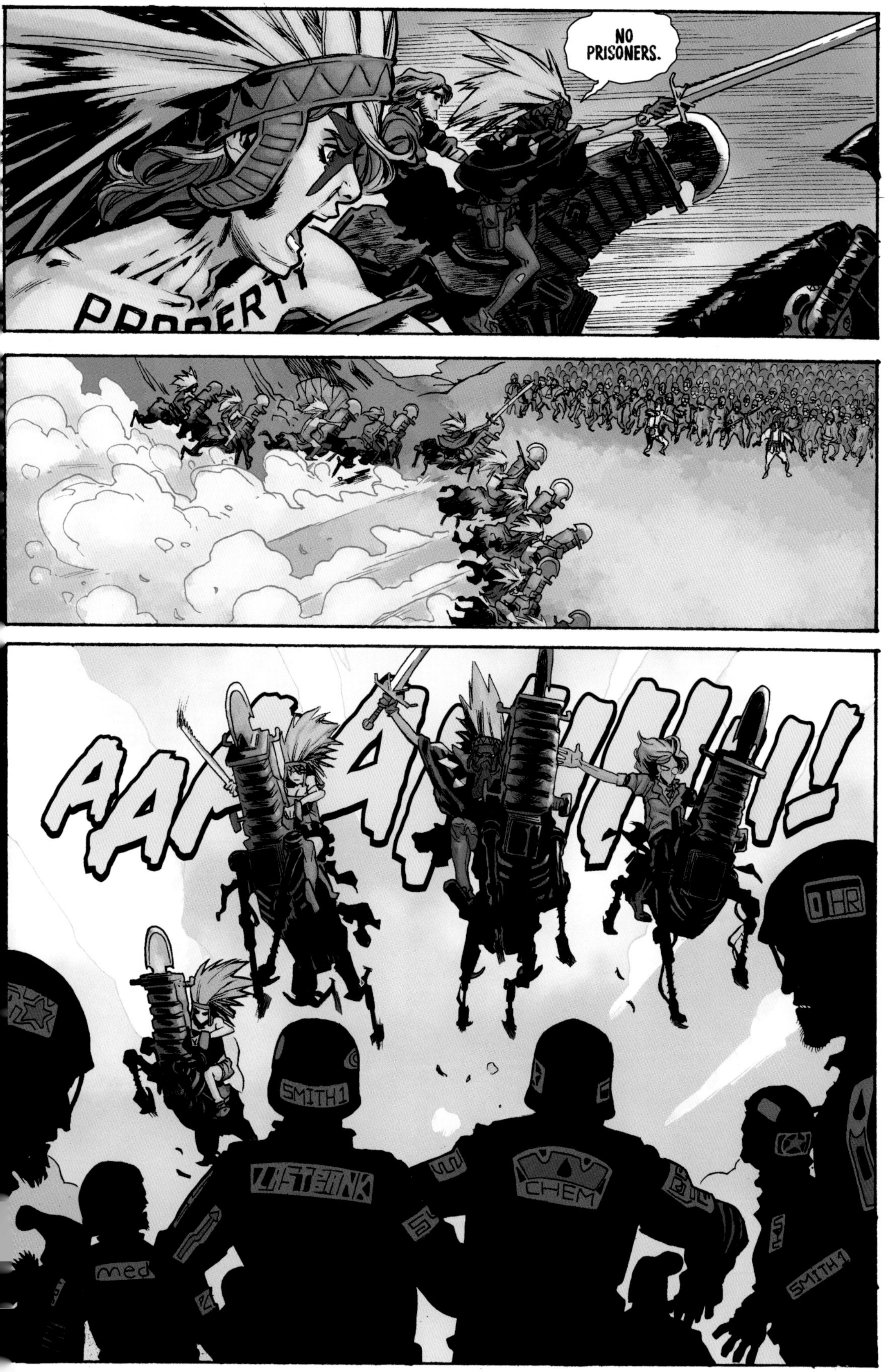
NO PRISONERS.
SMITH1
CHEM
med
SMITH1

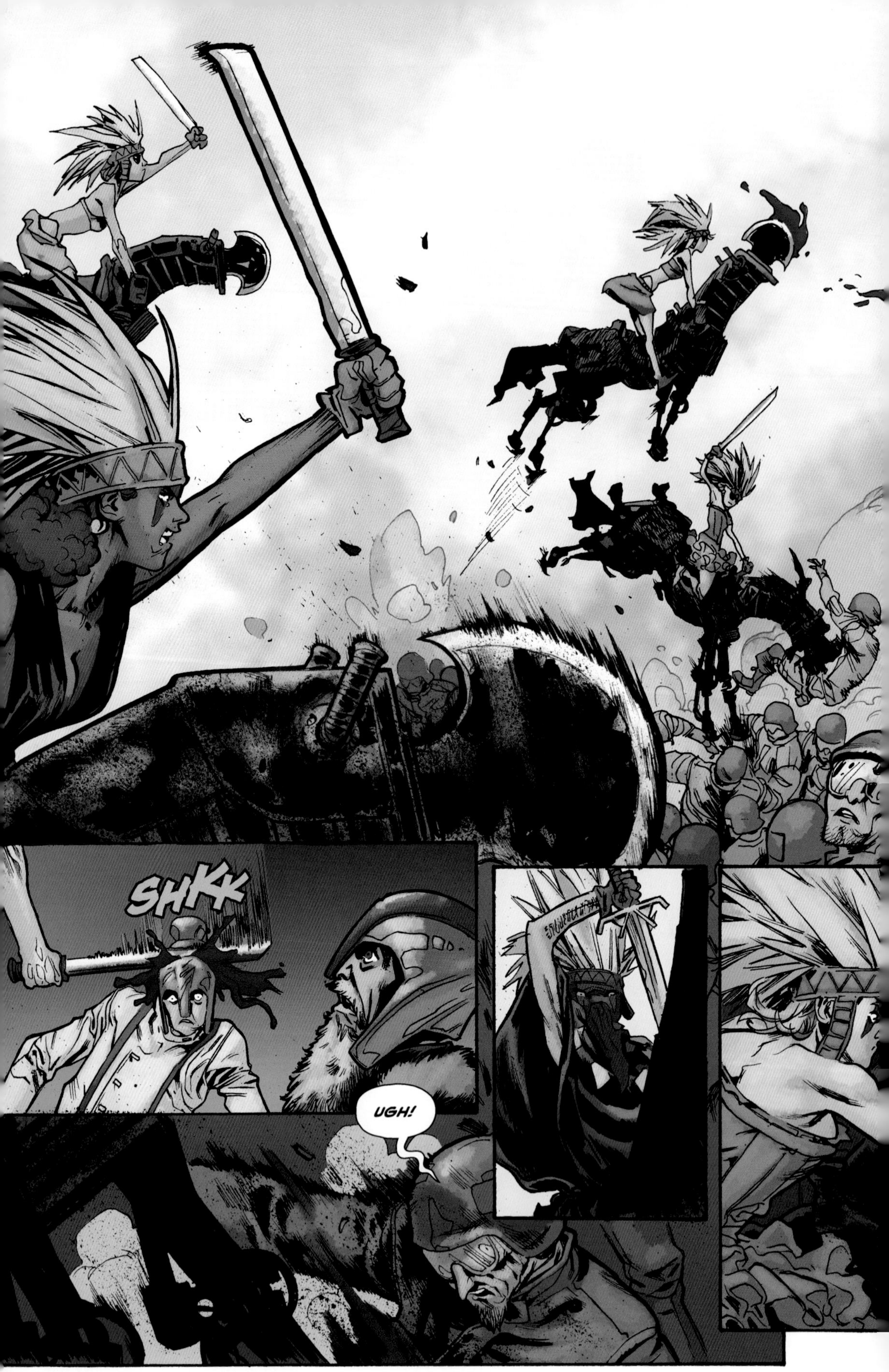
SHKK
UGH!

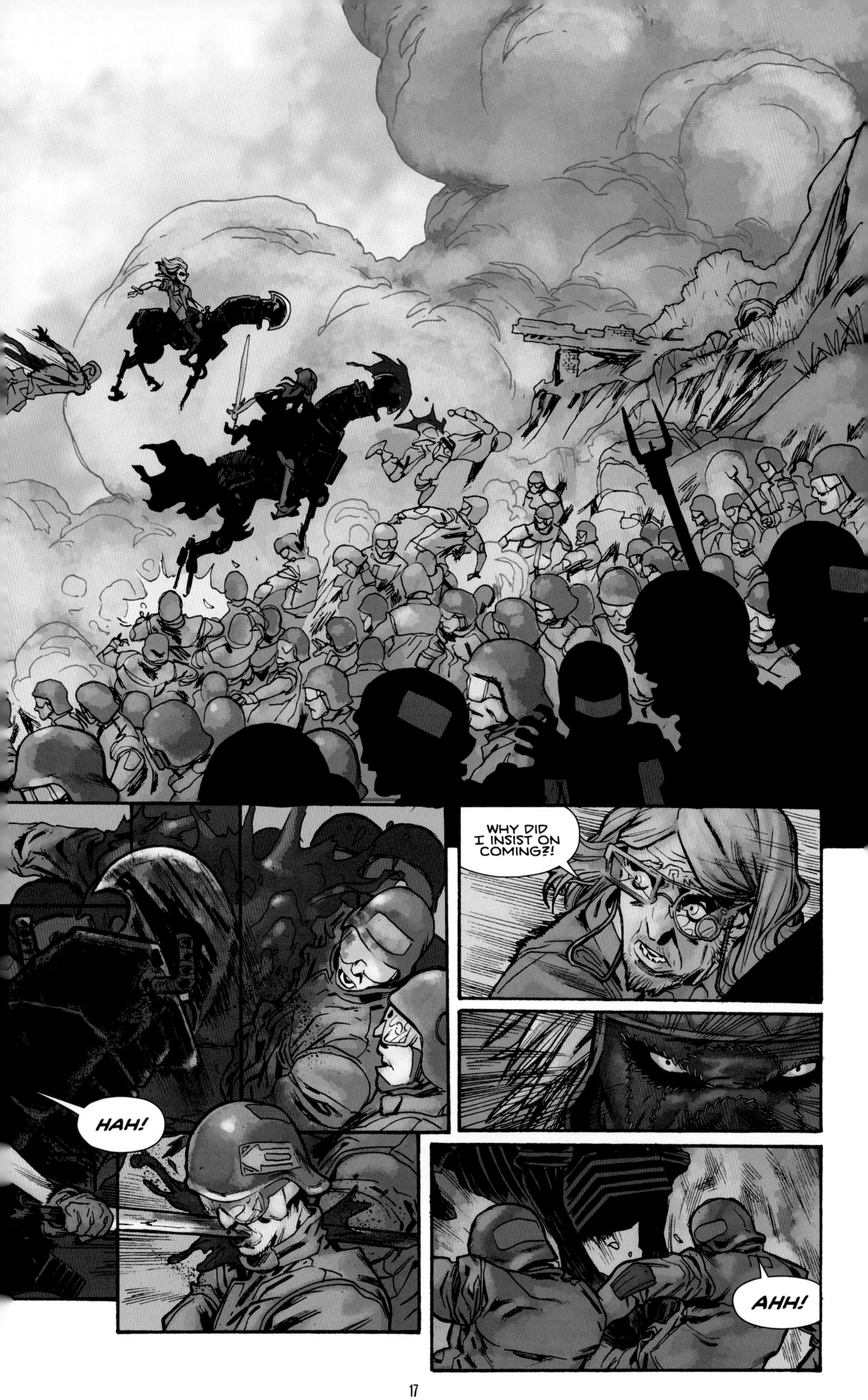

WHY DID I INSIST ON COMING?!
HAH!
AHH!

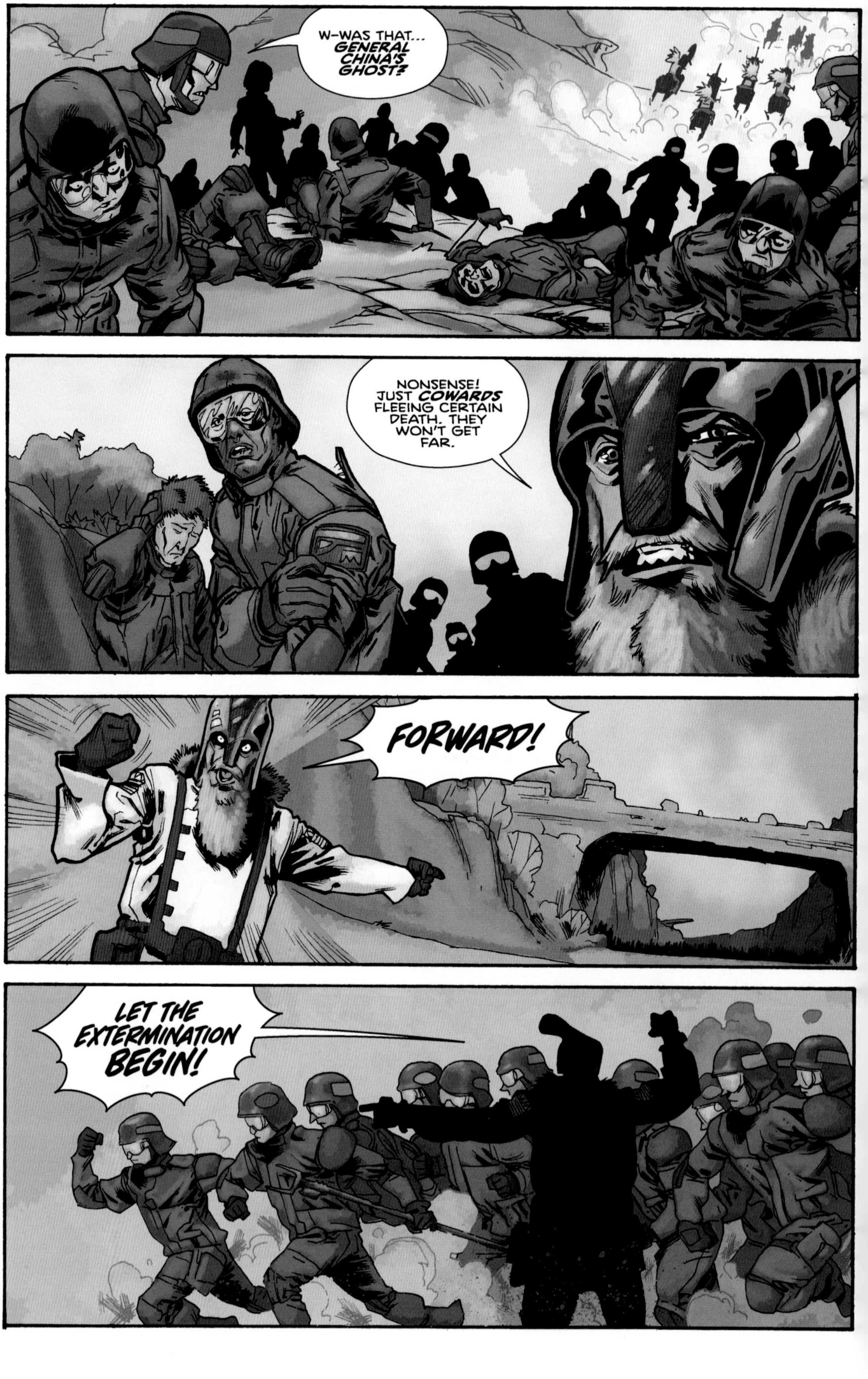

W-WAS THAT... GENERAL CHINA'S GHOST?
NONSENSE! JUST COWARDS FLEEING CERTAIN DEATH. THEY WON'T GET FAR.
FORWARD!
LET THE EXTERMINATION BEGIN!

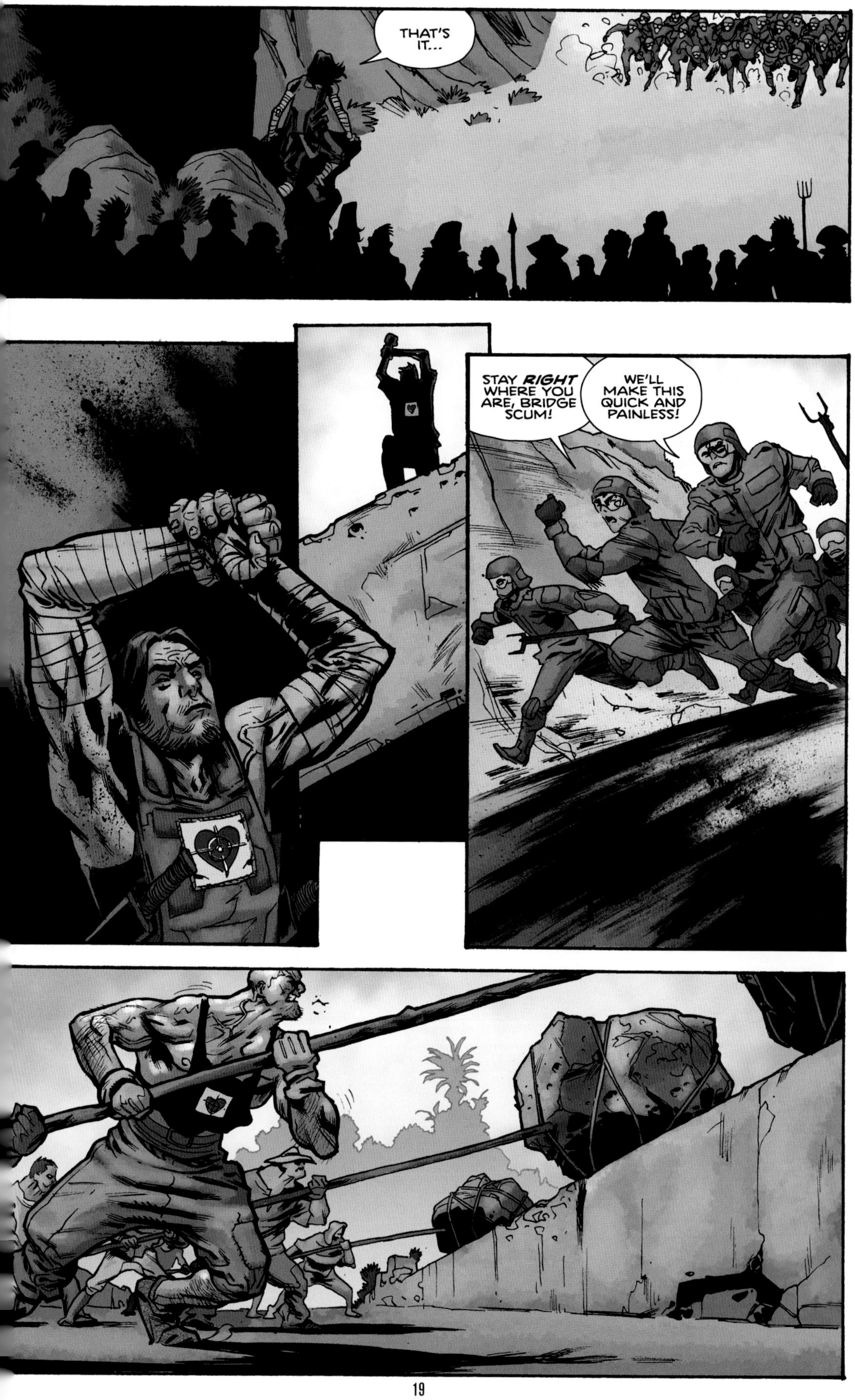
THAT'S IT...
STAY RIGHT WHERE YOU ARE, BRIDGE SCUM!
WE'LL MAKE THIS QUICK AND PAINLESS!

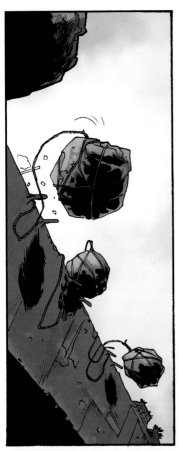

NO...

THOOM

THOOM THOOM

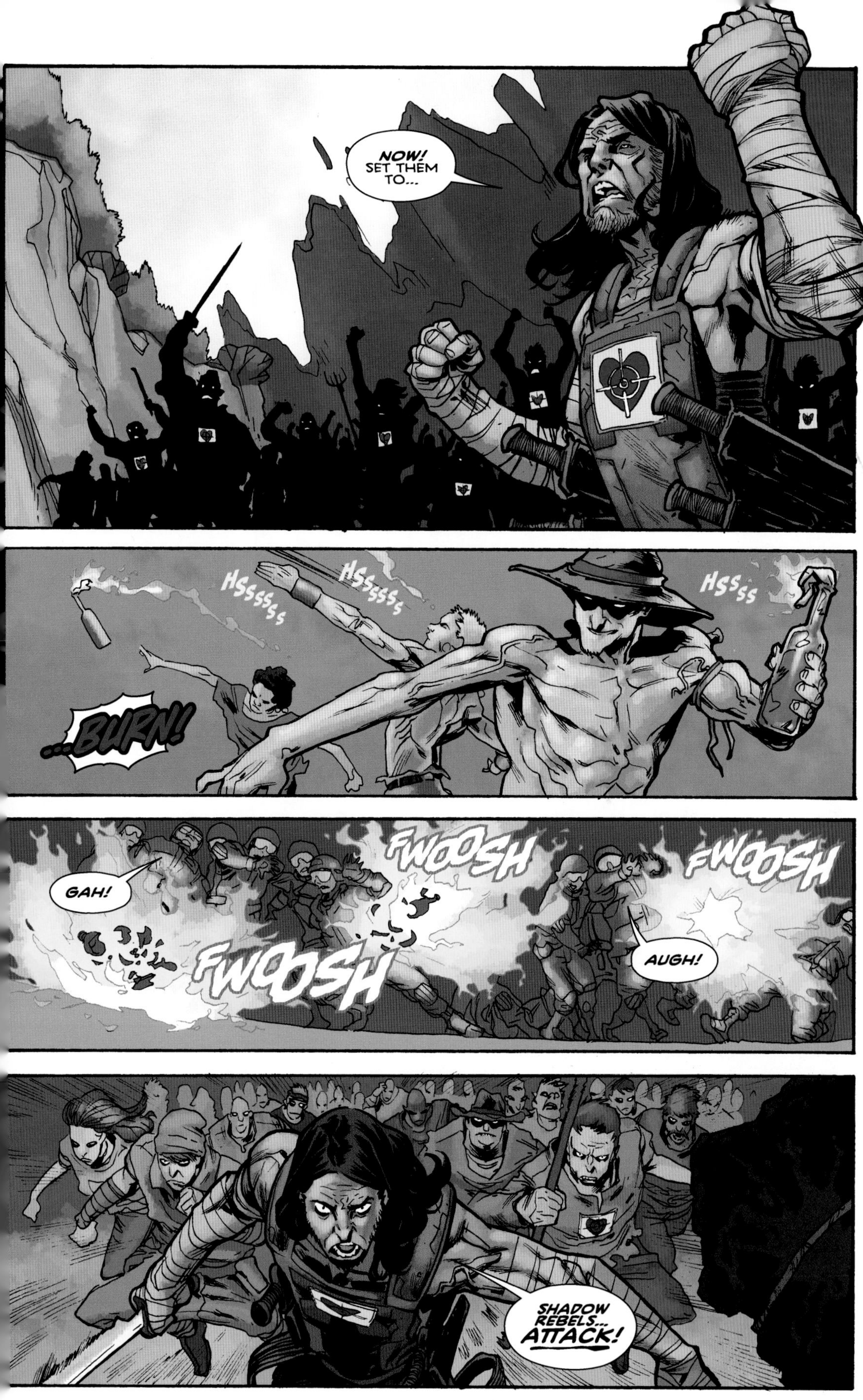
NOW! SET THEM TO...
HSSSSSS
HSSSSSS
HSSSS
...BURN!
FWOOSH
FWOOSH
GAH!
FWOOSH
AUGH!
SHADOW REBELS... ATTACK!

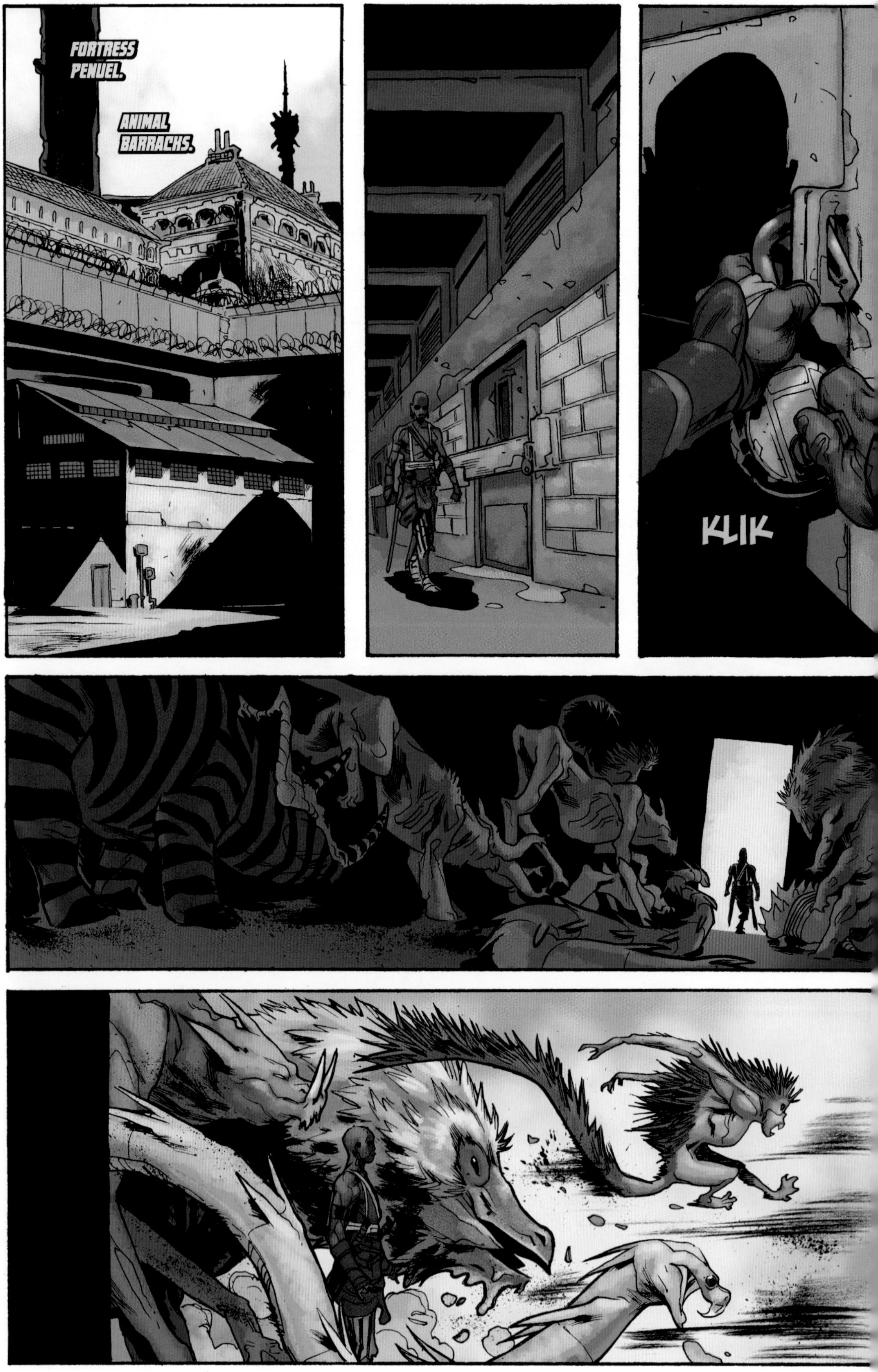

FORTRESS PENUEL.
ANIMAL BARRACKS.
KLIK

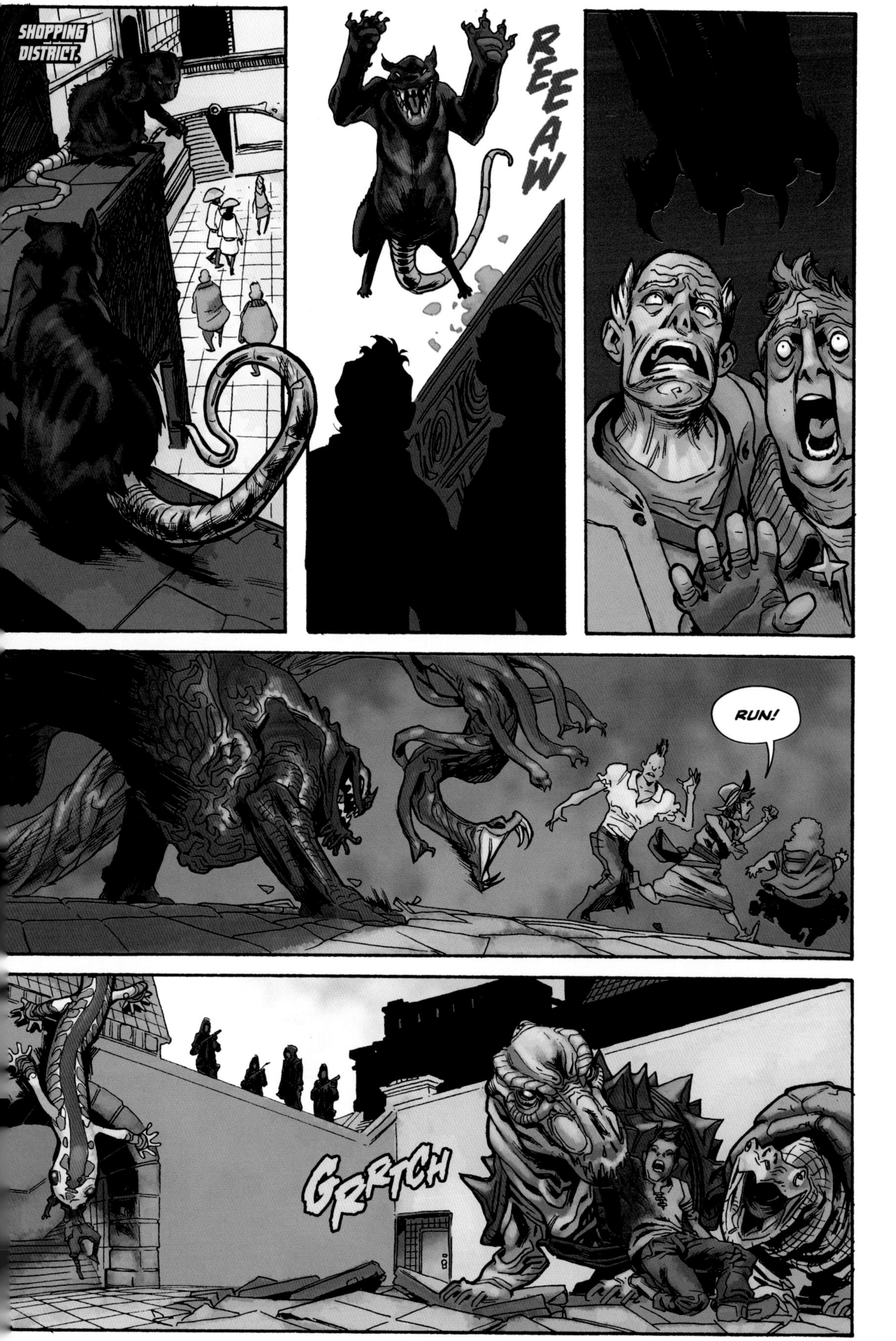

SHOPPING DISTRICT.
REEEAW
RUN!
GRRTCH

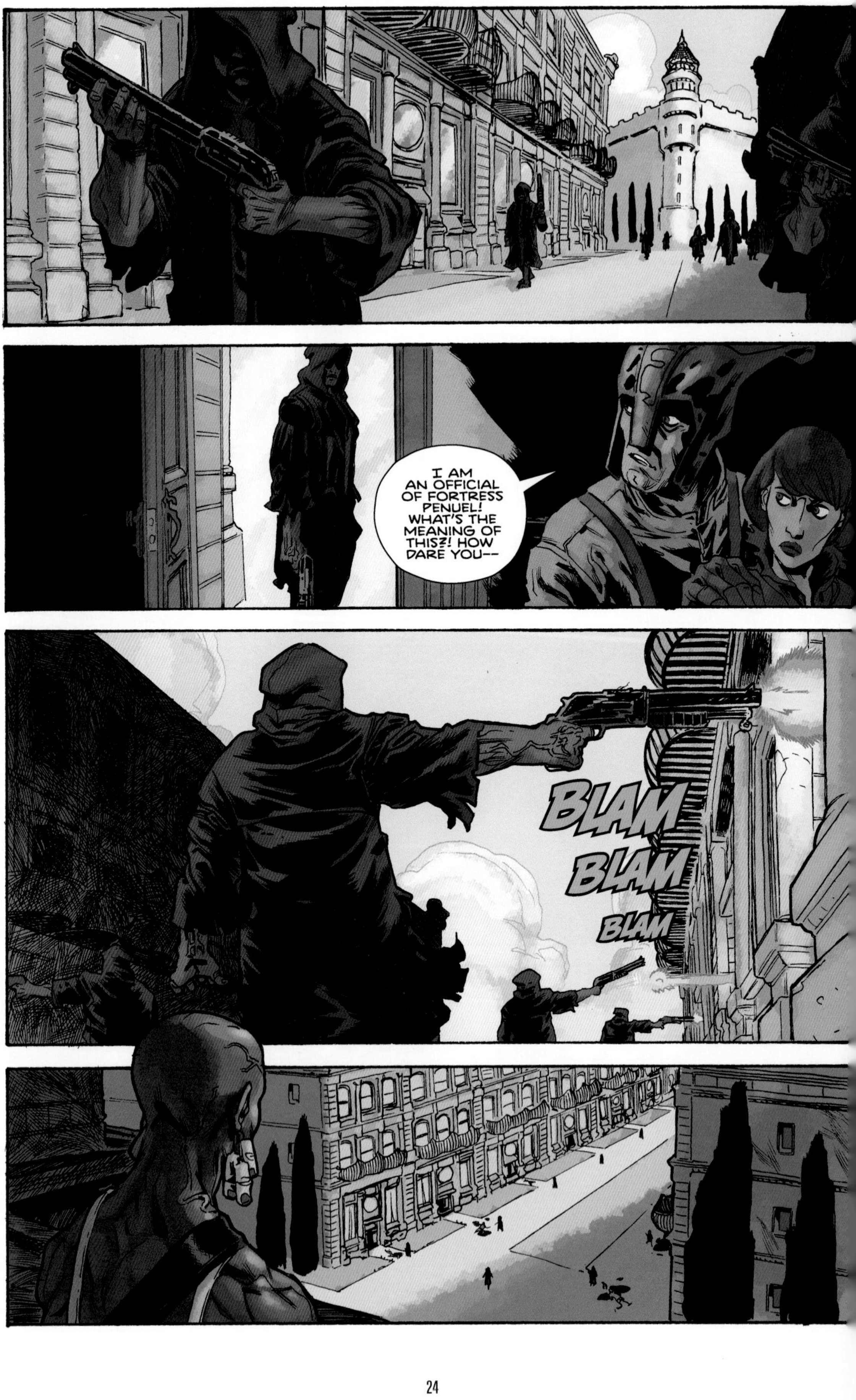
I AM AN OFFICIAL OF FORTRESS PENUEL! WHAT'S THE MEANING OF THIS?! HOW DARE YOU--
BLAM
BLAM
BLAM

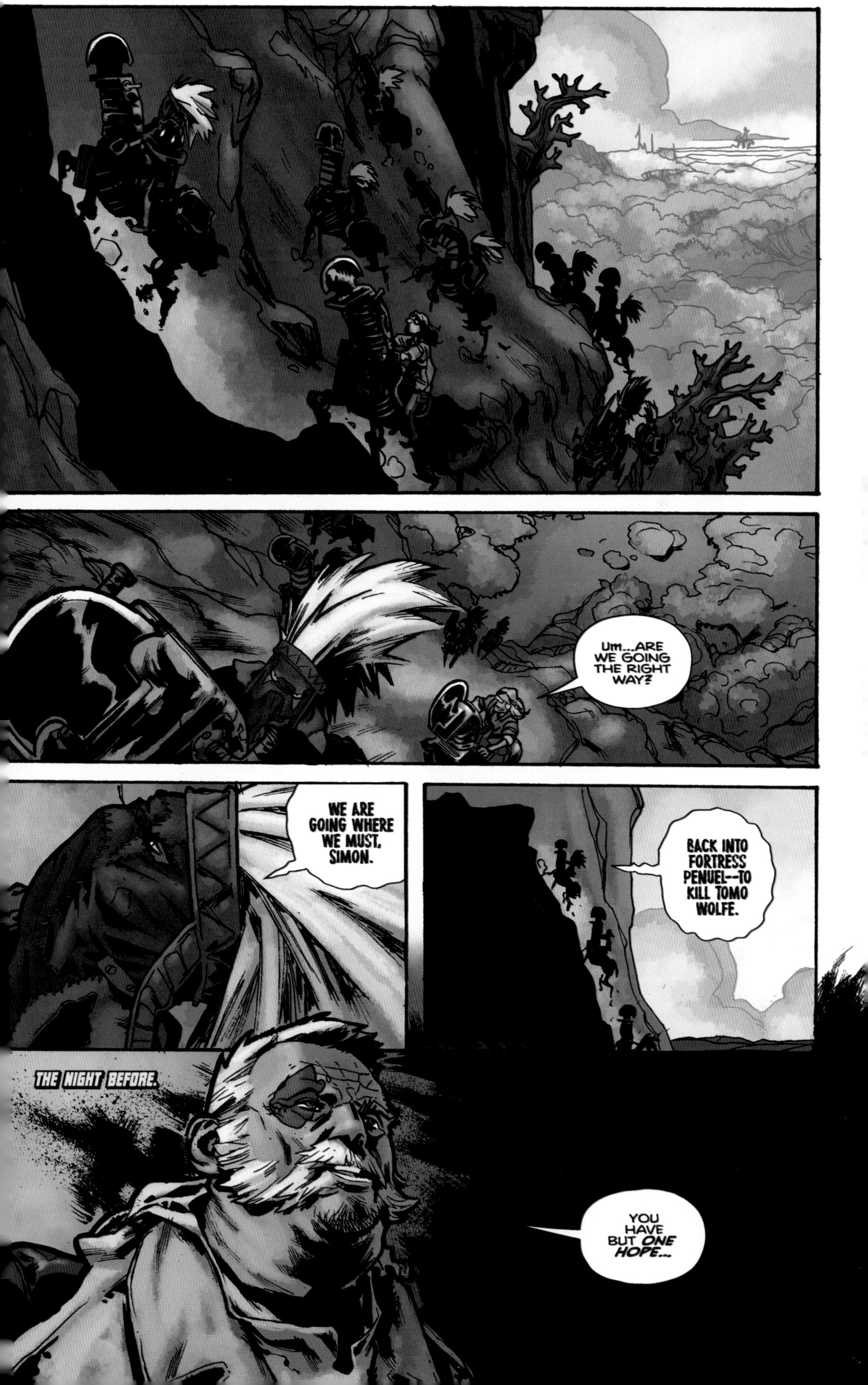
UM...ARE WE GOING THE RIGHT WAY?
WE ARE GOING WHERE WE MUST, SIMON.
BACK INTO FORTRESS PENUEL--TO KILL TOMO WOLFE.
THE NIGHT BEFORE.
YOU HAVE BUT *ONE HOPE*...

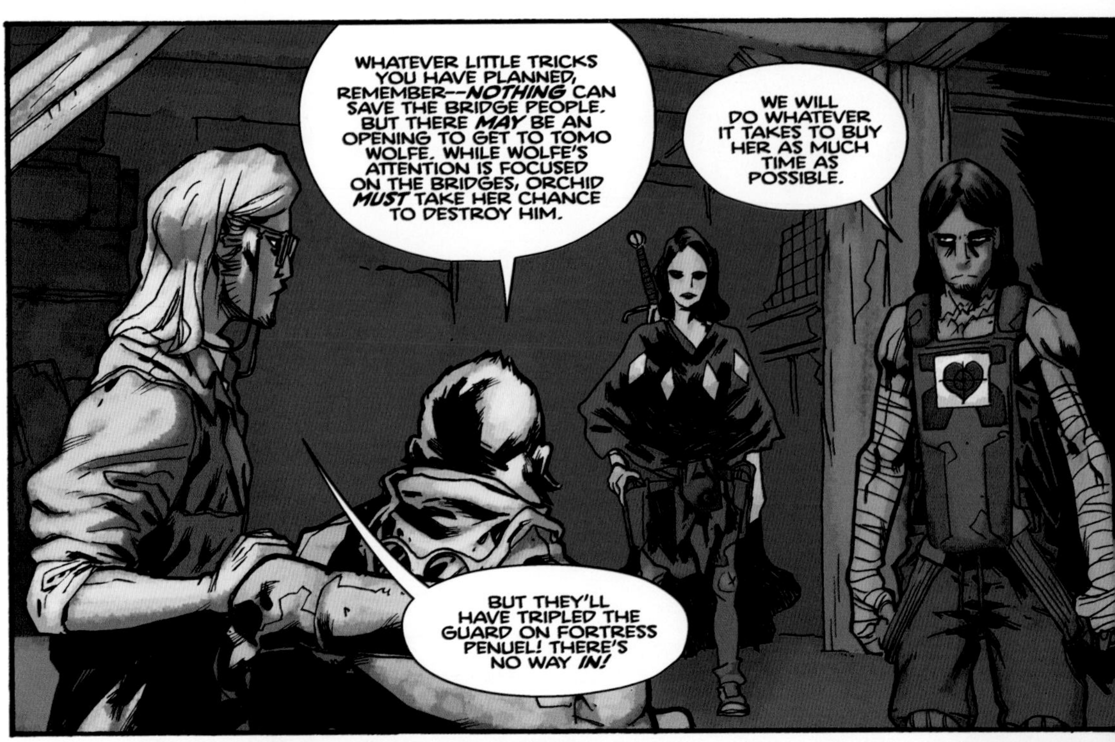
WHATEVER LITTLE TRICKS YOU HAVE PLANNED, REMEMBER--NOTHING CAN SAVE THE BRIDGE PEOPLE. BUT THERE MAY BE AN OPENING TO GET TO TOMO WOLFE. WHILE WOLFE'S ATTENTION IS FOCUSED ON THE BRIDGES, ORCHID MUST TAKE HER CHANCE TO DESTROY HIM.
WE WILL DO WHATEVER IT TAKES TO BUY HER AS MUCH TIME AS POSSIBLE.
BUT THEY'LL HAVE TRIPLED THE GUARD ON FORTRESS PENUEL! THERE'S NO WAY IN!

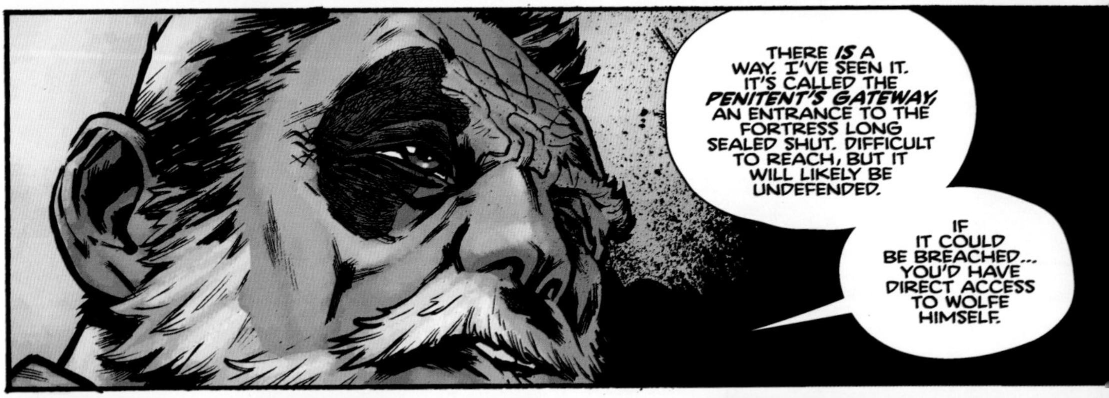
THERE IS A WAY. I'VE SEEN IT. IT'S CALLED THE PENITENT'S GATEWAY, AN ENTRANCE TO THE FORTRESS LONG SEALED SHUT. DIFFICULT TO REACH, BUT IT WILL LIKELY BE UNDEFENDED.
IF IT COULD BE BREACHED... YOU'D HAVE DIRECT ACCESS TO WOLFE HIMSELF.

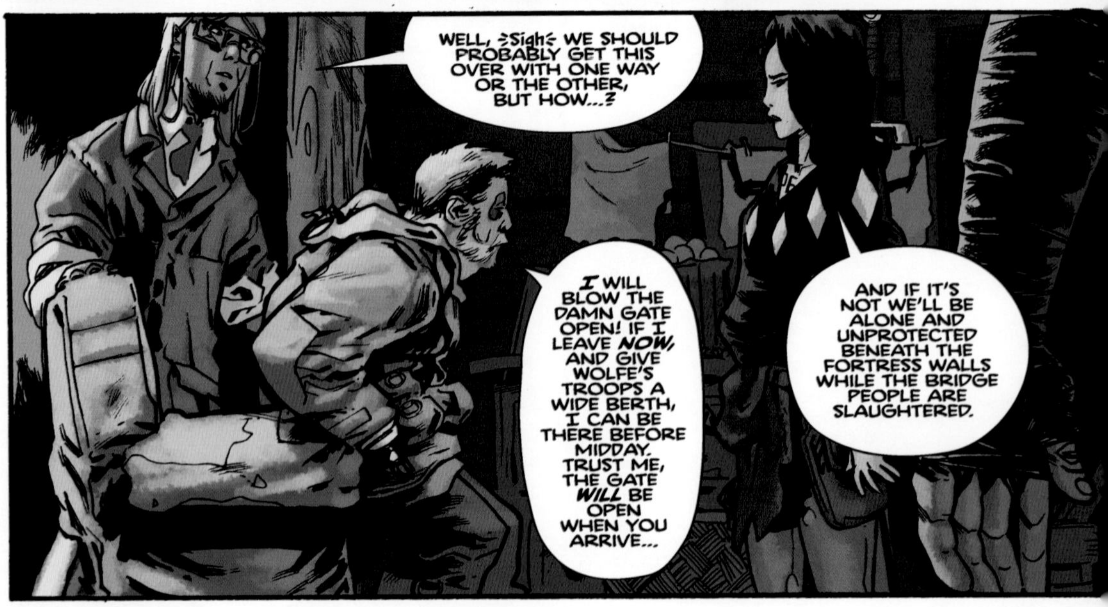
WELL, <Sigh> WE SHOULD PROBABLY GET THIS OVER WITH ONE WAY OR THE OTHER, BUT HOW...?
AND IF IT'S NOT WE'LL BE ALONE AND UNPROTECTED BENEATH THE FORTRESS WALLS WHILE THE BRIDGE PEOPLE ARE SLAUGHTERED.
I WILL BLOW THE DAMN GATE OPEN! IF I LEAVE NOW, AND GIVE WOLFE'S TROOPS A WIDE BERTH, I CAN BE THERE BEFORE MIDDAY. TRUST ME, THE GATE WILL BE OPEN WHEN YOU ARRIVE...

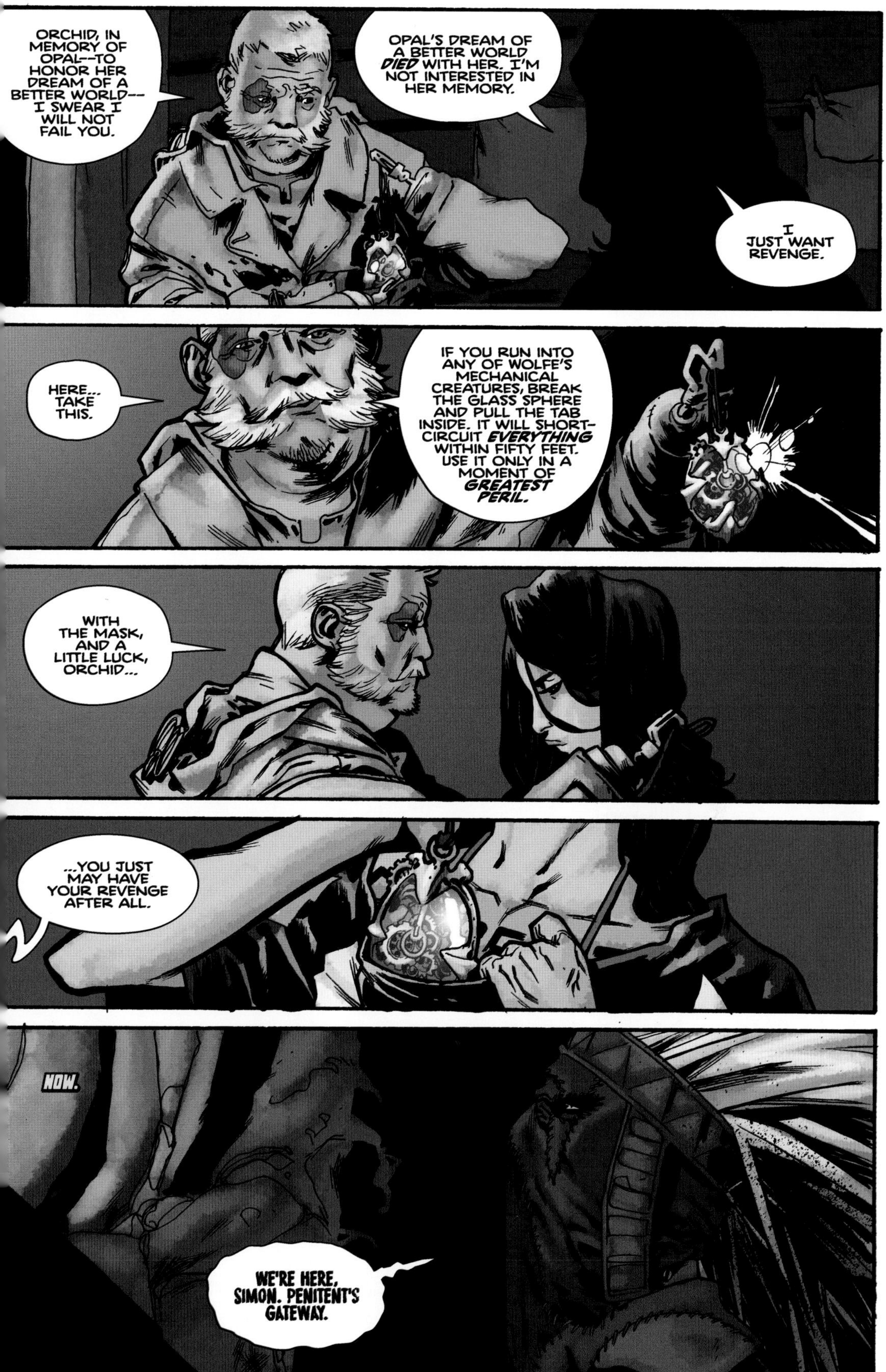
ORCHID, IN MEMORY OF OPAL--TO HONOR HER DREAM OF A BETTER WORLD-- I SWEAR I WILL NOT FAIL YOU.
OPAL'S DREAM OF A BETTER WORLD DIED WITH HER. I'M NOT INTERESTED IN HER MEMORY.
I JUST WANT REVENGE.
HERE... TAKE THIS.
IF YOU RUN INTO ANY OF WOLFE'S MECHANICAL CREATURES, BREAK THE GLASS SPHERE AND PULL THE TAB INSIDE. IT WILL SHORT-CIRCUIT EVERYTHING WITHIN FIFTY FEET. USE IT ONLY IN A MOMENT OF GREATEST PERIL.
WITH THE MASK, AND A LITTLE LUCK, ORCHID...
...YOU JUST MAY HAVE YOUR REVENGE AFTER ALL.
NOW.
WE'RE HERE, SIMON. PENITENT'S GATEWAY.

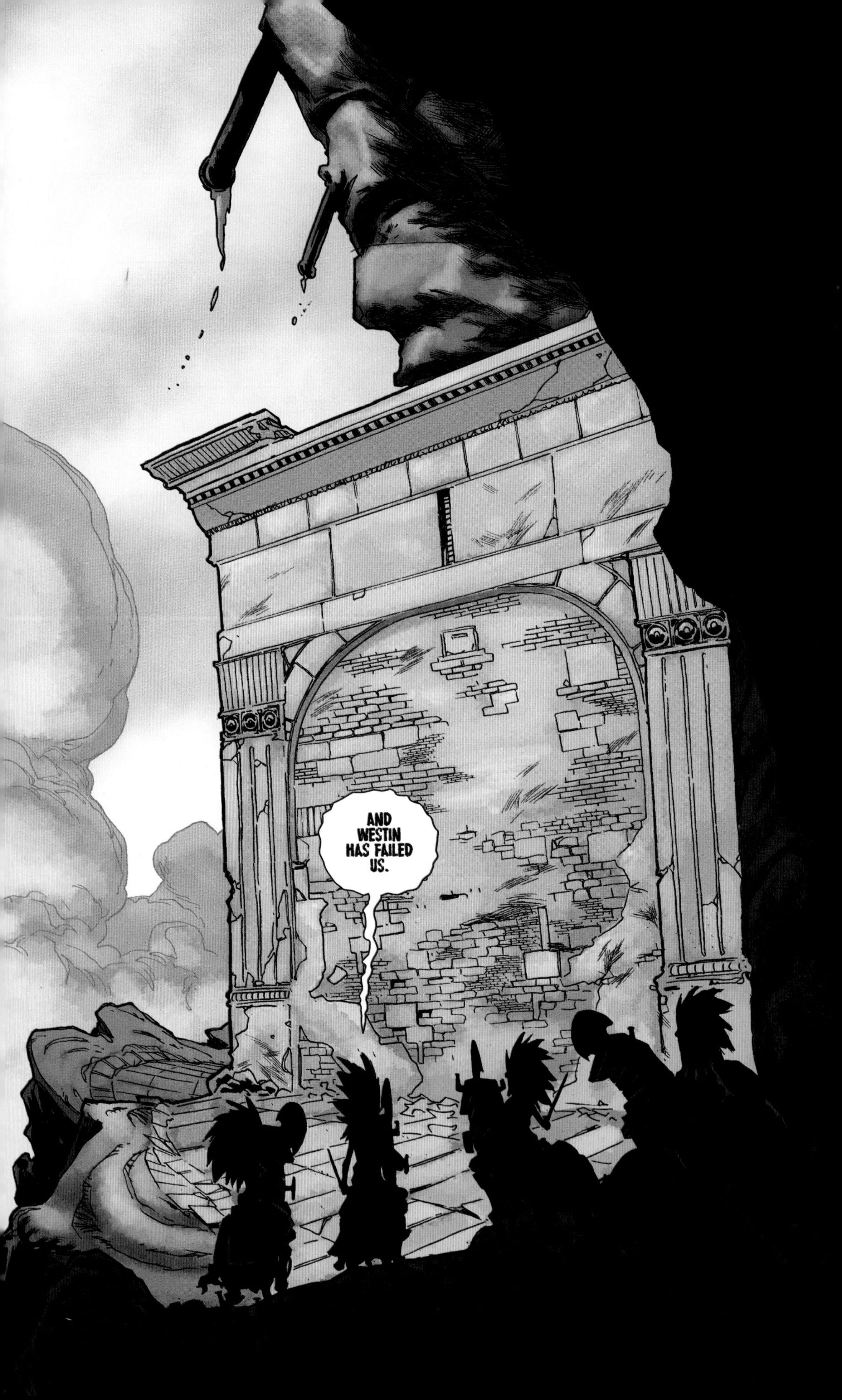
AND WESTIN HAS FAILED US.

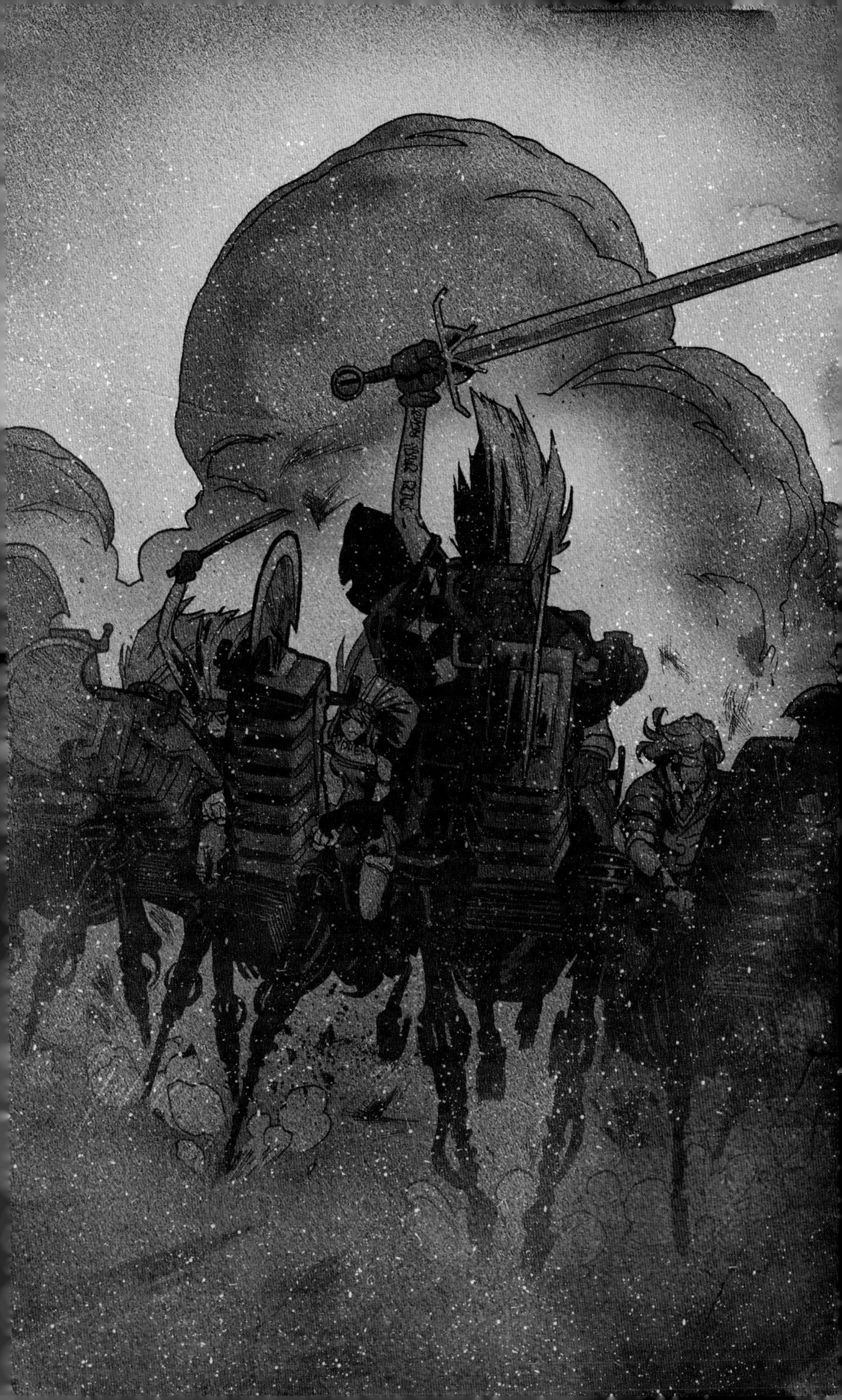

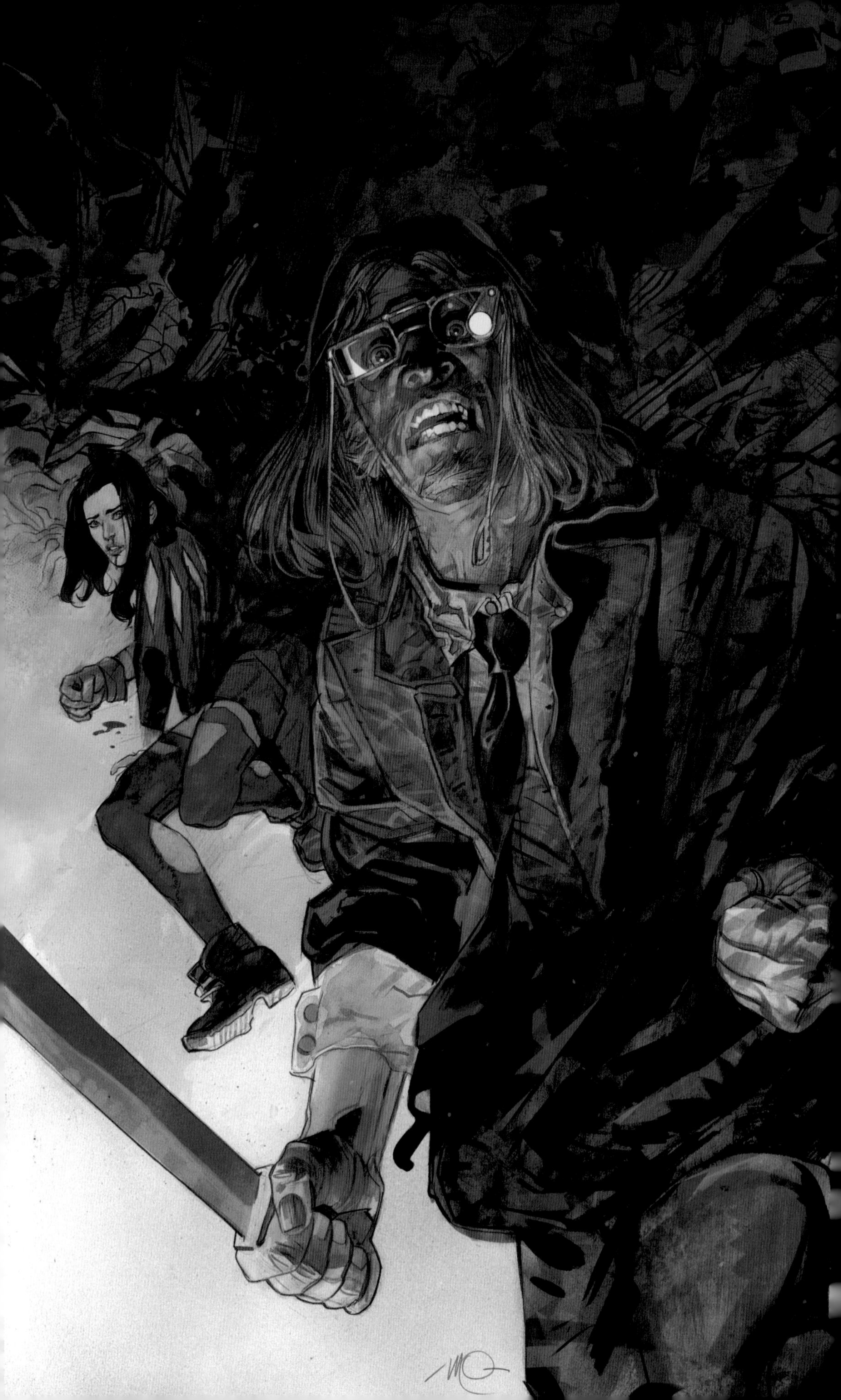

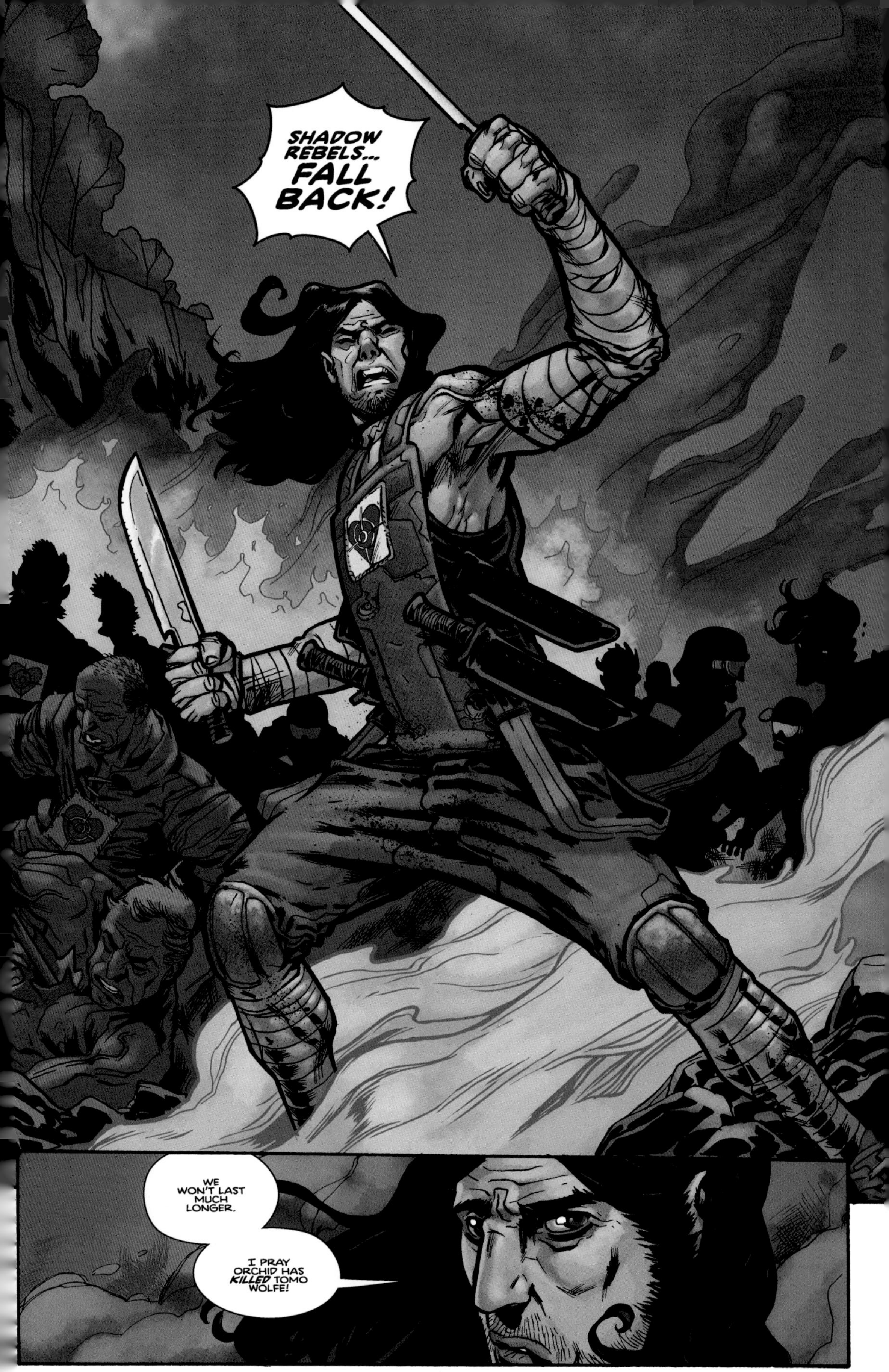
SHADOW REBELS... FALL BACK!
WE WON'T LAST MUCH LONGER.
I PRAY ORCHID HAS *KILLED* TOMO WOLFE!

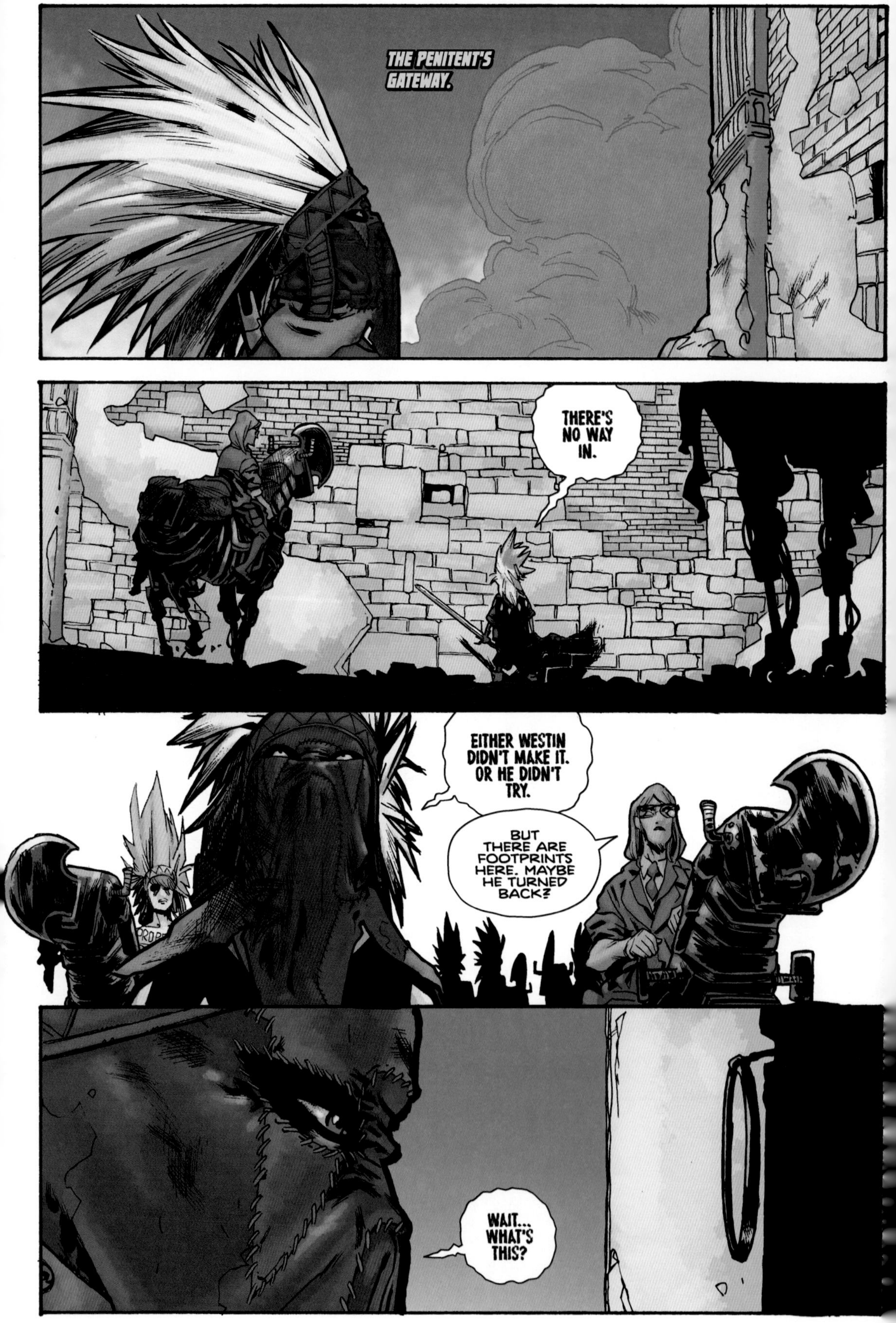
THE PENITENT'S GATEWAY.
THERE'S NO WAY IN.
EITHER WESTIN DIDN'T MAKE IT. OR HE DIDN'T TRY.
BUT THERE ARE FOOTPRINTS HERE. MAYBE HE TURNED BACK?
WAIT... WHAT'S THIS?

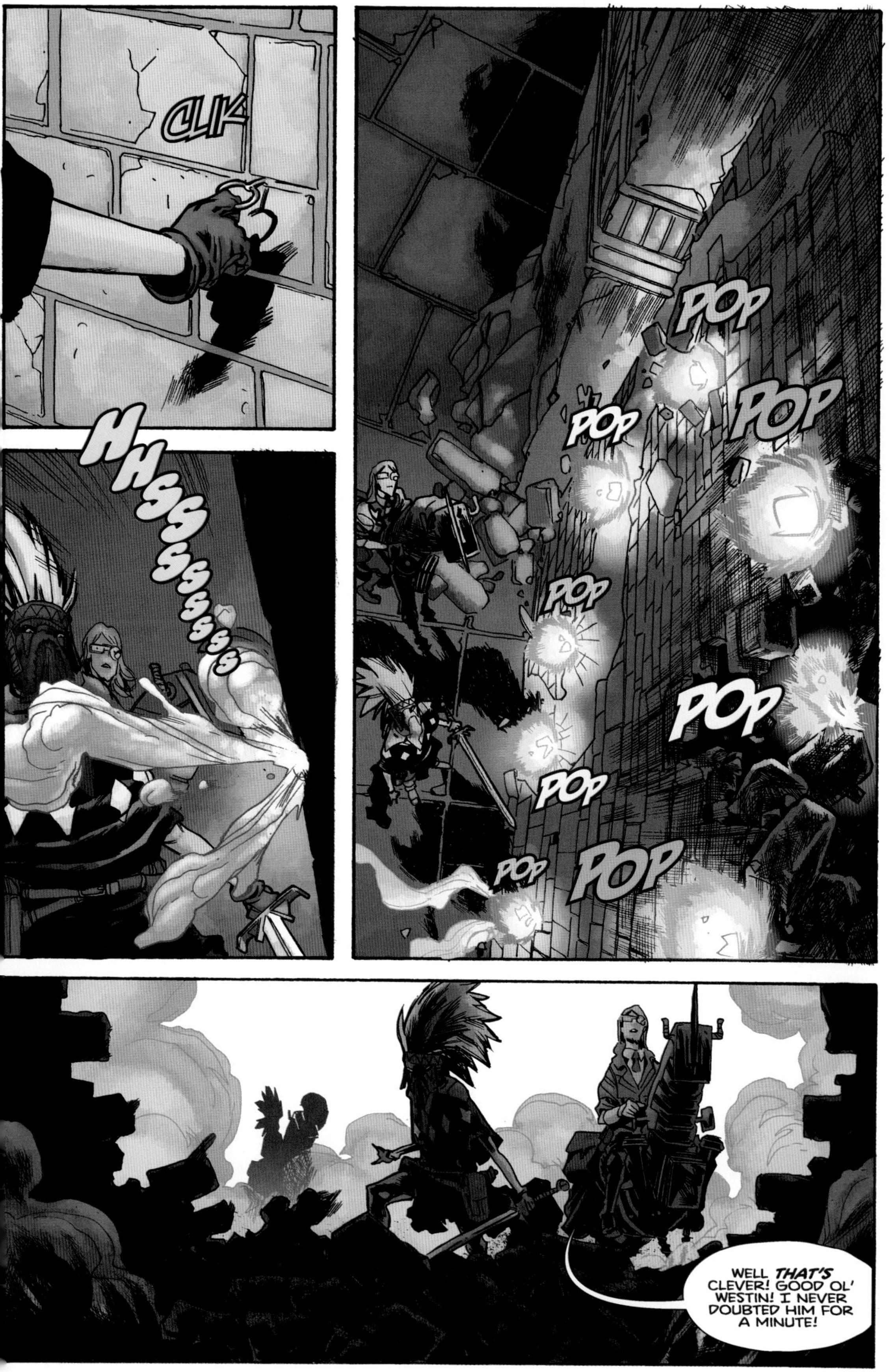
CLIK
HHSSSSSSS
POP
POP
POP
POP
POP
POP
POP
POP
WELL THAT'S CLEVER! GOOD OL' WESTIN! I NEVER DOUBTED HIM FOR A MINUTE!

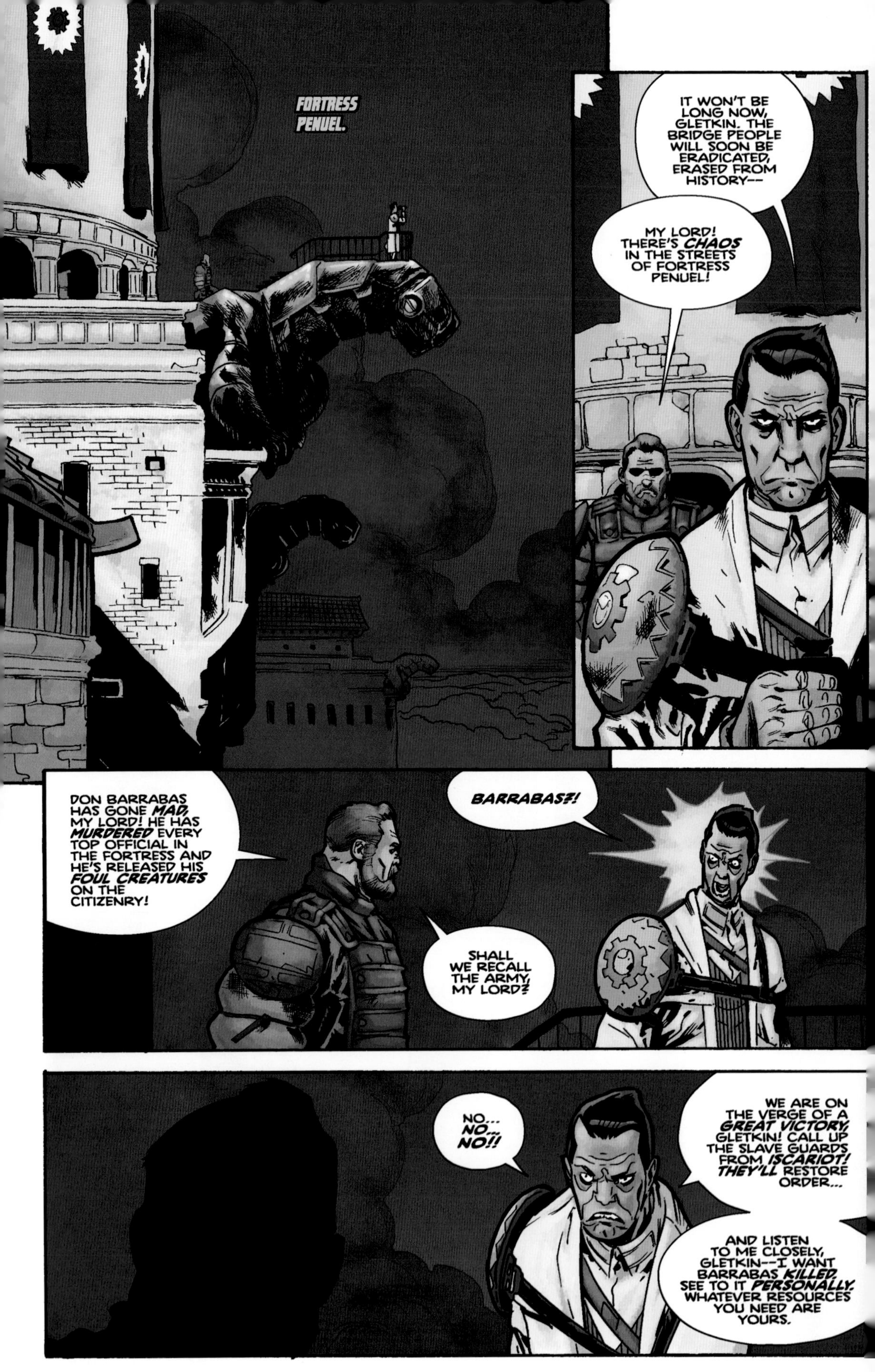
FORTRESS PENUEL.
IT WON'T BE LONG NOW, GLETKIN. THE BRIDGE PEOPLE WILL SOON BE ERADICATED, ERASED FROM HISTORY--
MY LORD! THERE'S CHAOS IN THE STREETS OF FORTRESS PENUEL!
DON BARRABAS HAS GONE MAD, MY LORD! HE HAS MURDERED EVERY TOP OFFICIAL IN THE FORTRESS AND HE'S RELEASED HIS FOUL CREATURES ON THE CITIZENRY!
BARRABAS?!
SHALL WE RECALL THE ARMY, MY LORD?
NO... NO... NO!!
WE ARE ON THE VERGE OF A GREAT VICTORY, GLETKIN! CALL UP THE SLAVE GUARDS FROM ISCARIOT! THEY'LL RESTORE ORDER...
AND LISTEN TO ME CLOSELY, GLETKIN--I WANT BARRABAS KILLED. SEE TO IT PERSONALLY. WHATEVER RESOURCES YOU NEED ARE YOURS.

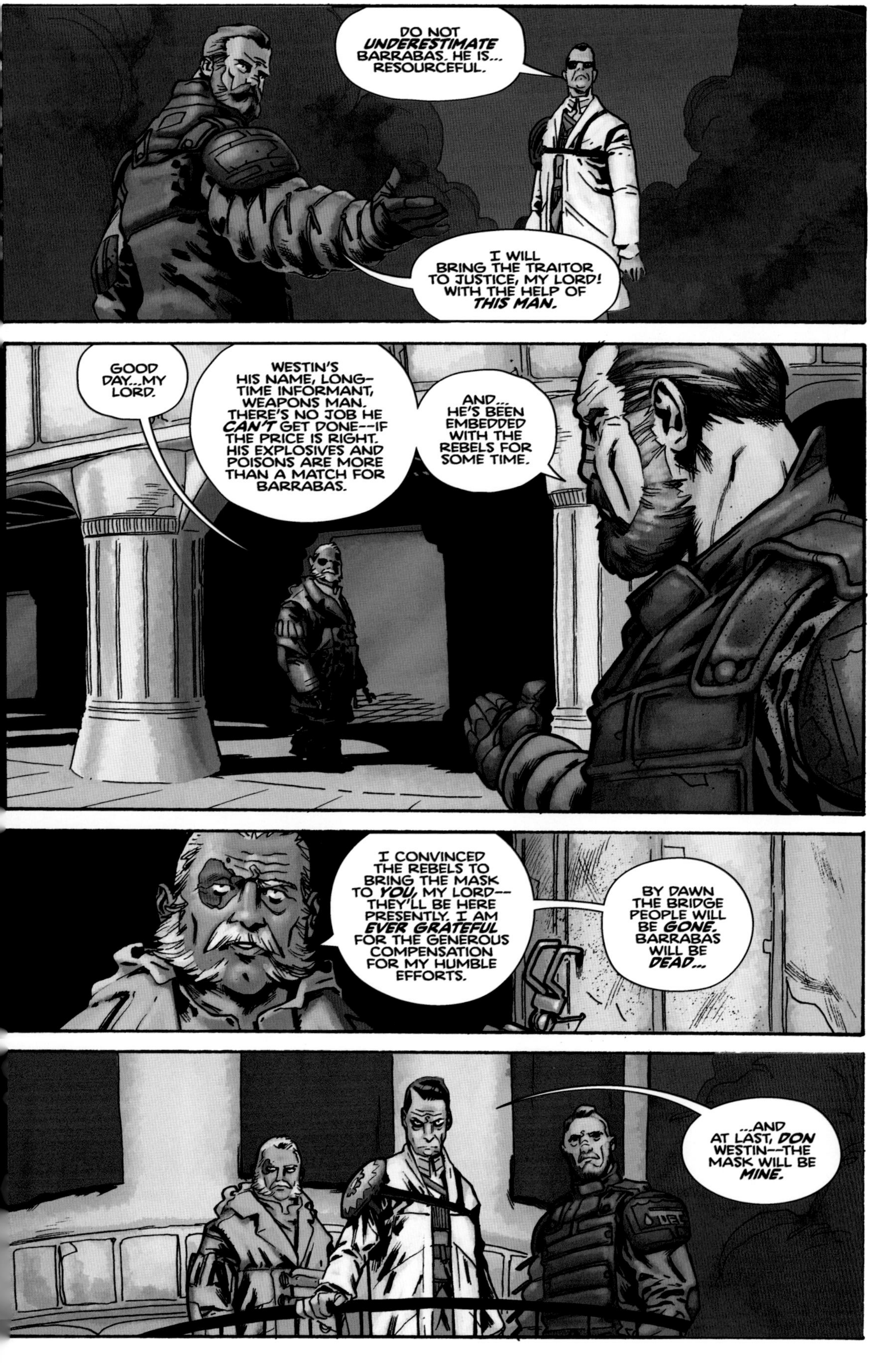
DO NOT UNDERESTIMATE BARRABAS. HE IS... RESOURCEFUL.
I WILL BRING THE TRAITOR TO JUSTICE, MY LORD! WITH THE HELP OF THIS MAN.
GOOD DAY...MY LORD.
WESTIN'S HIS NAME, LONG-TIME INFORMANT, WEAPONS MAN. THERE'S NO JOB HE CAN'T GET DONE--IF THE PRICE IS RIGHT. HIS EXPLOSIVES AND POISONS ARE MORE THAN A MATCH FOR BARRABAS.
AND... HE'S BEEN EMBEDDED WITH THE REBELS FOR SOME TIME.
I CONVINCED THE REBELS TO BRING THE MASK TO YOU, MY LORD-- THEY'LL BE HERE PRESENTLY. I AM EVER GRATEFUL FOR THE GENEROUS COMPENSATION FOR MY HUMBLE EFFORTS.
BY DAWN THE BRIDGE PEOPLE WILL BE GONE. BARRABAS WILL BE DEAD...
...AND AT LAST, DON WESTIN--THE MASK WILL BE MINE.

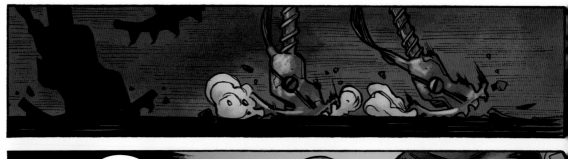

Huh...?

AYYIIII!

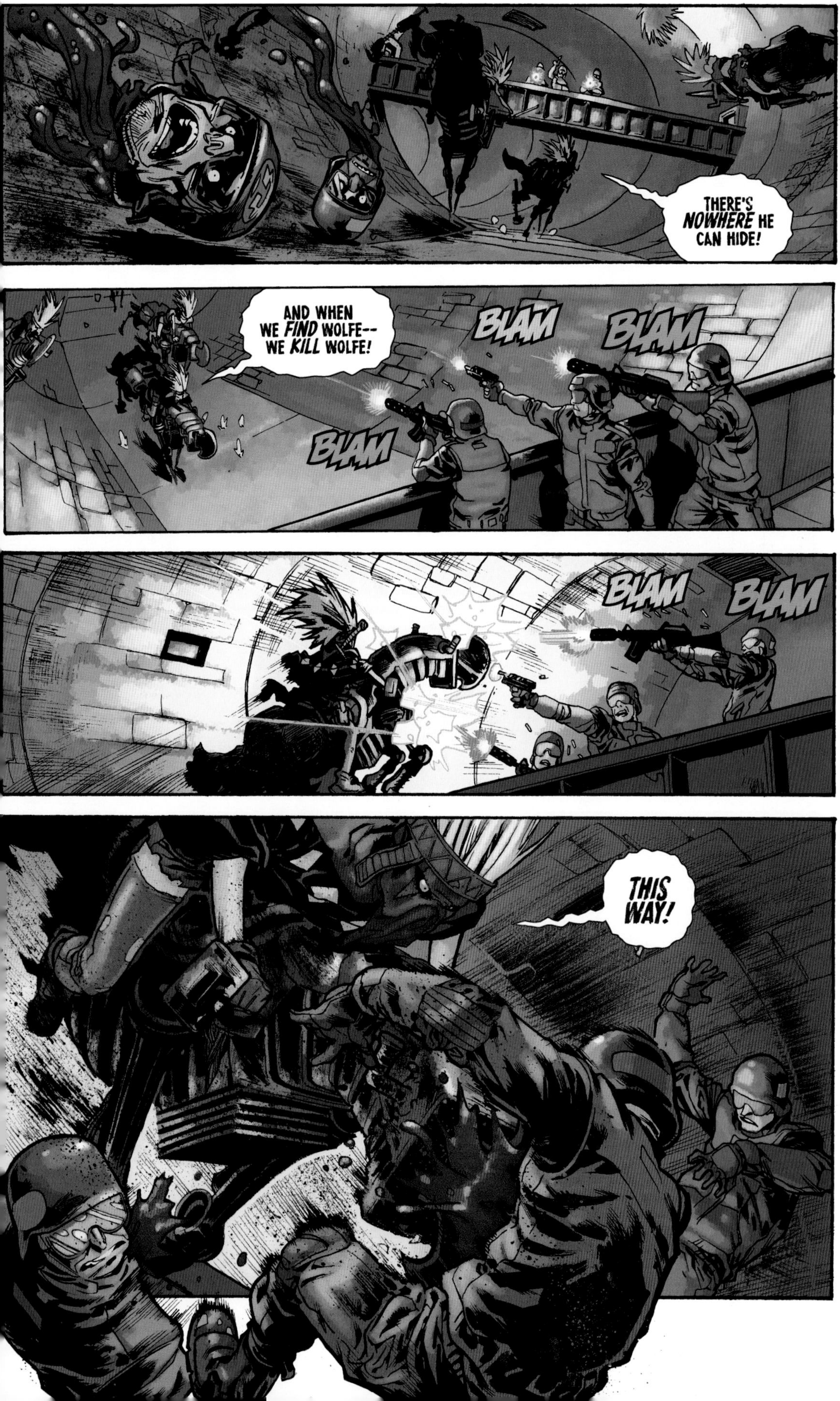
THERE'S NOWHERE HE CAN HIDE!
AND WHEN WE FIND WOLFE-- WE KILL WOLFE!
BLAM
BLAM
BLAM
BLAM
BLAM
THIS WAY!

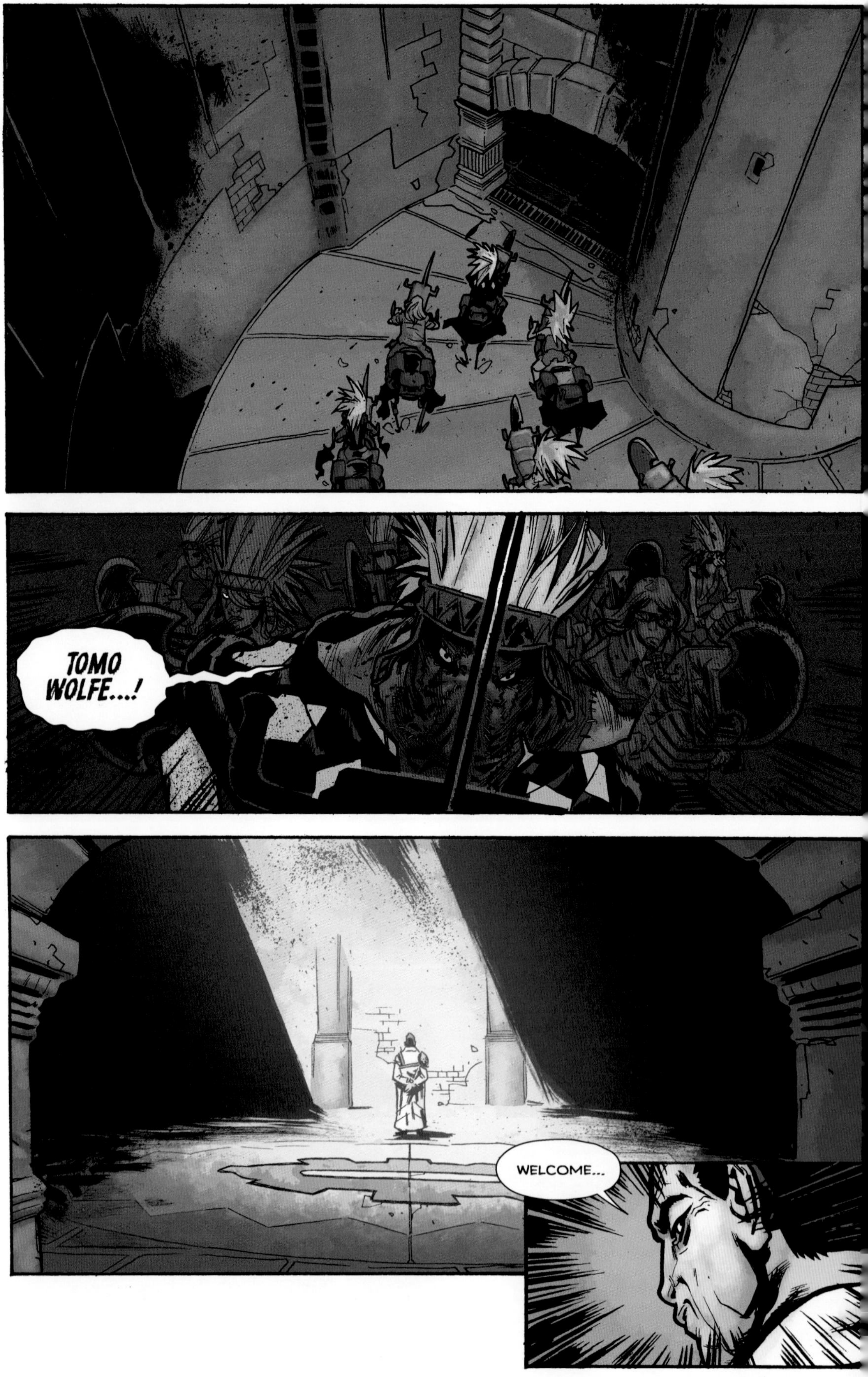
TOMO WOLFE...!
WELCOME...

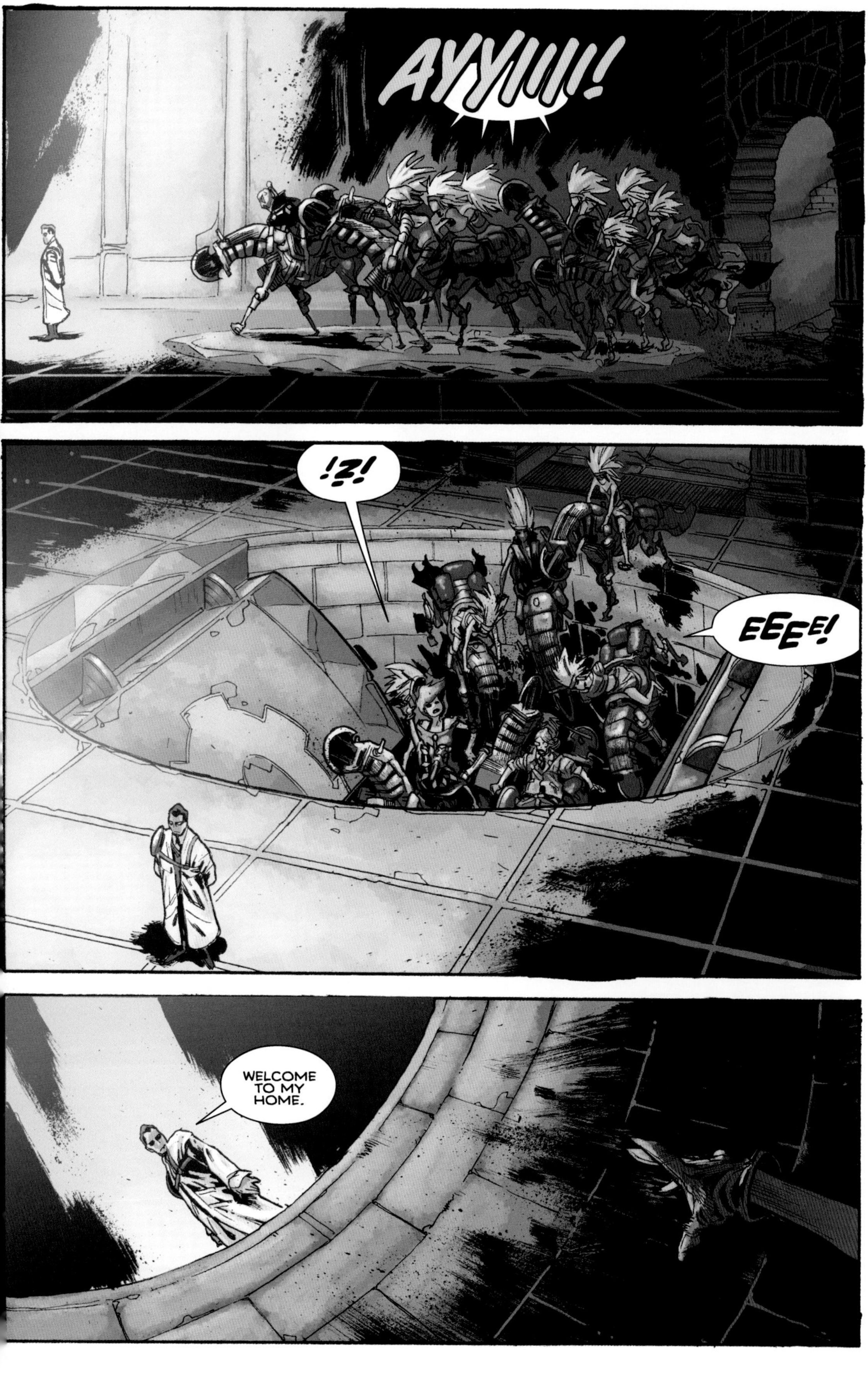
AYYIIII!
!Z!
EEEE!
WELCOME TO MY HOME.

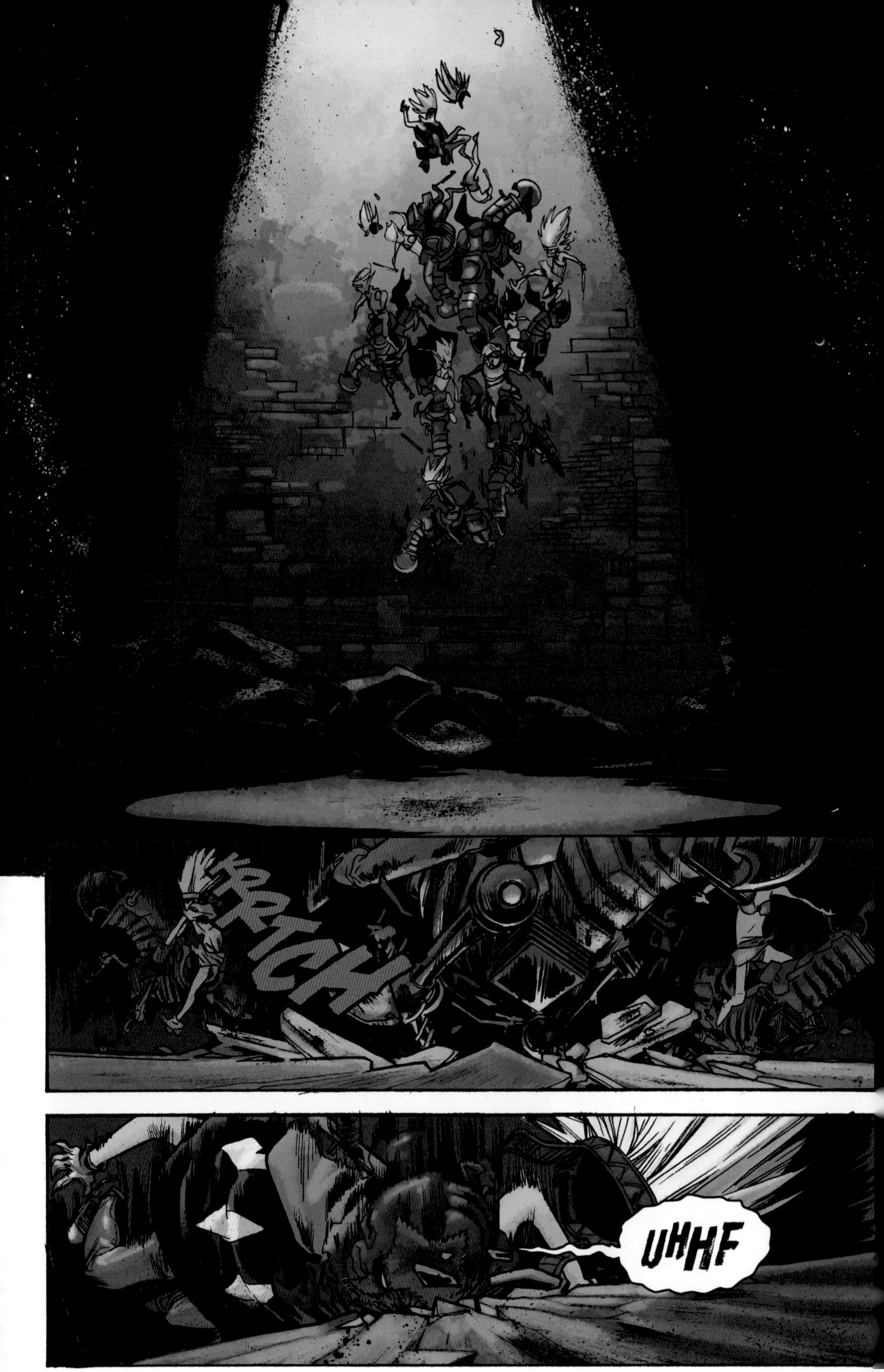
KRTCH
UHHF

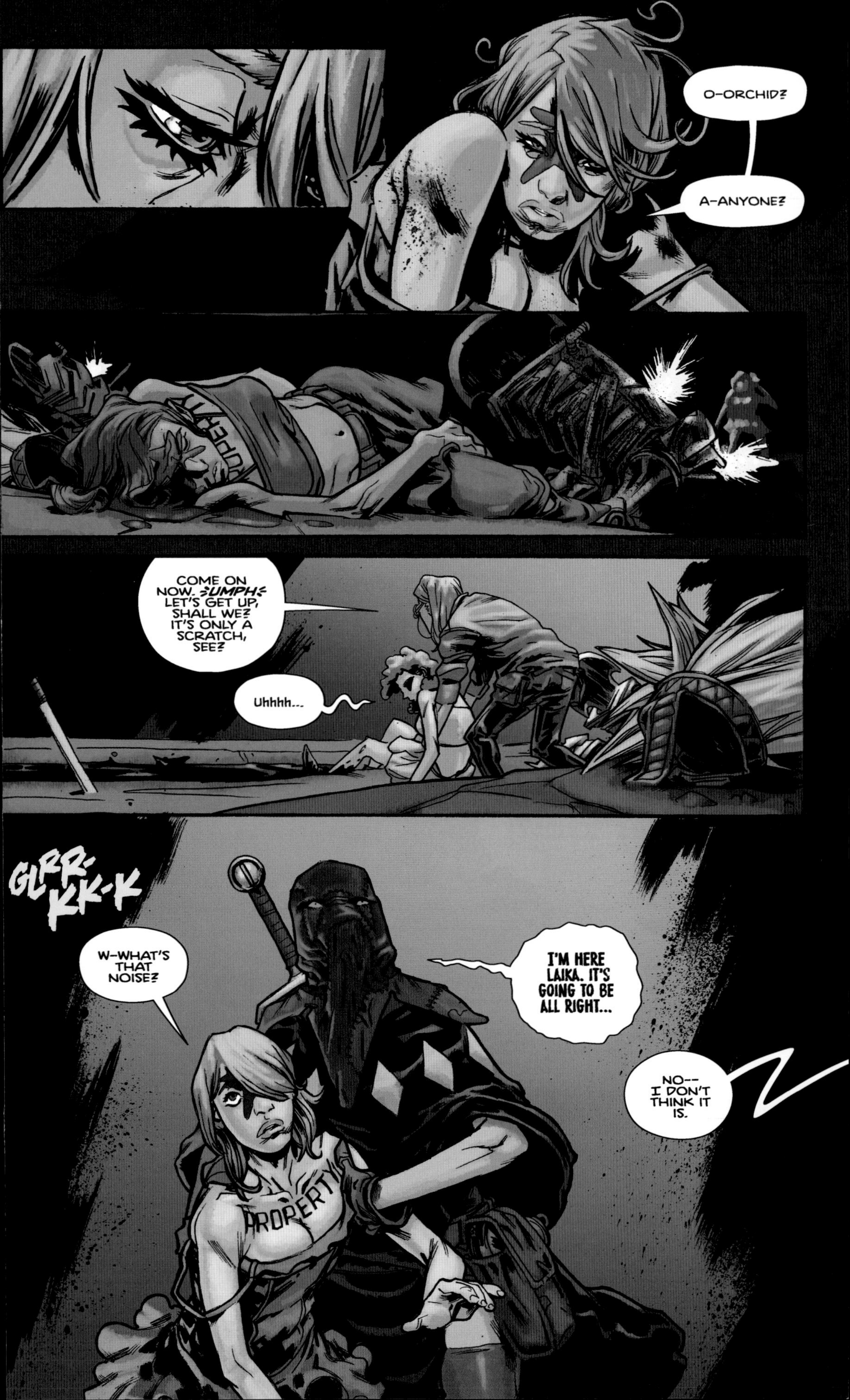
O-ORCHID?
A-ANYONE?
COME ON NOW. *UMPH* LET'S GET UP, SHALL WE? IT'S ONLY A SCRATCH, SEE?
Uhhhh...
GLRR-KK-K
W-WHAT'S THAT NOISE?
I'M HERE LAIKA. IT'S GOING TO BE ALL RIGHT...
NO-- I DON'T THINK IT IS.

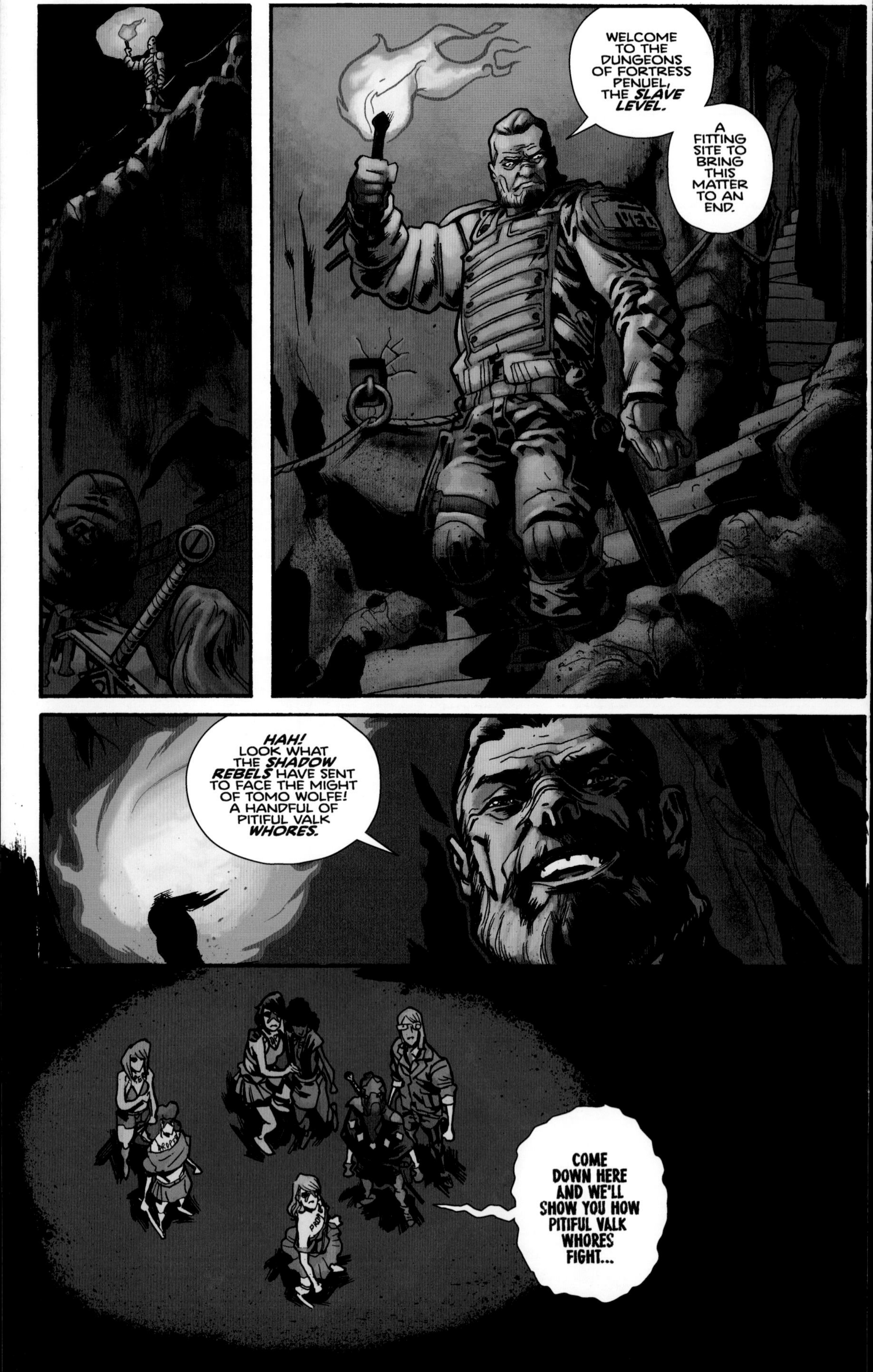
WELCOME TO THE DUNGEONS OF FORTRESS PENUEL, THE SLAVE LEVEL.
A FITTING SITE TO BRING THIS MATTER TO AN END.
HAH! LOOK WHAT THE SHADOW REBELS HAVE SENT TO FACE THE MIGHT OF TOMO WOLFE! A HANDFUL OF PITIFUL VALK WHORES.
COME DOWN HERE AND WE'LL SHOW YOU HOW PITIFUL VALK WHORES FIGHT...

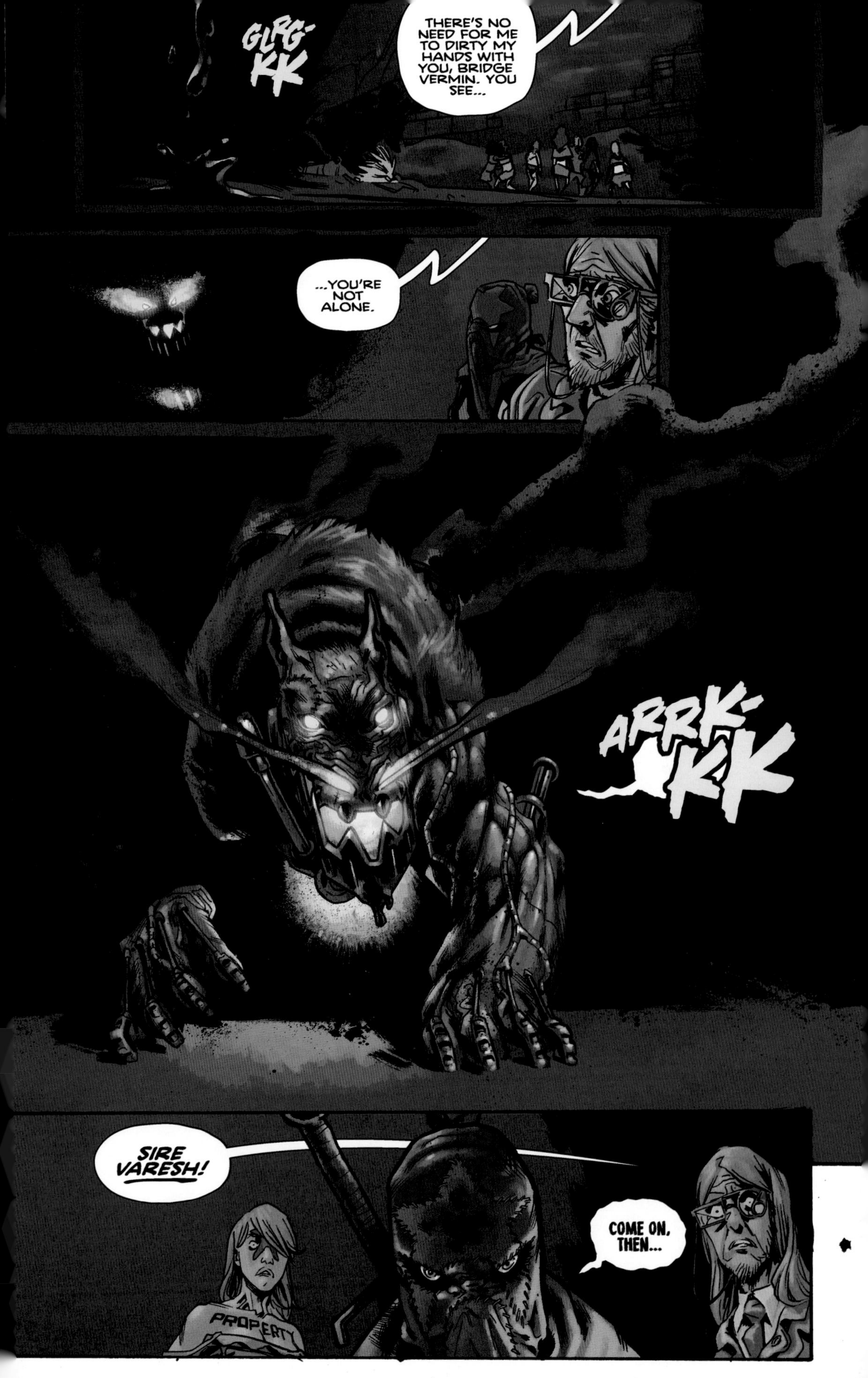
GLRG-KK
THERE'S NO NEED FOR ME TO DIRTY MY HANDS WITH YOU, BRIDGE VERMIN. YOU SEE...
...YOU'RE NOT ALONE.
ARRK-KK
SIRE VARESH!
COME ON, THEN...
PROPERTY

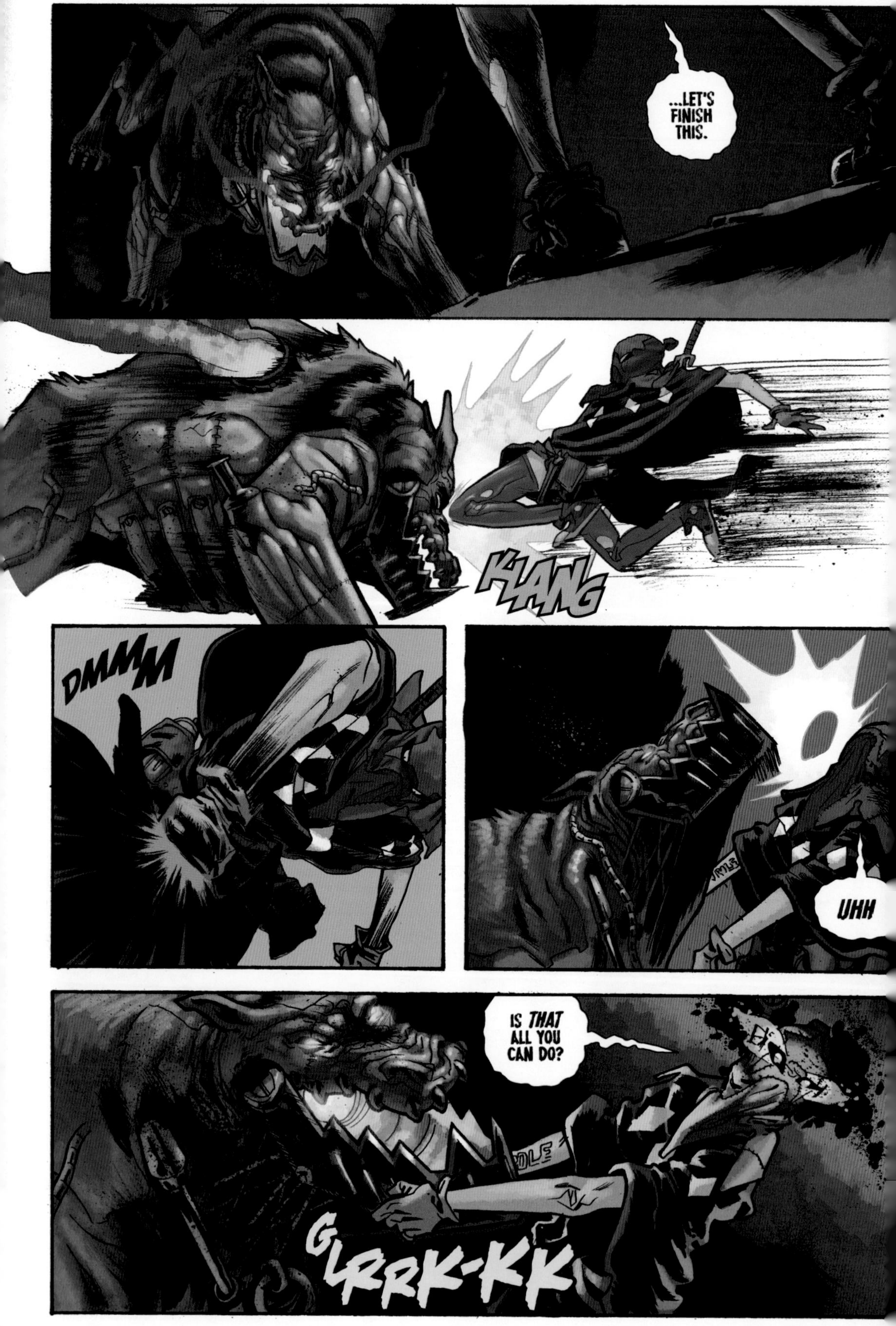
...LET'S FINISH THIS.
KLANG
DMMM
UHH
IS THAT ALL YOU CAN DO?
GLRRK-KK

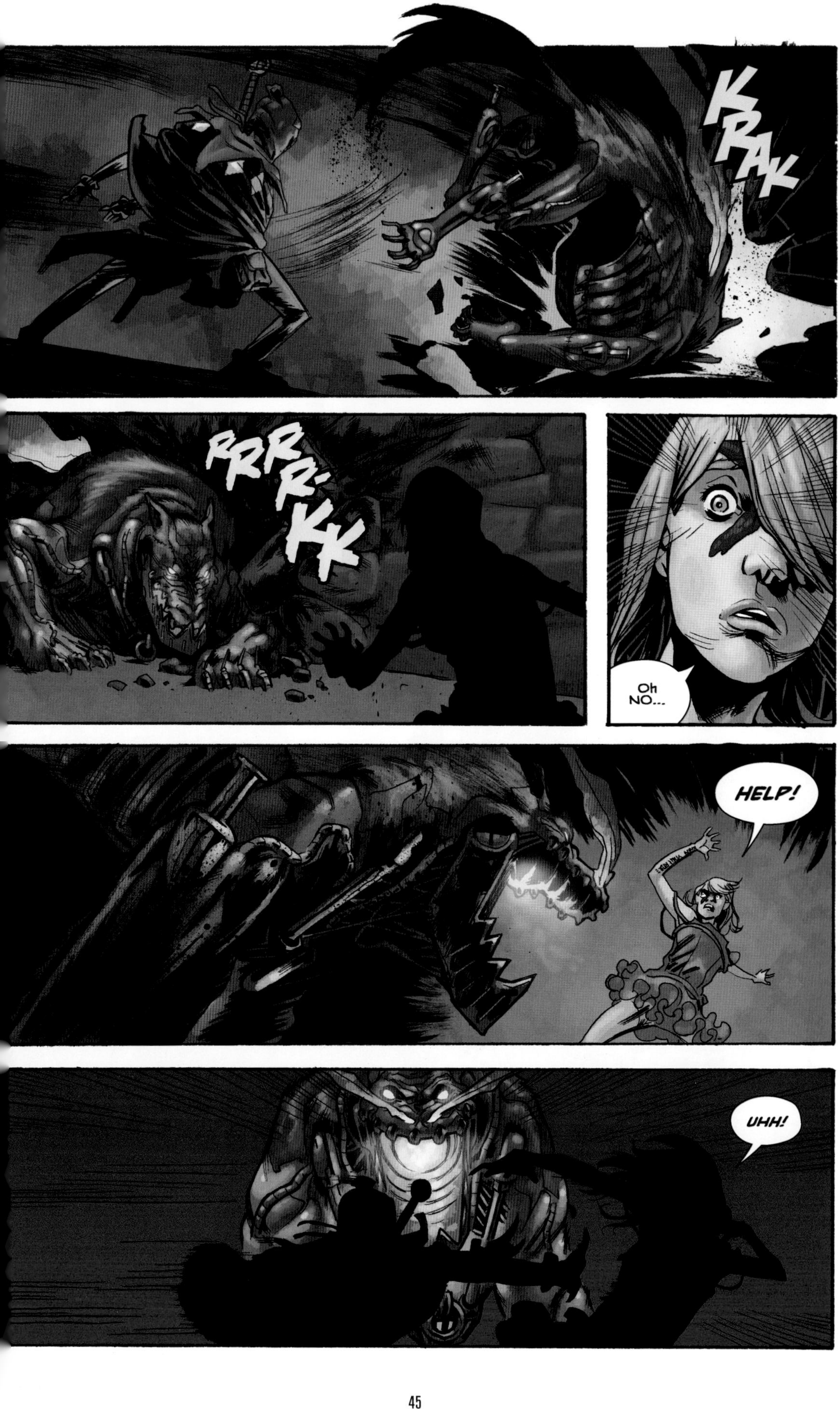
KRAK
RRRR-KK
Oh NO...
HELP!
UHH!

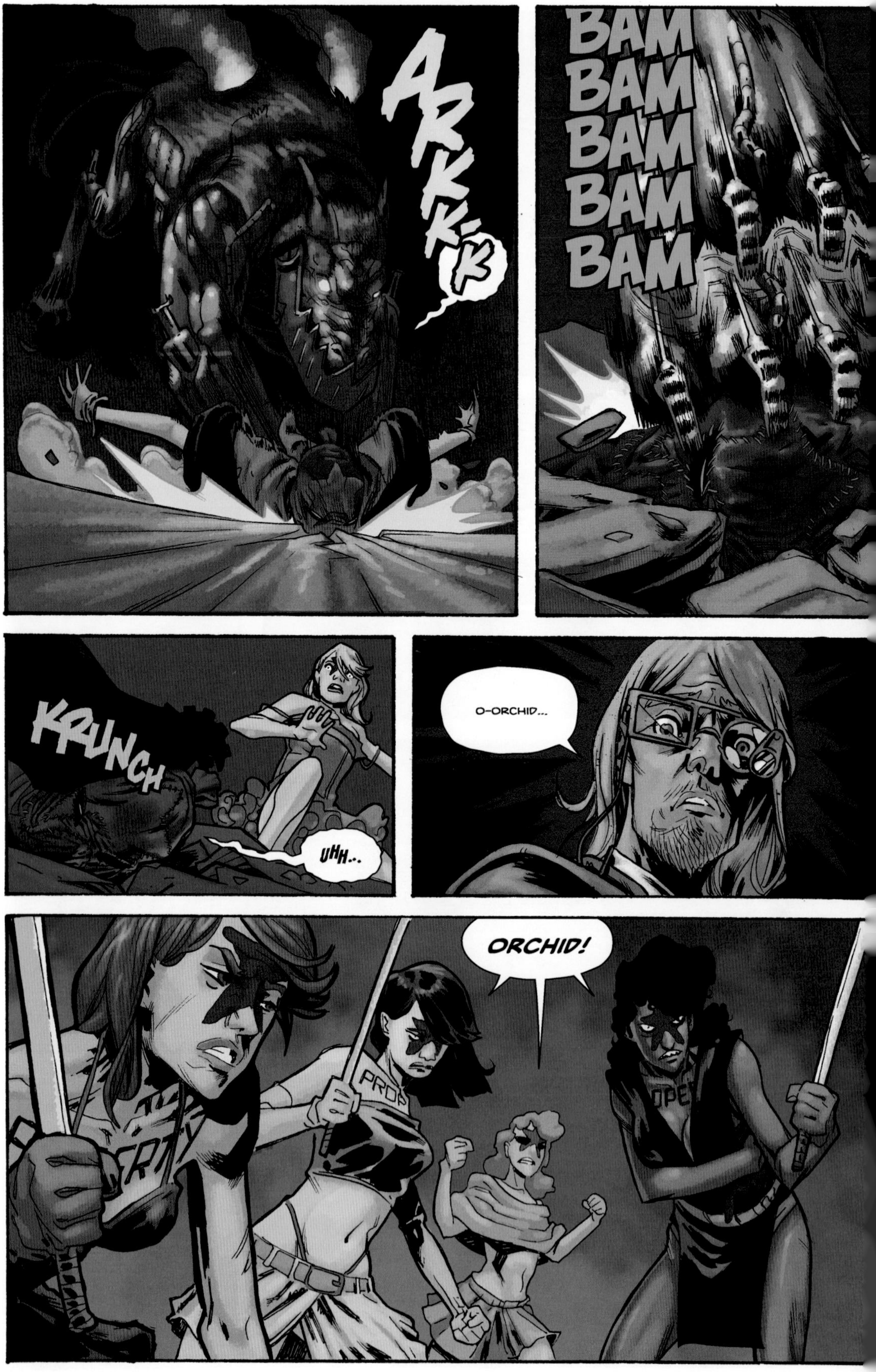
ARKKKK
BAM
BAM
BAM
BAM
BAM
KRUNCH
UHH...
O-ORCHID...
ORCHID!

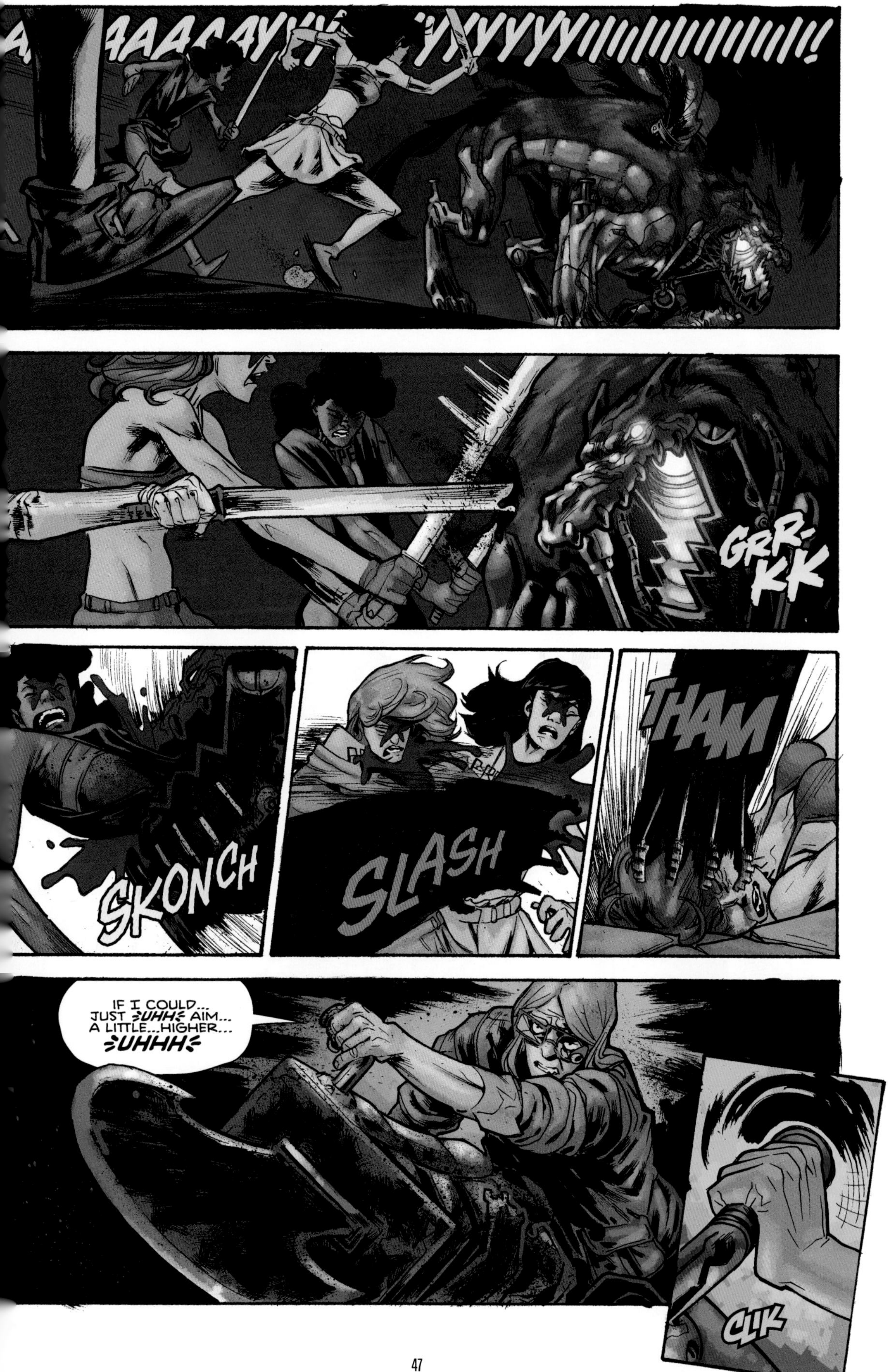
AAAAAAAYYYYYYYYYYIIIIIIIIIIIIIIII!!
GRR-KK
SKONCH
SLASH
THAM
IF I COULD... JUST ~UHH~ AIM... A LITTLE...HIGHER... ~UHHH~
CLIK

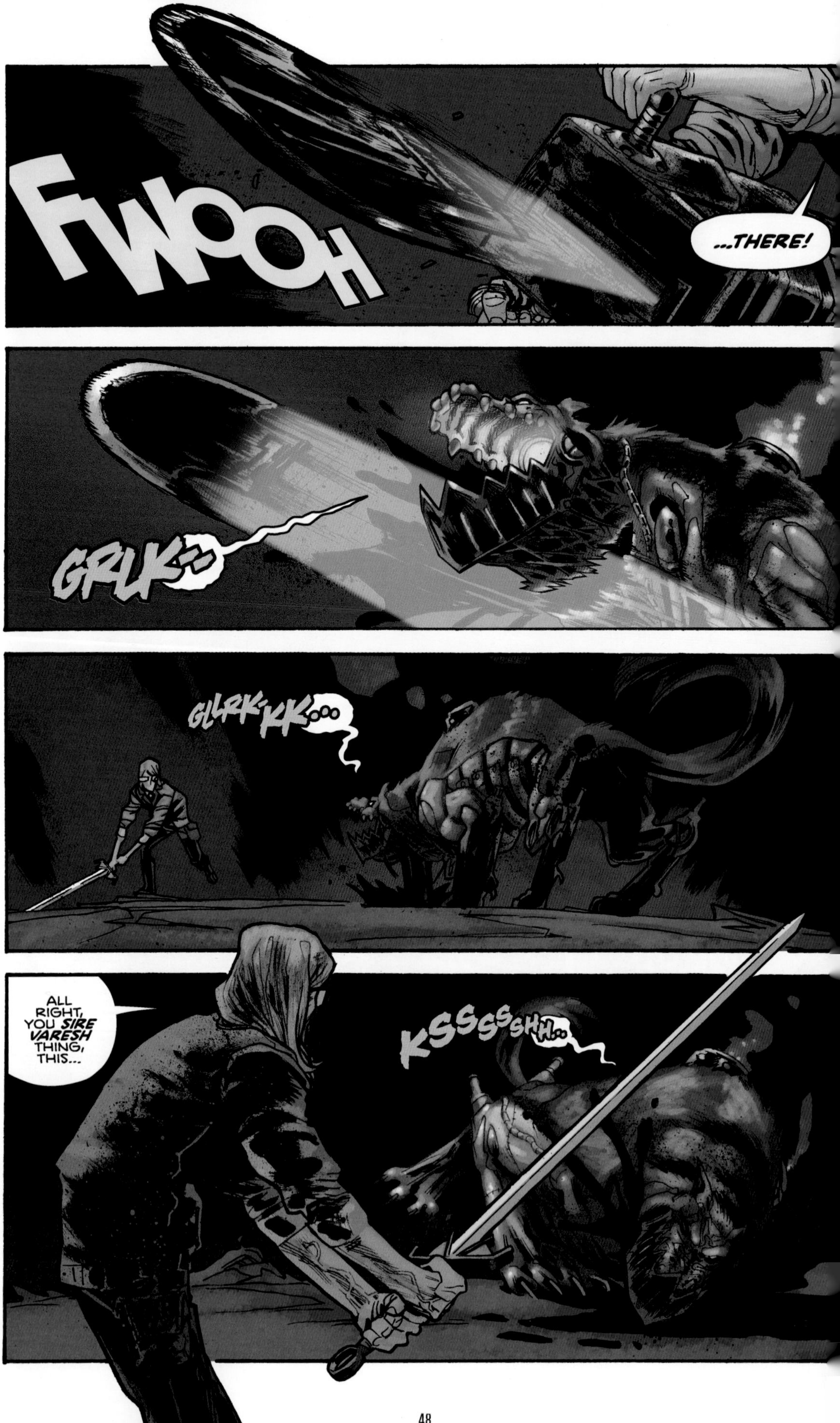
FWOOH
...THERE!
GRUK..
GLURK-KK...
ALL RIGHT, YOU SIRE VARESH THING, THIS...
KSSSSSHH..

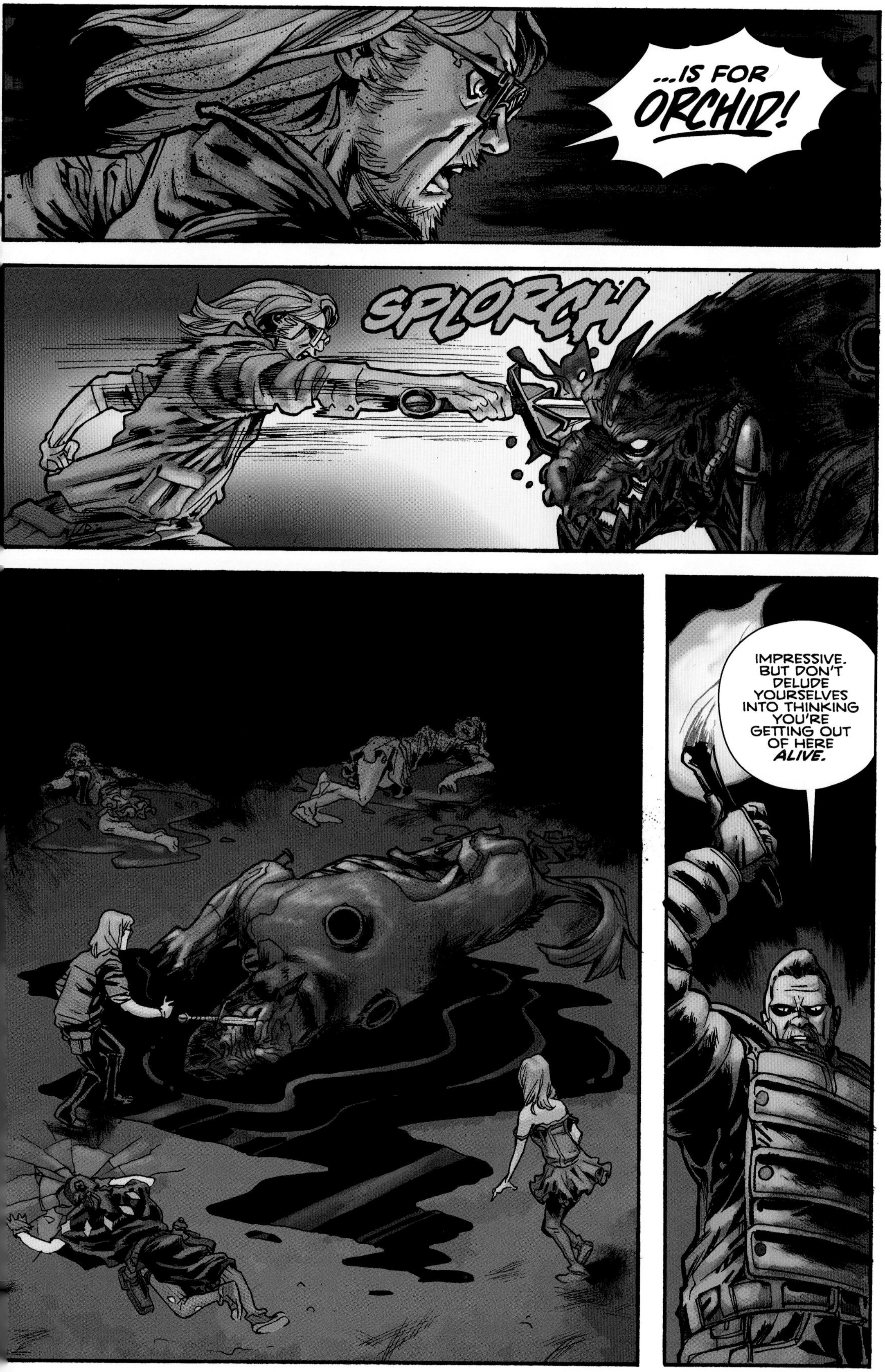

...IS FOR ORCHID!
SPLORCH
IMPRESSIVE. BUT DON'T DELUDE YOURSELVES INTO THINKING YOU'RE GETTING OUT OF HERE ALIVE.

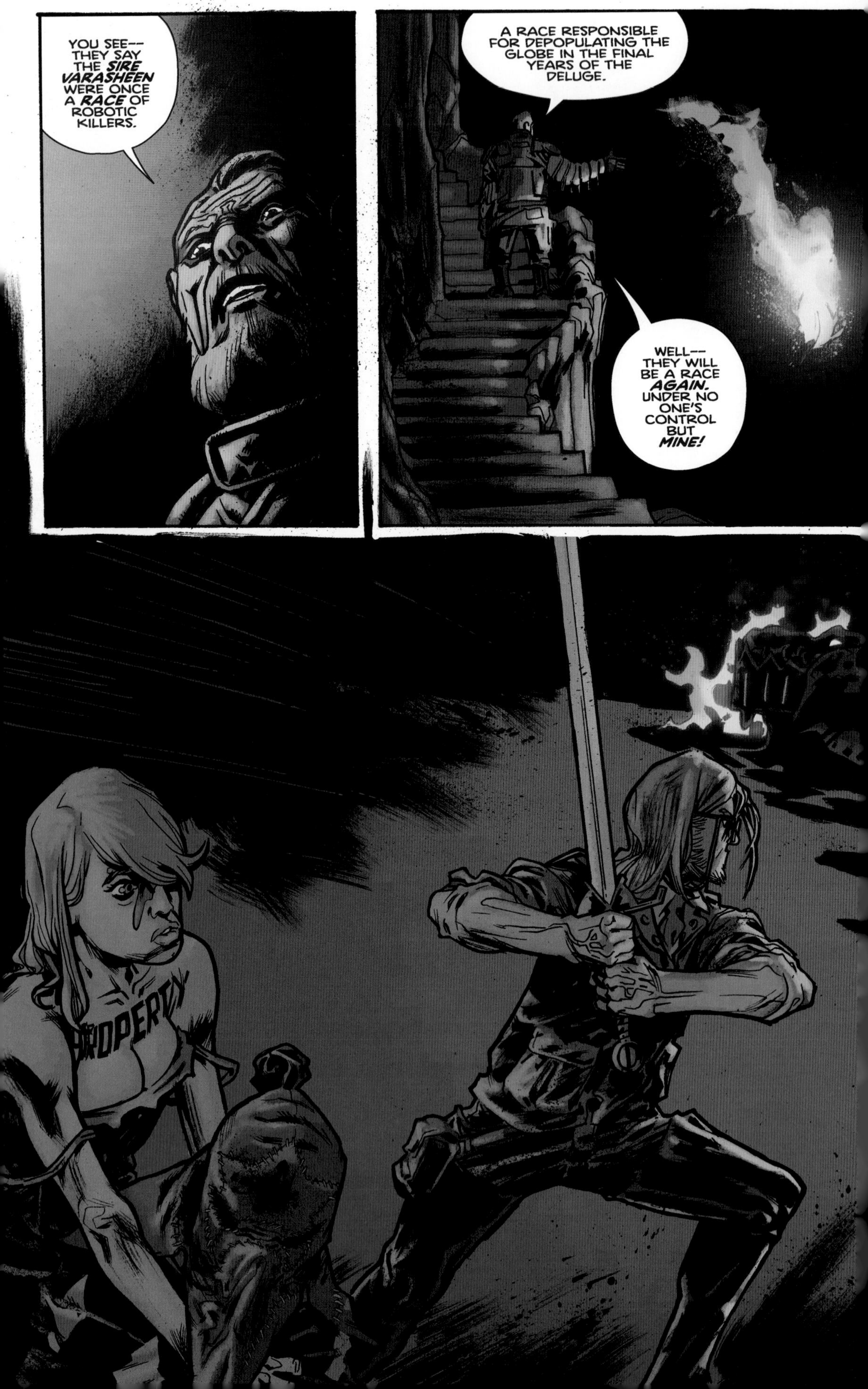
YOU SEE-- THEY SAY THE SIRE VARASHEEN WERE ONCE A RACE OF ROBOTIC KILLERS.
A RACE RESPONSIBLE FOR DEPOPULATING THE GLOBE IN THE FINAL YEARS OF THE DELUGE.
WELL-- THEY WILL BE A RACE AGAIN. UNDER NO ONE'S CONTROL BUT MINE!
PROPERTY

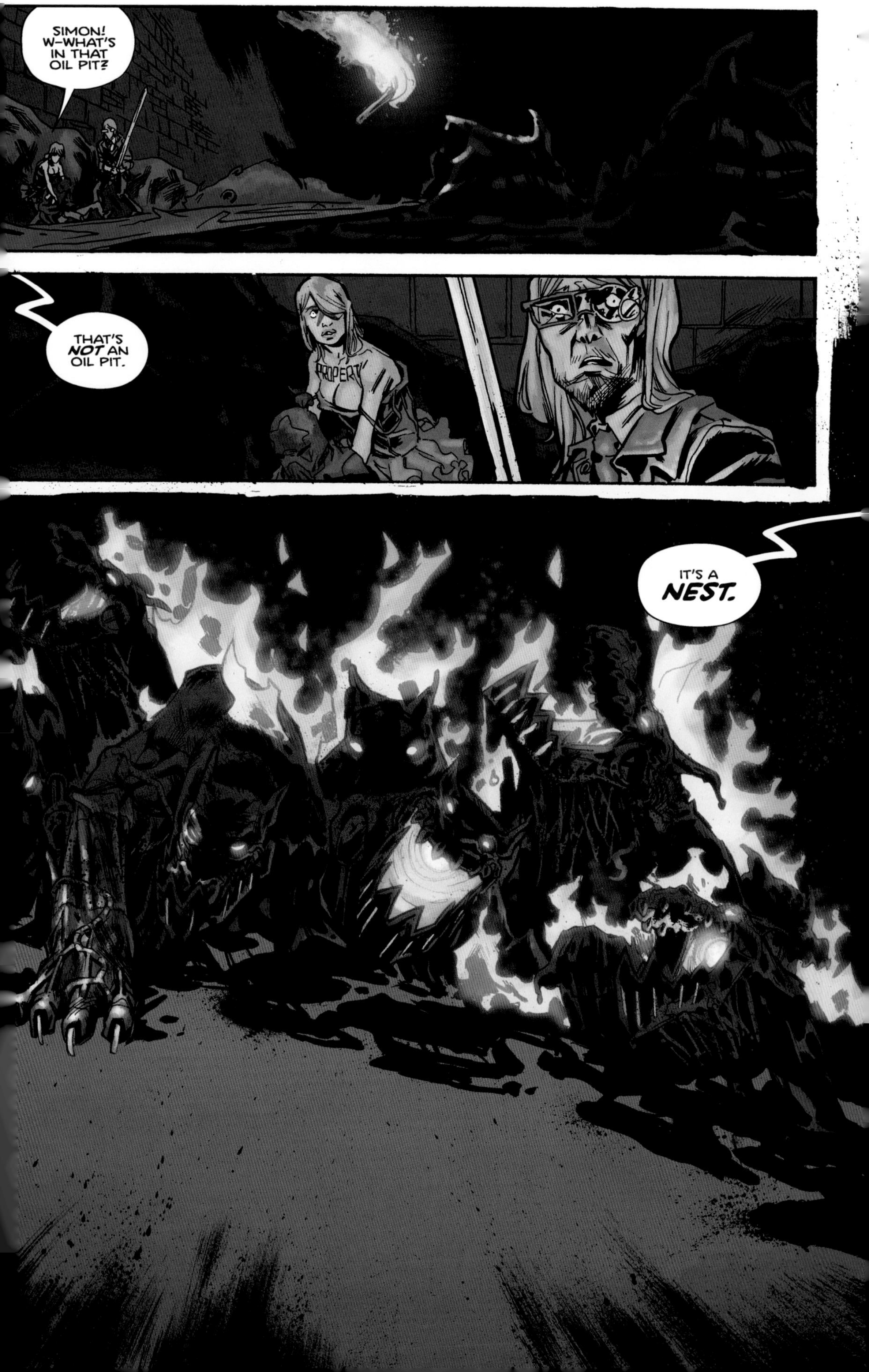
SIMON! W-WHAT'S IN THAT OIL PIT?
THAT'S NOT AN OIL PIT.
IT'S A NEST.

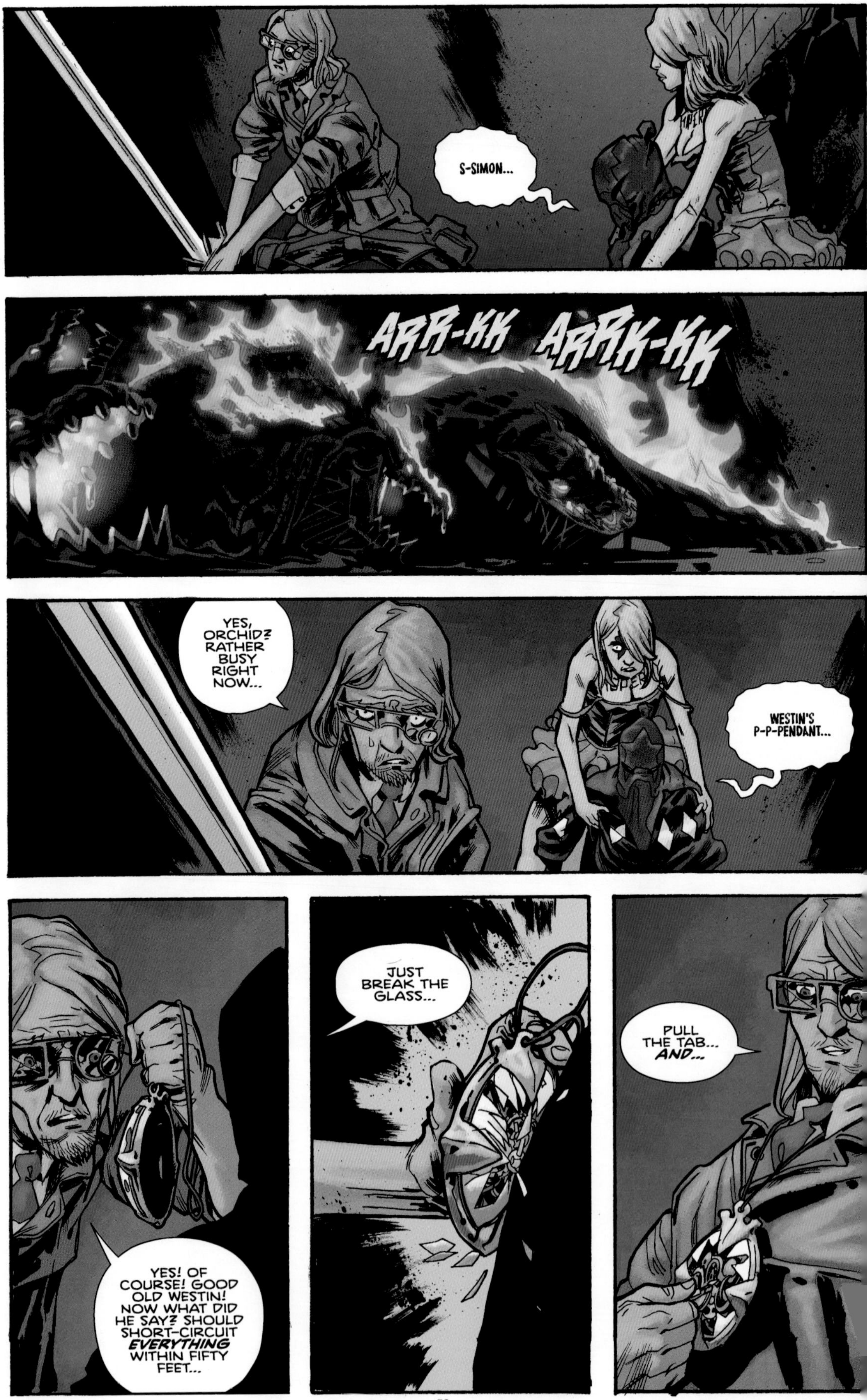
S-SIMON...
ARR-KK ARRK-KK
YES, ORCHID? RATHER BUSY RIGHT NOW...
WESTIN'S P-P-PENDANT...
YES! OF COURSE! GOOD OLD WESTIN! NOW WHAT DID HE SAY? SHOULD SHORT-CIRCUIT EVERYTHING WITHIN FIFTY FEET...
JUST BREAK THE GLASS...
PULL THE TAB... AND...

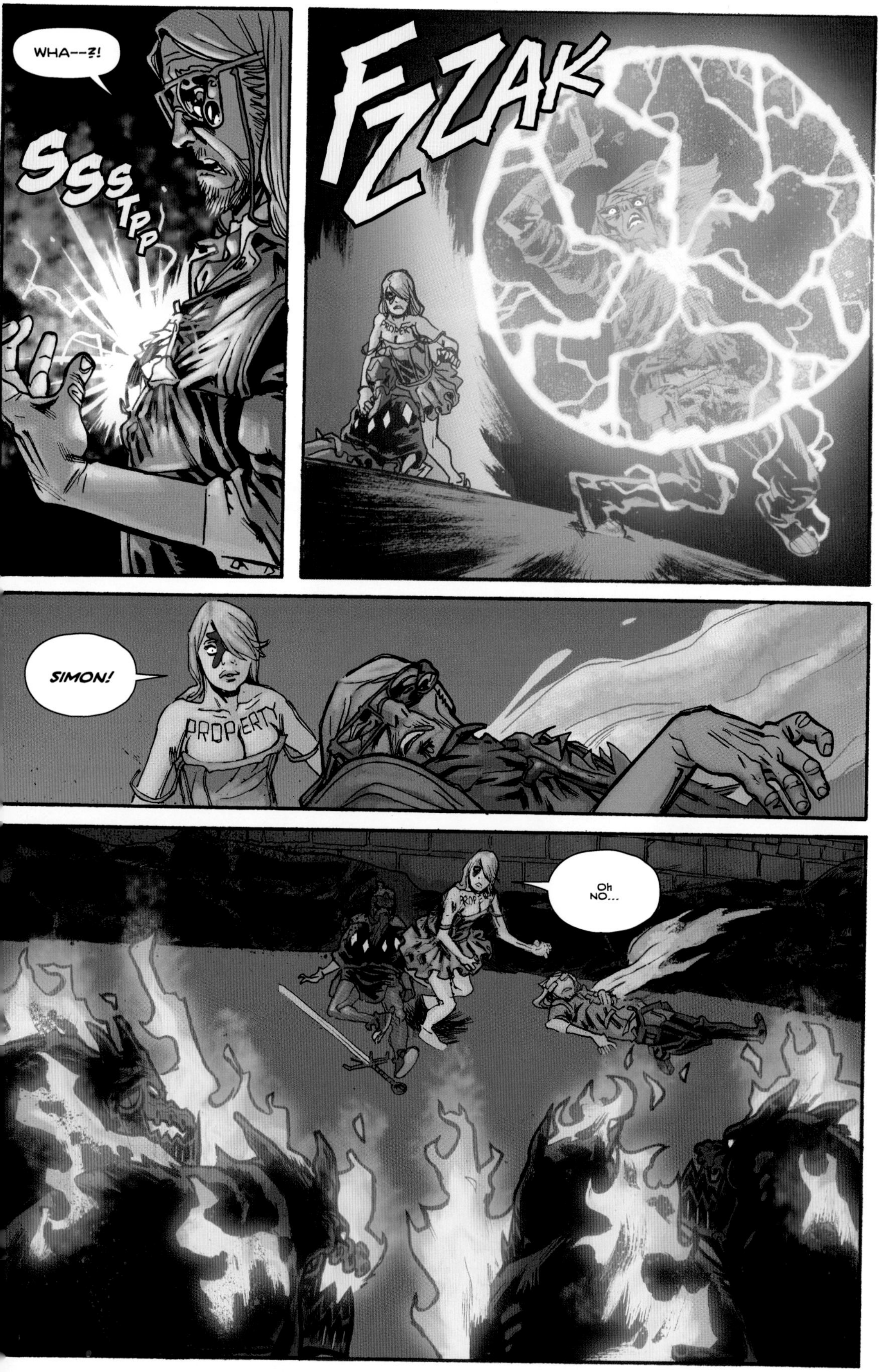

WHA--?!
SSSTPP
FZZAK
PROPERT
SIMON!
PROPERT
Oh
NO...

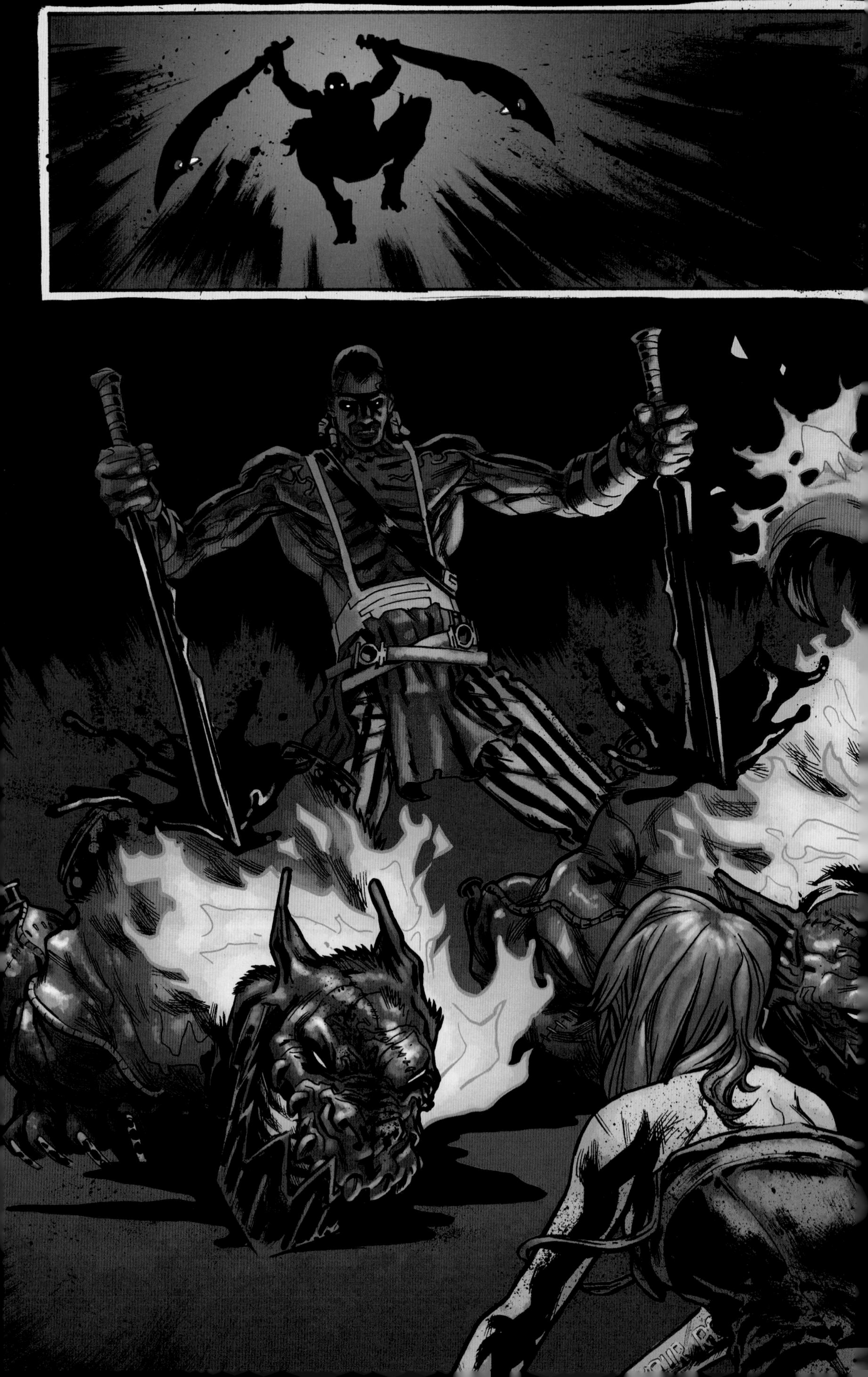

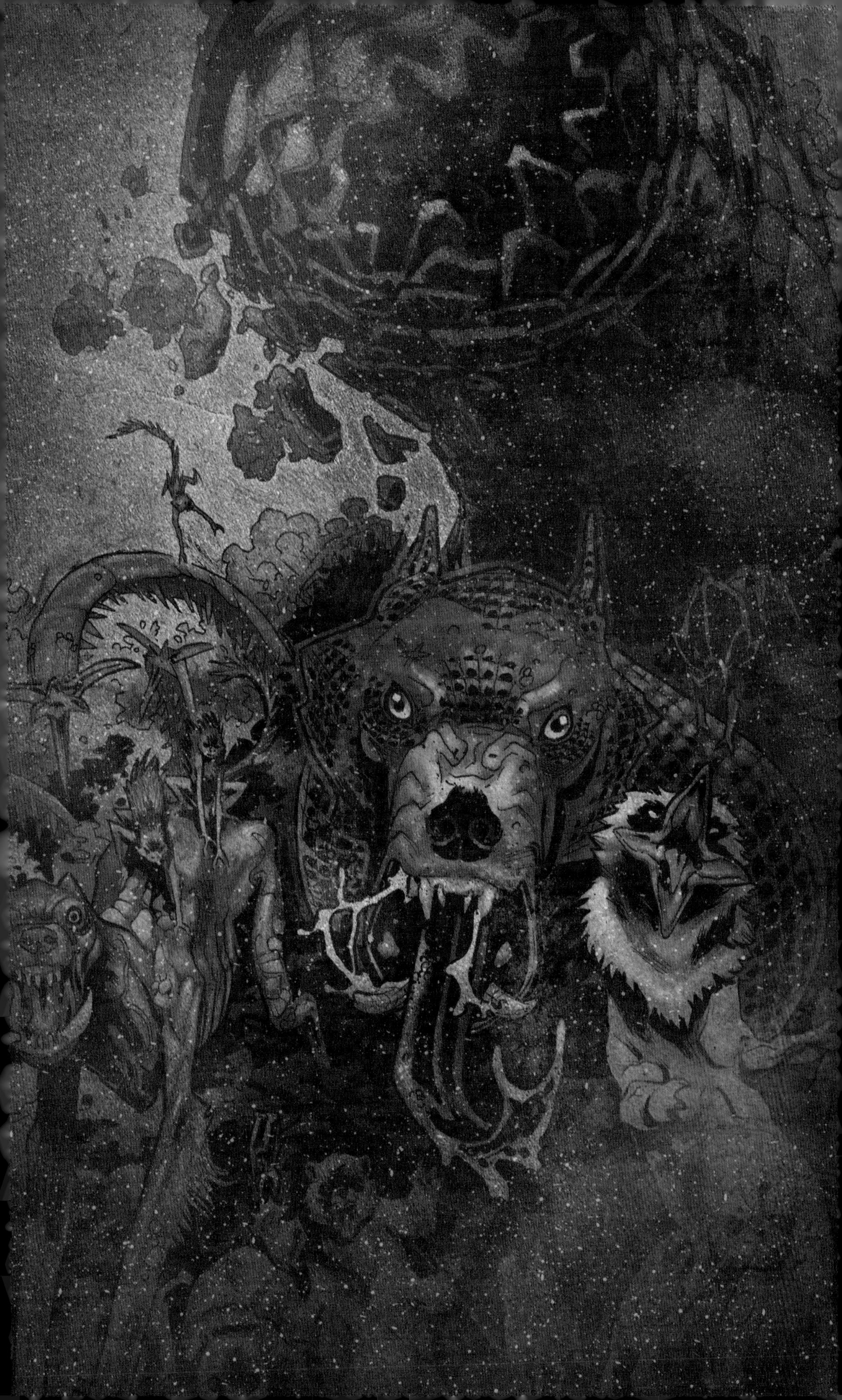

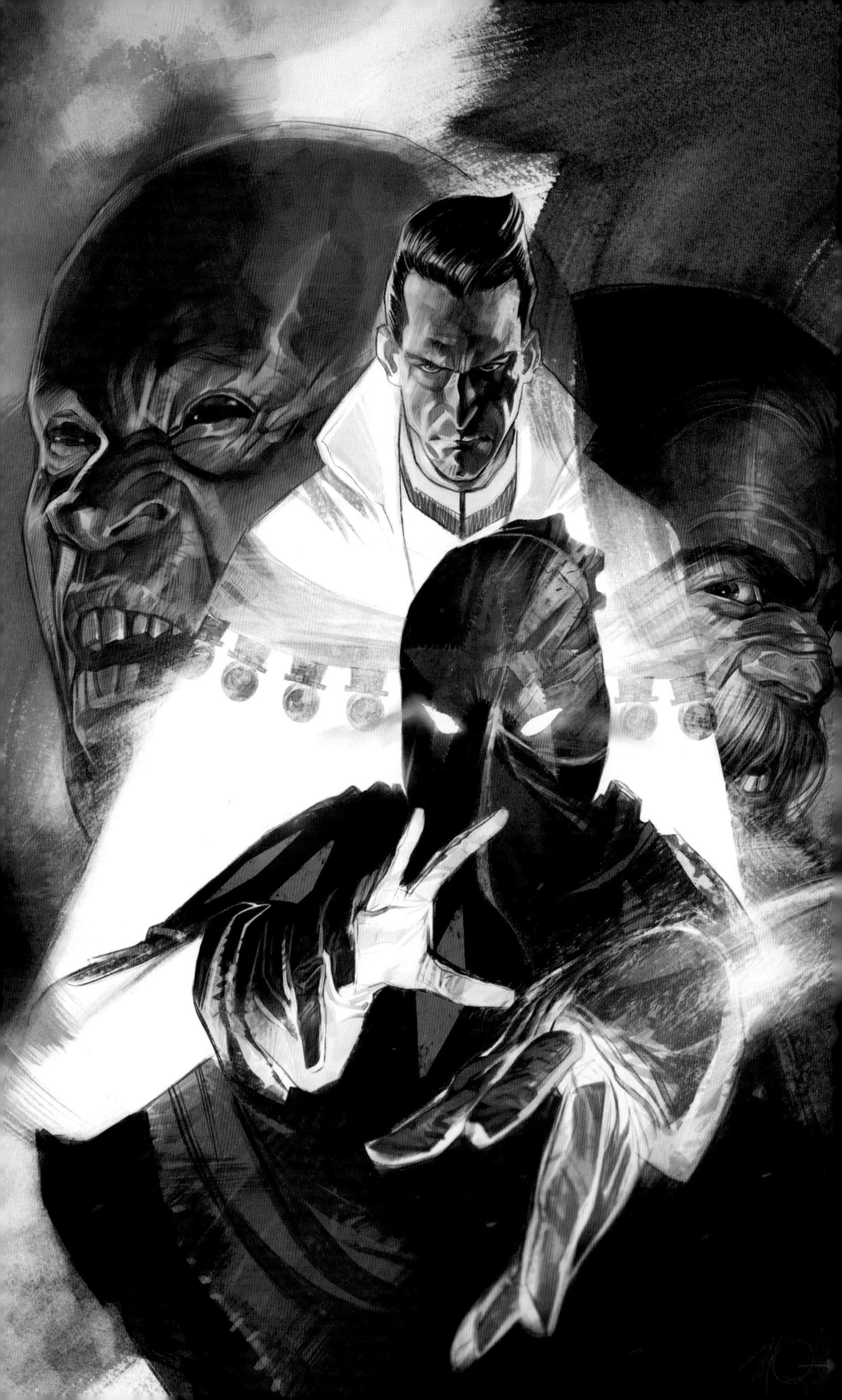

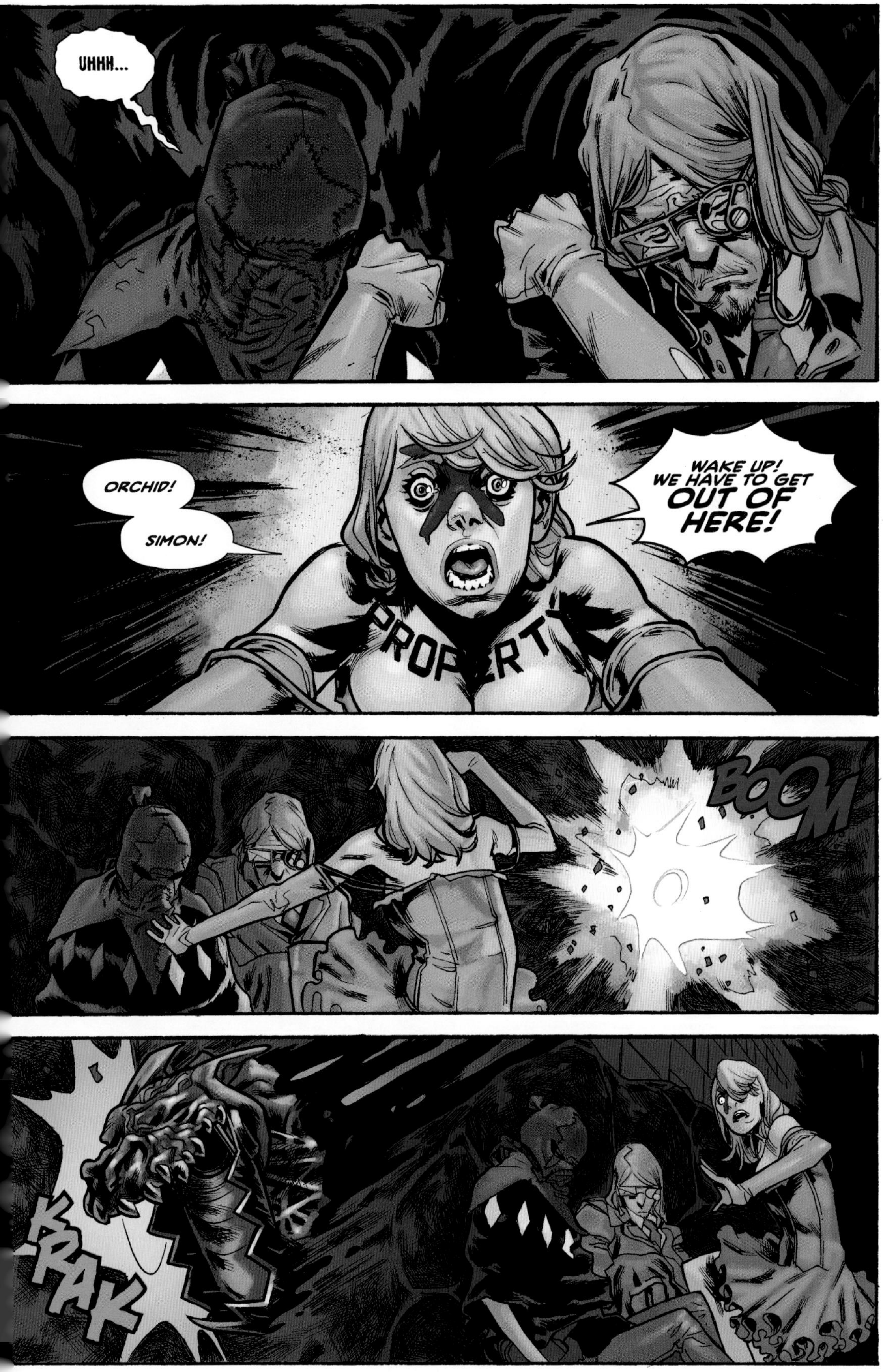
UHHH...
ORCHID!
SIMON!
WAKE UP! WE HAVE TO GET OUT OF HERE!
PROPERTY
BOOM
KRAK

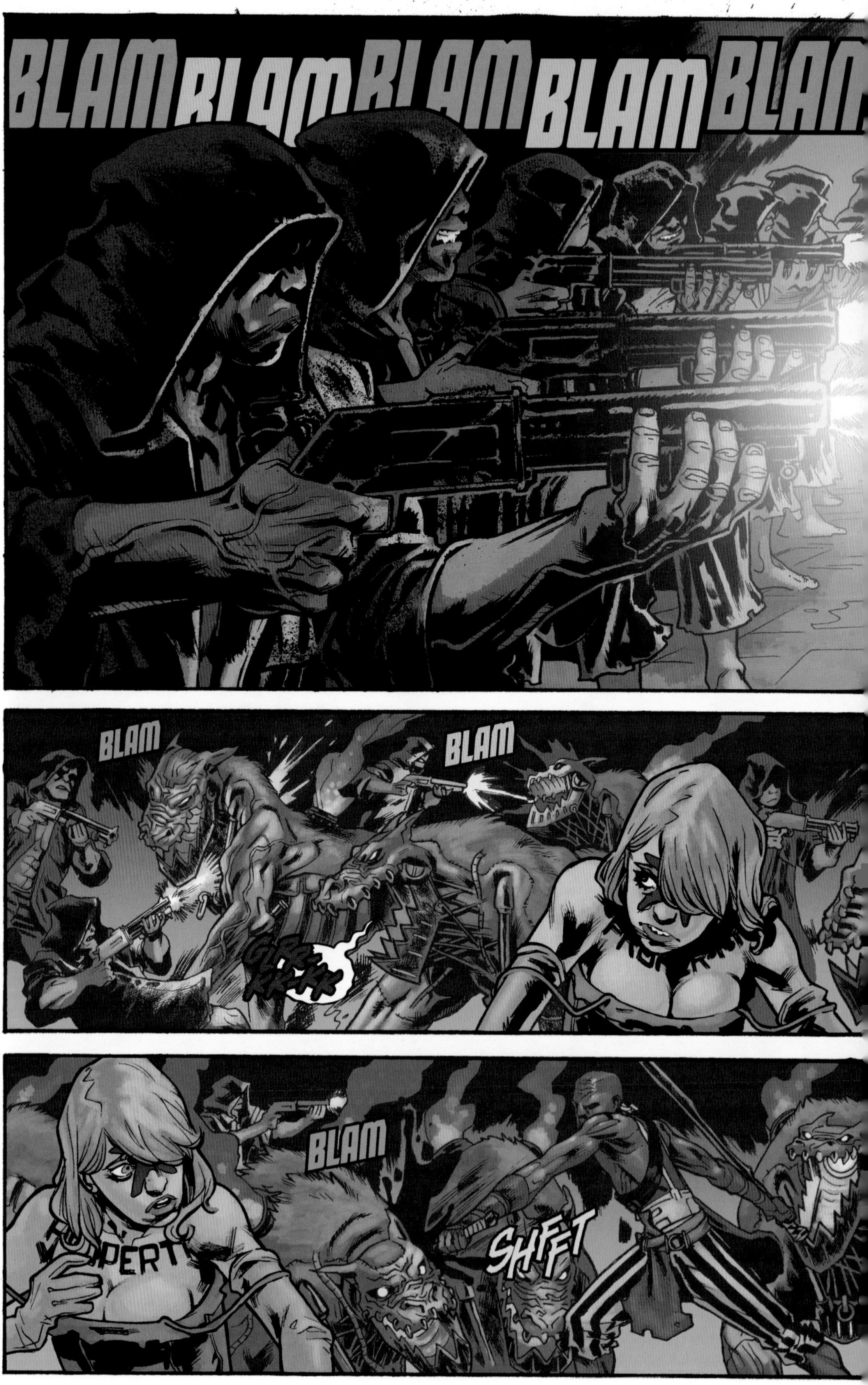
BLAM BLAM BLAM BLAM BLAM
BLAM
BLAM
BLAM
SHFFT

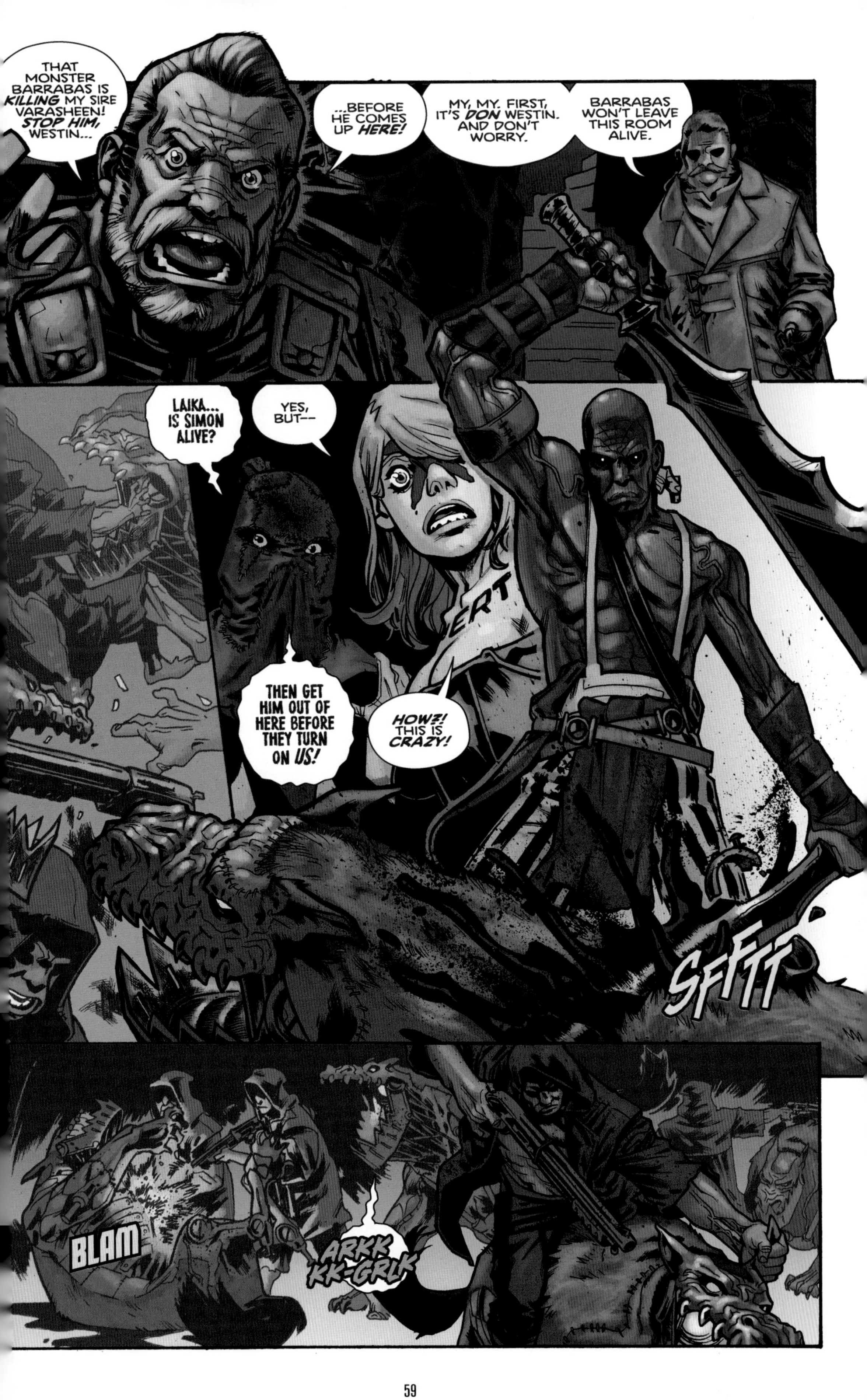

THAT MONSTER BARRABAS IS KILLING MY SIRE VARASHEEN! STOP HIM, WESTIN...
...BEFORE HE COMES UP HERE!
MY, MY. FIRST, IT'S DON WESTIN. AND DON'T WORRY.
BARRABAS WON'T LEAVE THIS ROOM ALIVE.
LAIKA... IS SIMON ALIVE?
YES, BUT--
THEN GET HIM OUT OF HERE BEFORE THEY TURN ON US!
HOW?! THIS IS CRAZY!
SFFTT
BLAM
ARKK KK-GRLK

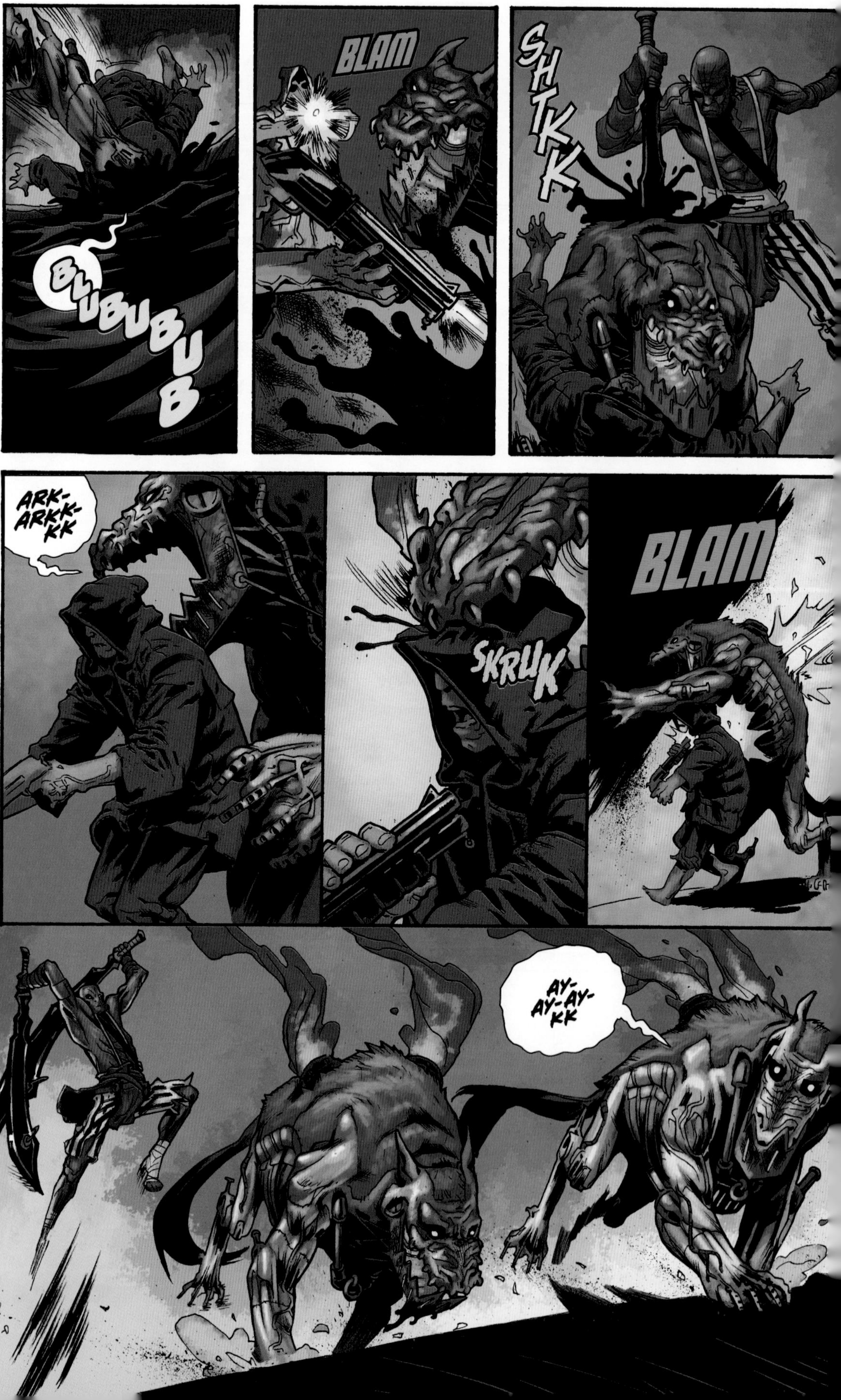
BLUBUBUBUB
BLAM
SHTKK
ARK-ARK-K-KK
SKRUK
BLAM
AY-AY-AY-KK

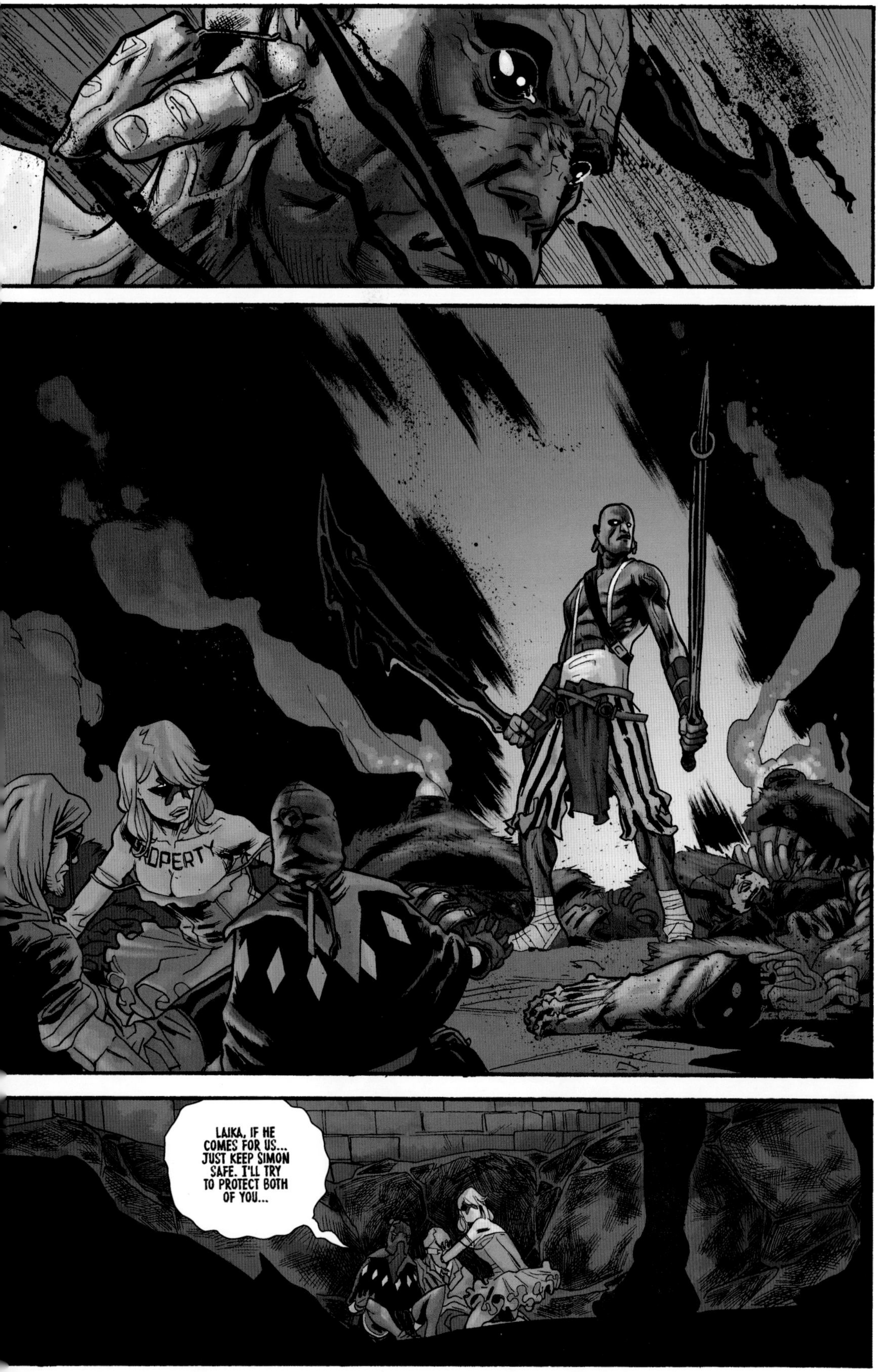
LAIKA, IF HE COMES FOR US... JUST KEEP SIMON SAFE. I'LL TRY TO PROTECT BOTH OF YOU...

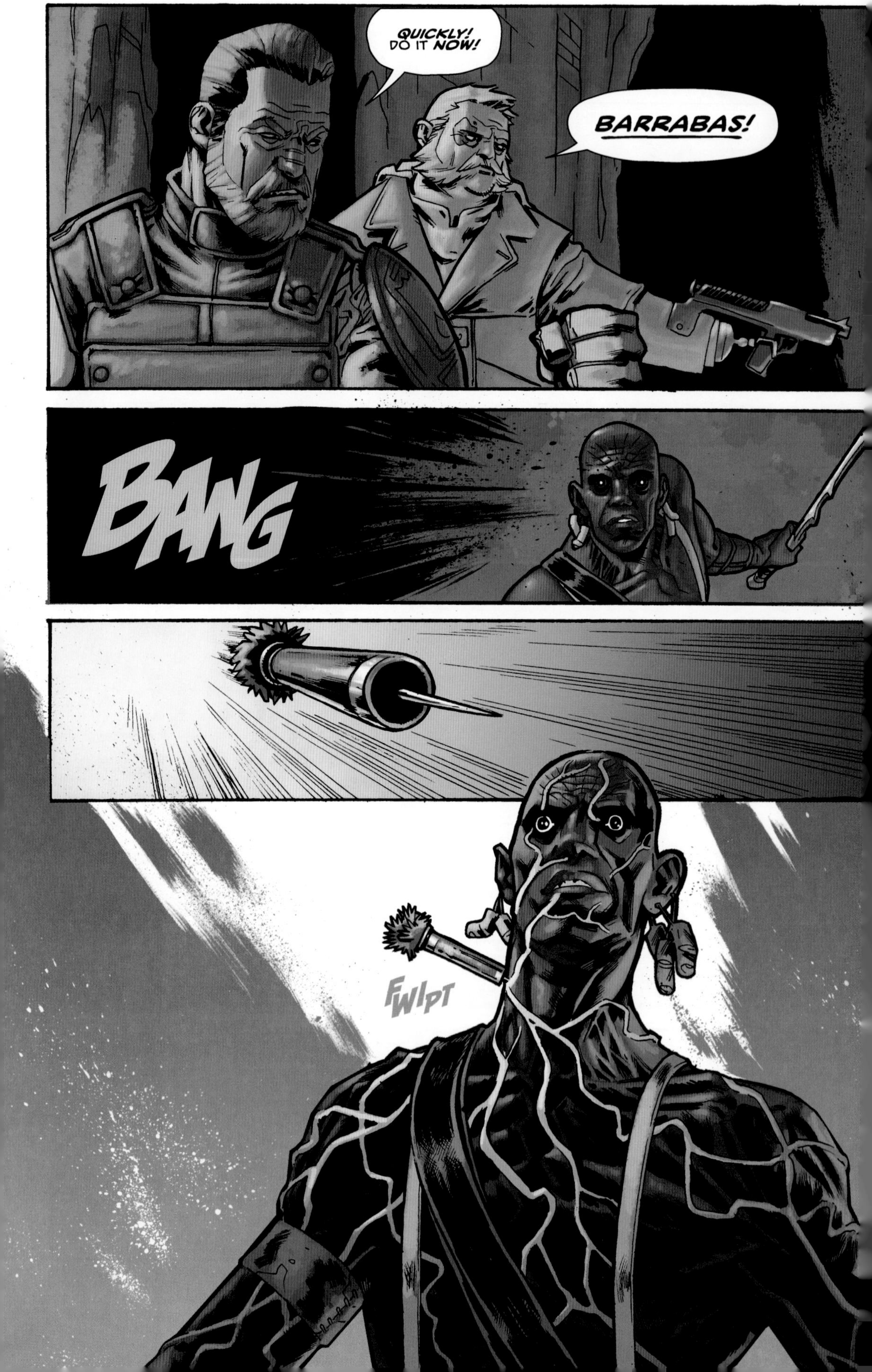
QUICKLY! DO IT NOW!
BARRABAS!
BANG
FWIPT

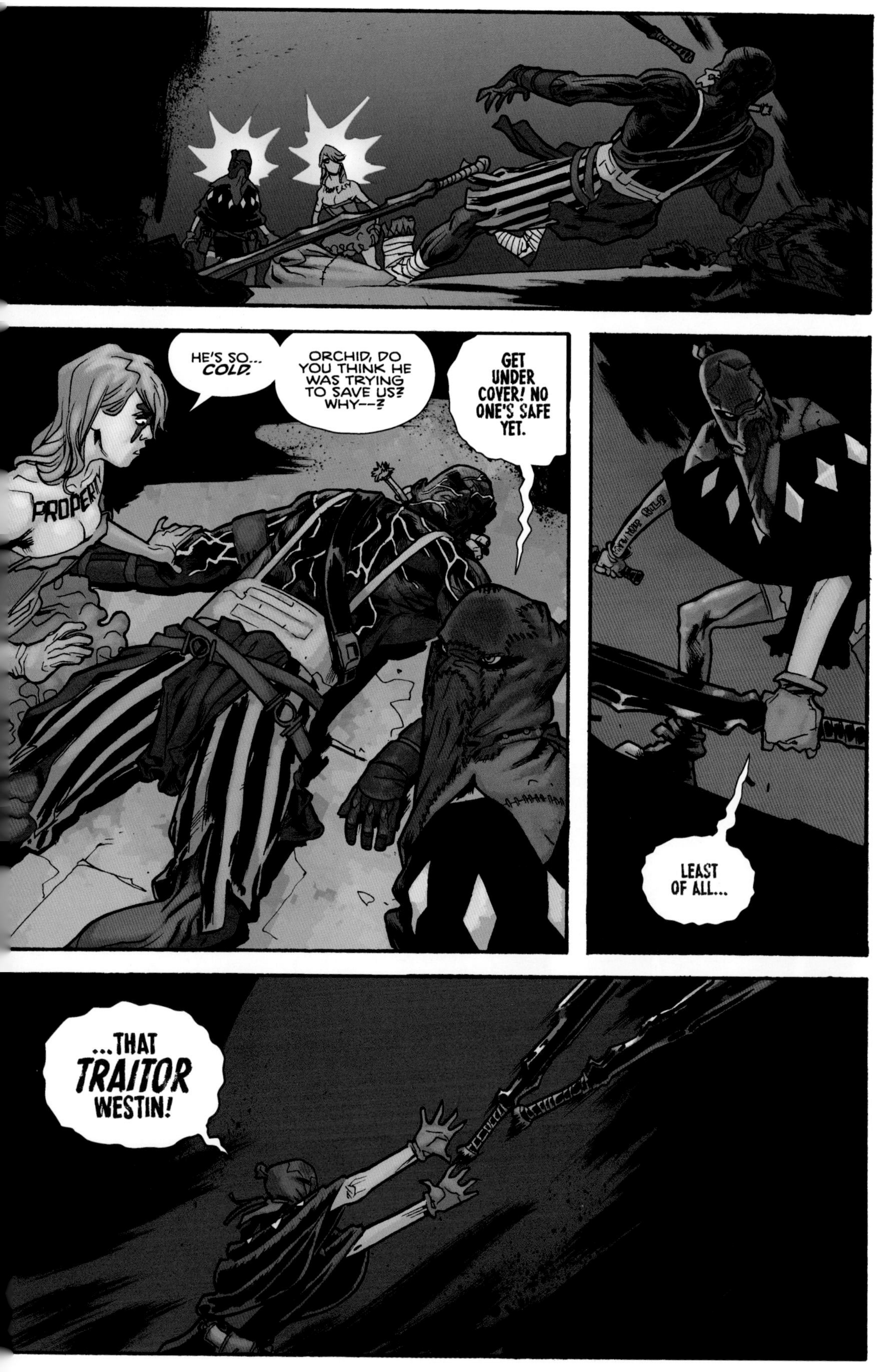
HE'S SO... COLD.
ORCHID, DO YOU THINK HE WAS TRYING TO SAVE US? WHY--?
GET UNDER COVER! NO ONE'S SAFE YET.
LEAST OF ALL...
...THAT TRAITOR WESTIN!

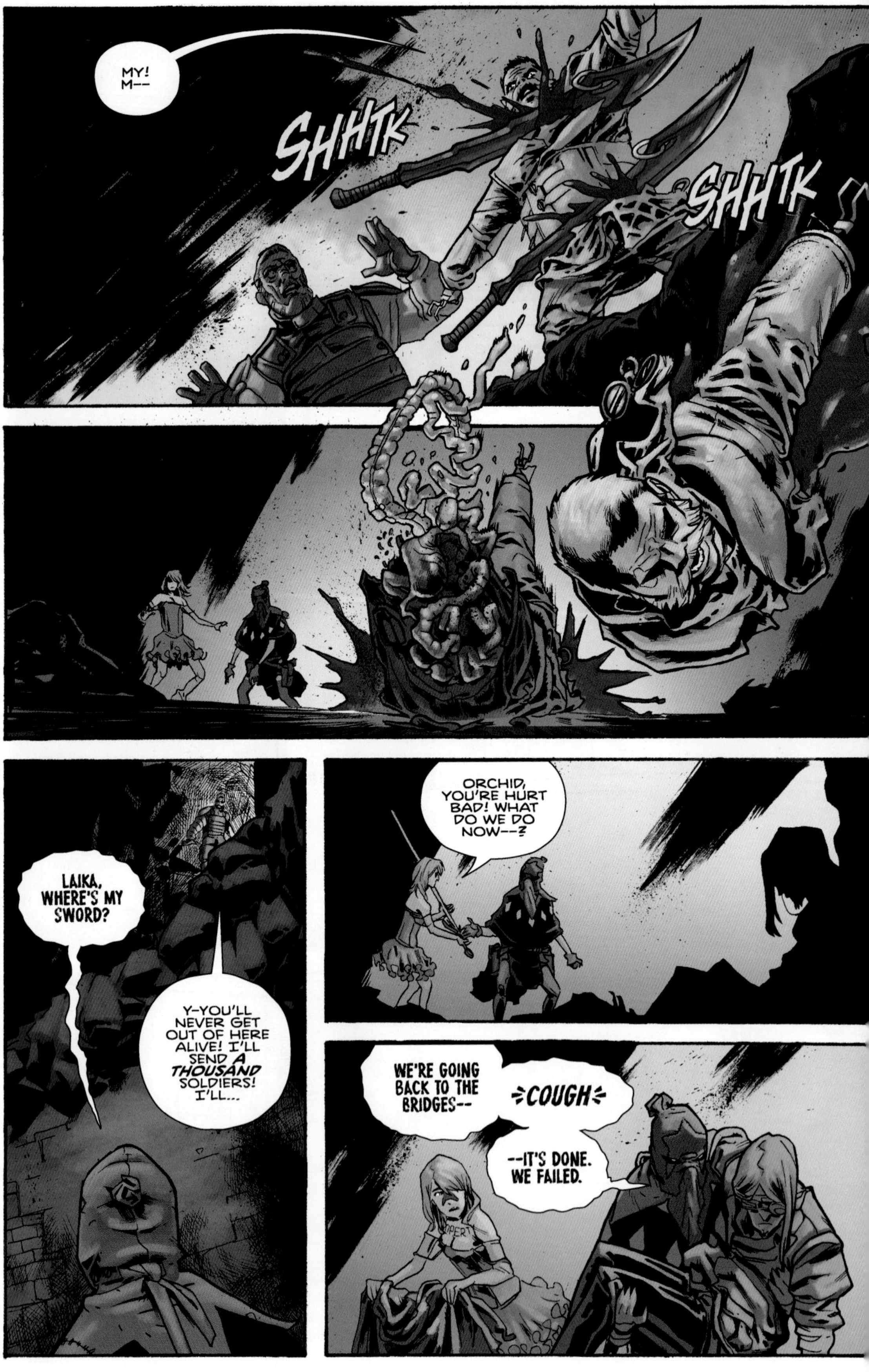
MY! M--
SHHTK
SHHTK
LAIKA, WHERE'S MY SWORD?
Y-YOU'LL NEVER GET OUT OF HERE ALIVE! I'LL SEND *A THOUSAND* SOLDIERS! I'LL...
ORCHID, YOU'RE HURT BAD! WHAT DO WE DO NOW--?
WE'RE GOING BACK TO THE BRIDGES--
COUGH
--IT'S DONE. WE FAILED.

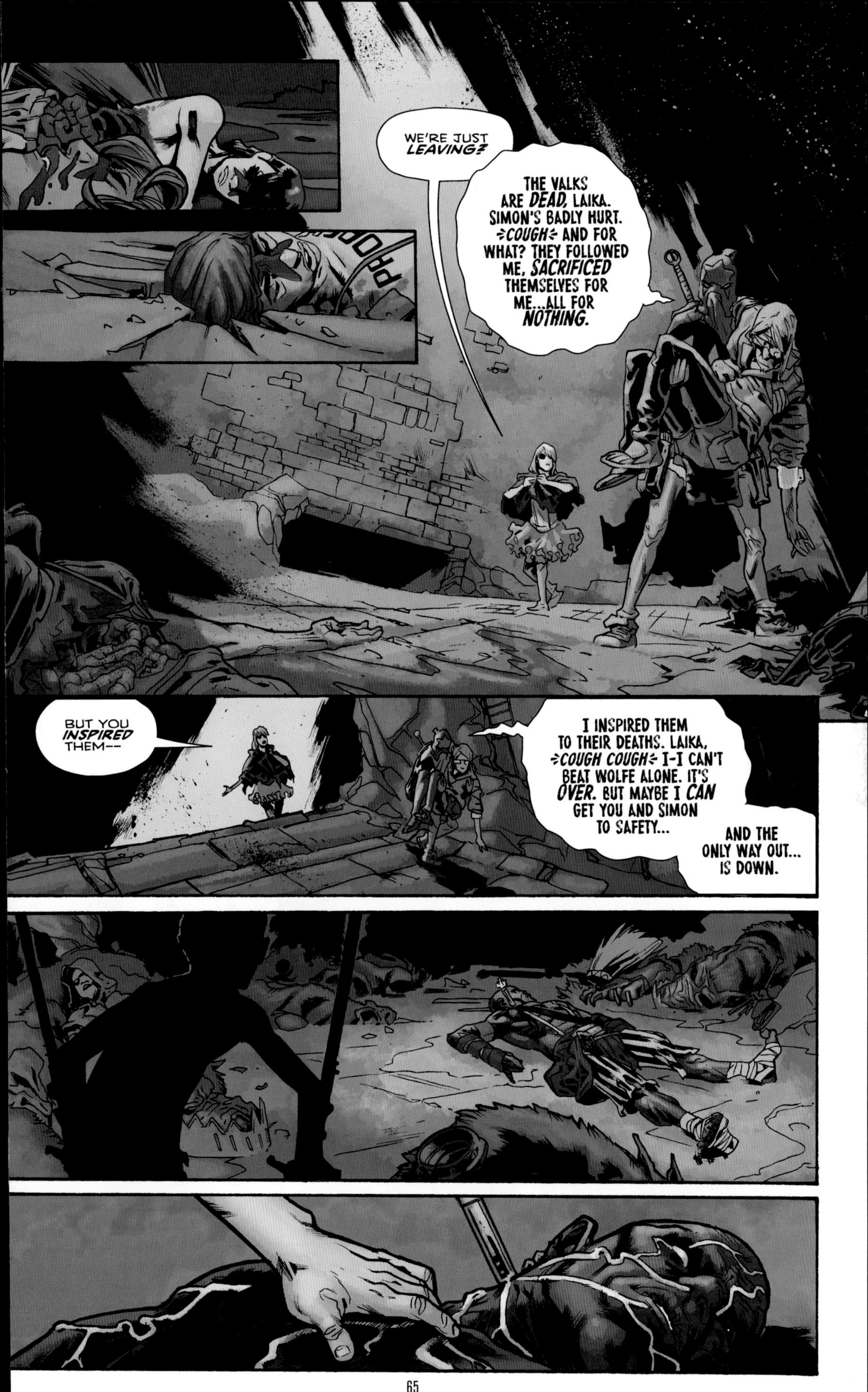
WE'RE JUST LEAVING?
THE VALKS ARE DEAD, LAIKA. SIMON'S BADLY HURT. *COUGH* AND FOR WHAT? THEY FOLLOWED ME, SACRIFICED THEMSELVES FOR ME...ALL FOR NOTHING.
BUT YOU INSPIRED THEM--
I INSPIRED THEM TO THEIR DEATHS. LAIKA, *COUGH COUGH* I-I CAN'T BEAT WOLFE ALONE. IT'S OVER. BUT MAYBE I CAN GET YOU AND SIMON TO SAFETY...
AND THE ONLY WAY OUT... IS DOWN.

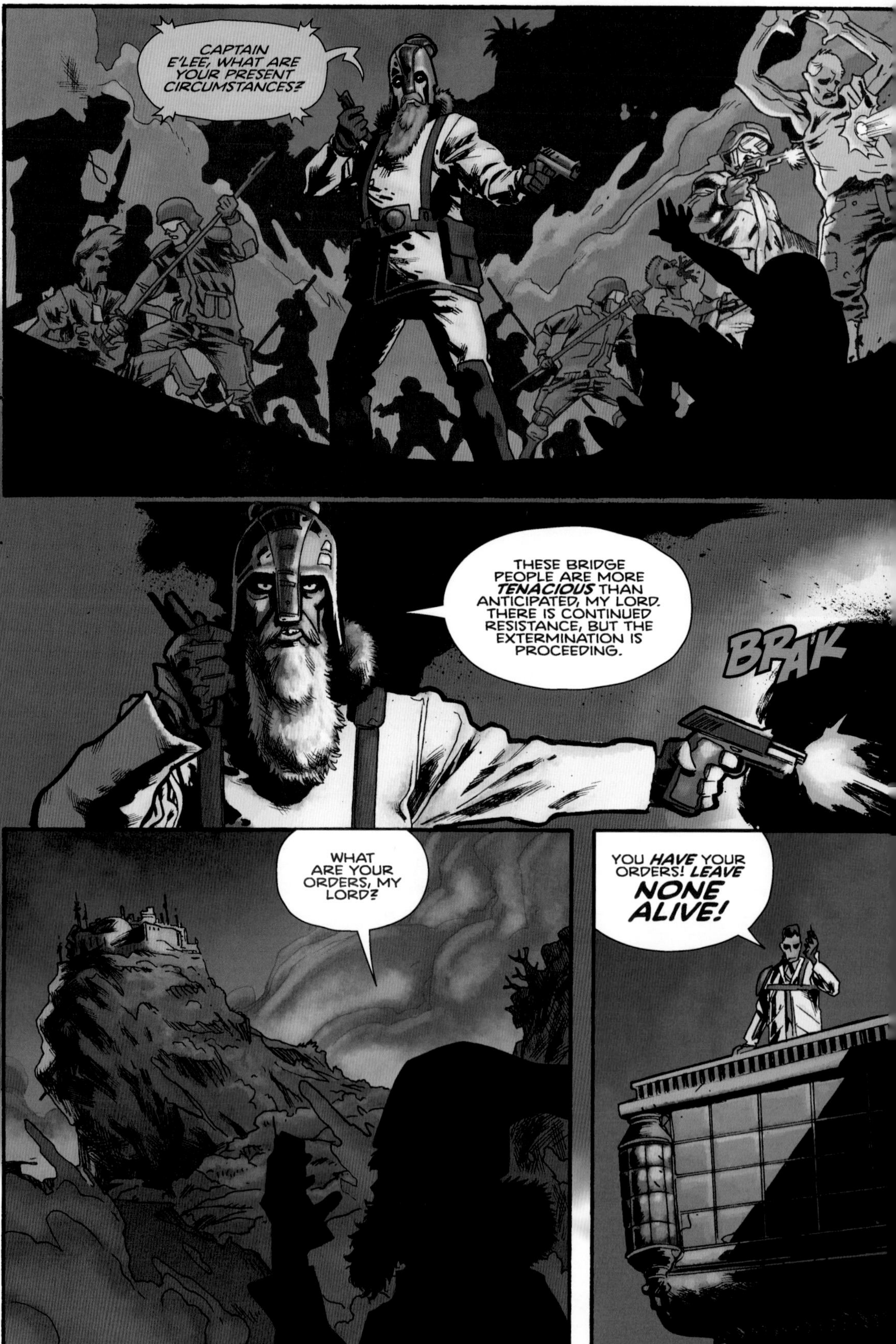

CAPTAIN E'LEE, WHAT ARE YOUR PRESENT CIRCUMSTANCES?
THESE BRIDGE PEOPLE ARE MORE TENACIOUS THAN ANTICIPATED, MY LORD. THERE IS CONTINUED RESISTANCE, BUT THE EXTERMINATION IS PROCEEDING.
BRAK
WHAT ARE YOUR ORDERS, MY LORD?
YOU HAVE YOUR ORDERS! LEAVE NONE ALIVE!

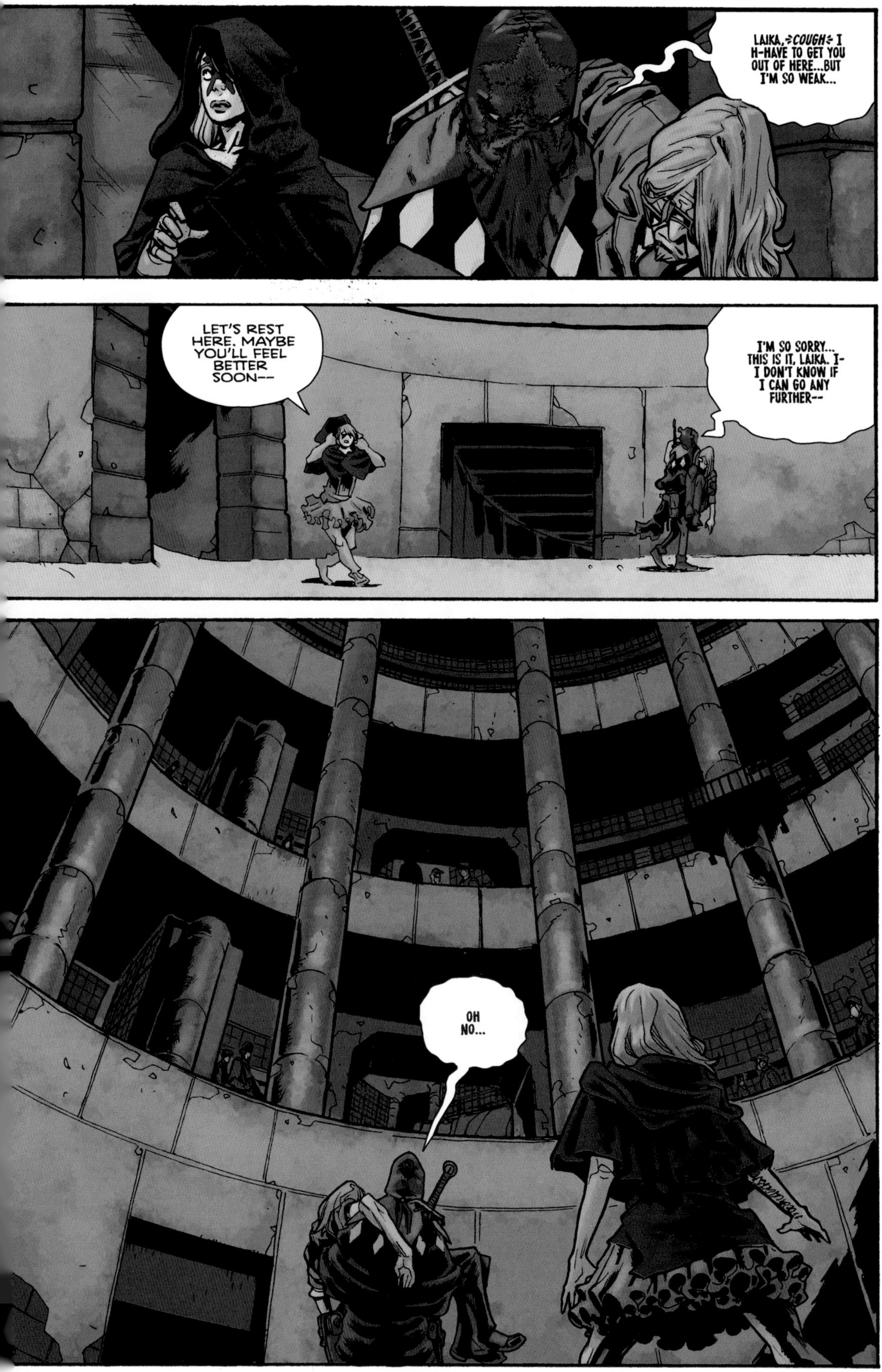

LAIKA, ≑COUGH≑ I H-HAVE TO GET YOU OUT OF HERE...BUT I'M SO WEAK...
LET'S REST HERE. MAYBE YOU'LL FEEL BETTER SOON--
I'M SO SORRY... THIS IS IT, LAIKA. I- I DON'T KNOW IF I CAN GO ANY FURTHER--
OH NO...

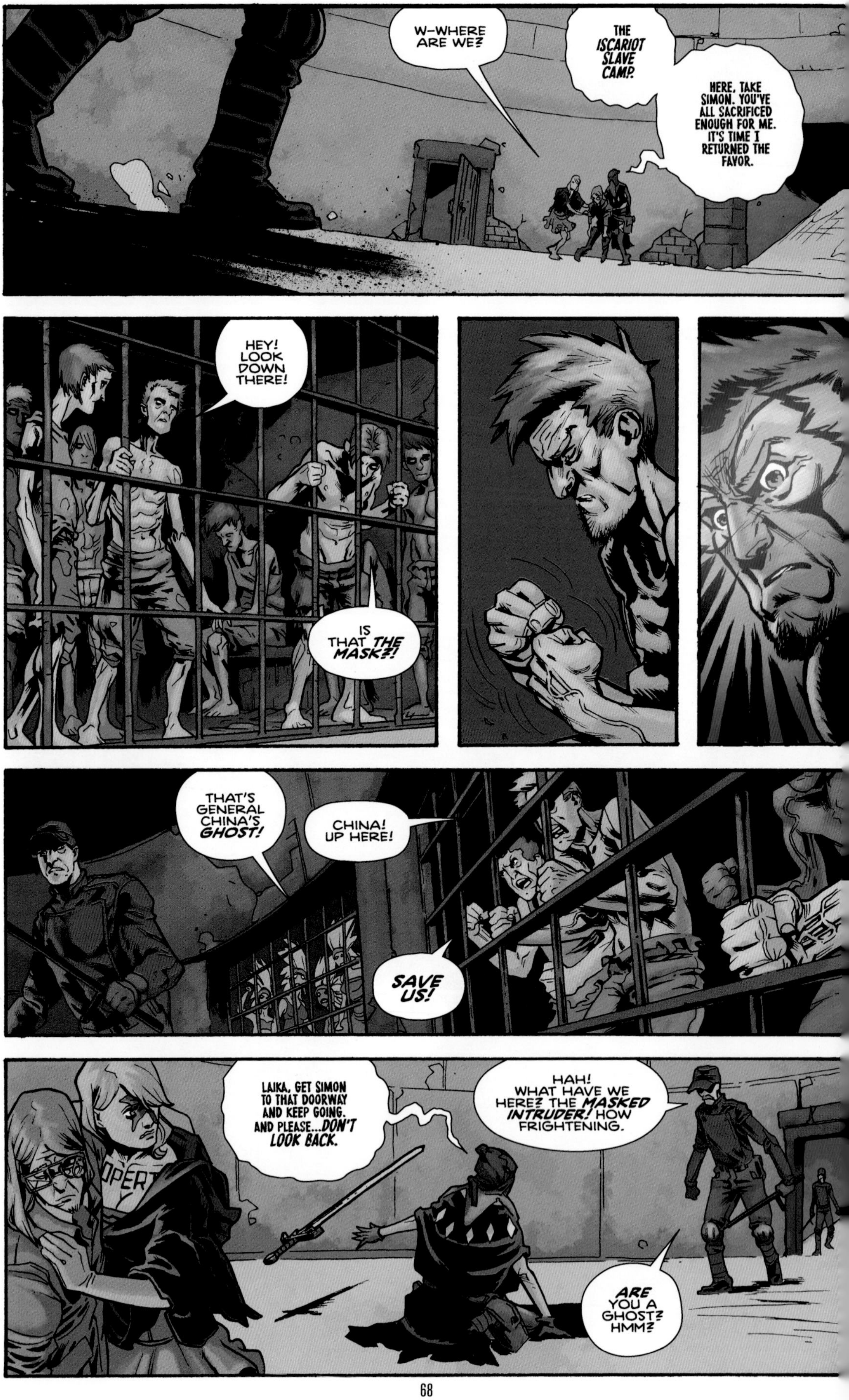
W-WHERE ARE WE?
THE ISCARIOT SLAVE CAMP.
HERE, TAKE SIMON. YOU'VE ALL SACRIFICED ENOUGH FOR ME. IT'S TIME I RETURNED THE FAVOR.
HEY! LOOK DOWN THERE!
IS THAT THE MASK?!
THAT'S GENERAL CHINA'S GHOST!
CHINA! UP HERE!
SAVE US!
LAIKA, GET SIMON TO THAT DOORWAY AND KEEP GOING. AND PLEASE...DON'T LOOK BACK.
HAH! WHAT HAVE WE HERE? THE MASKED INTRUDER! HOW FRIGHTENING.
ARE YOU A GHOST? HMM?

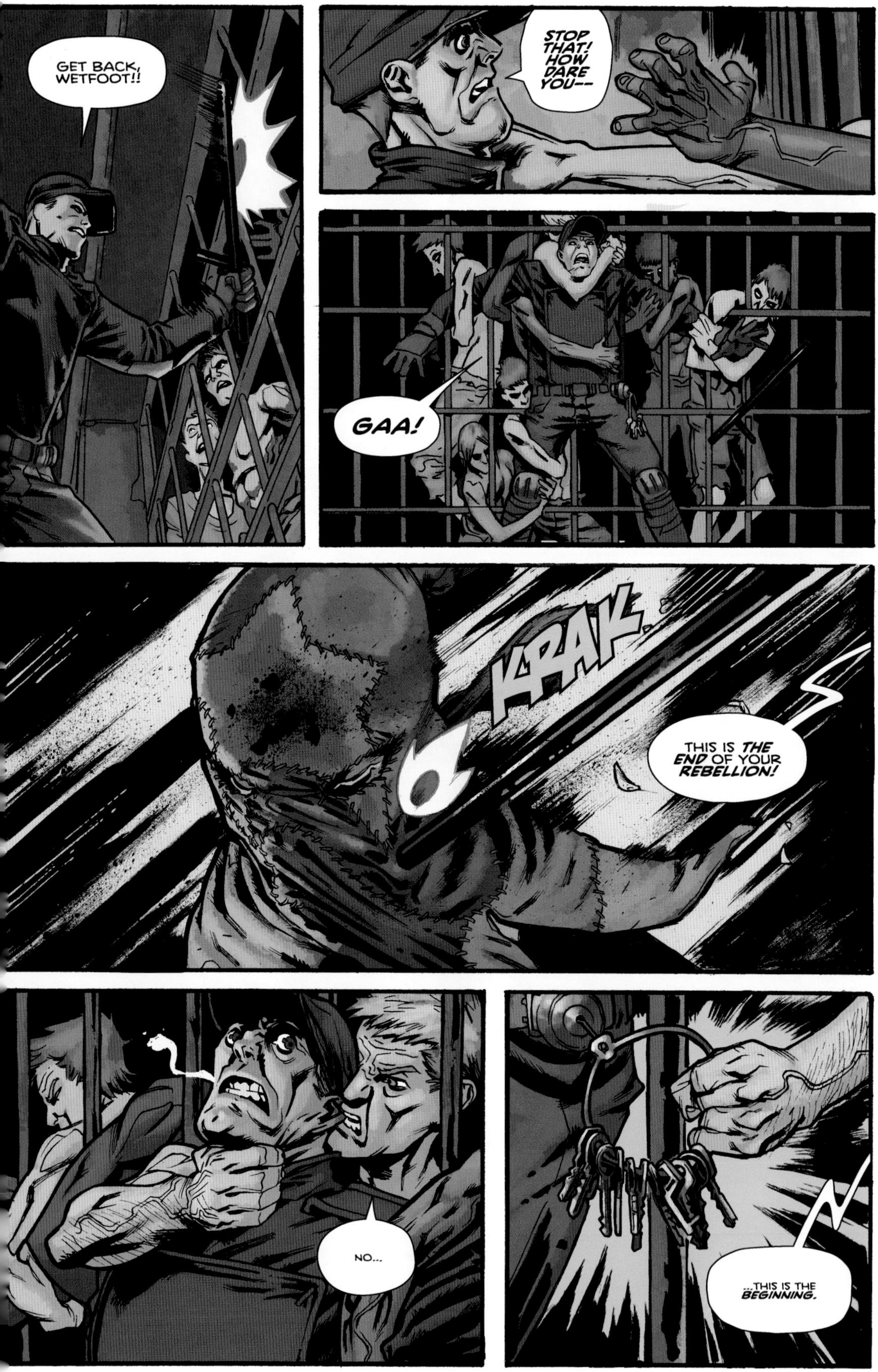
GET BACK, WETFOOT!!
STOP THAT! HOW DARE YOU--
GAA!
KRAK
THIS IS THE END OF YOUR REBELLION!
NO...
...THIS IS THE BEGINNING.

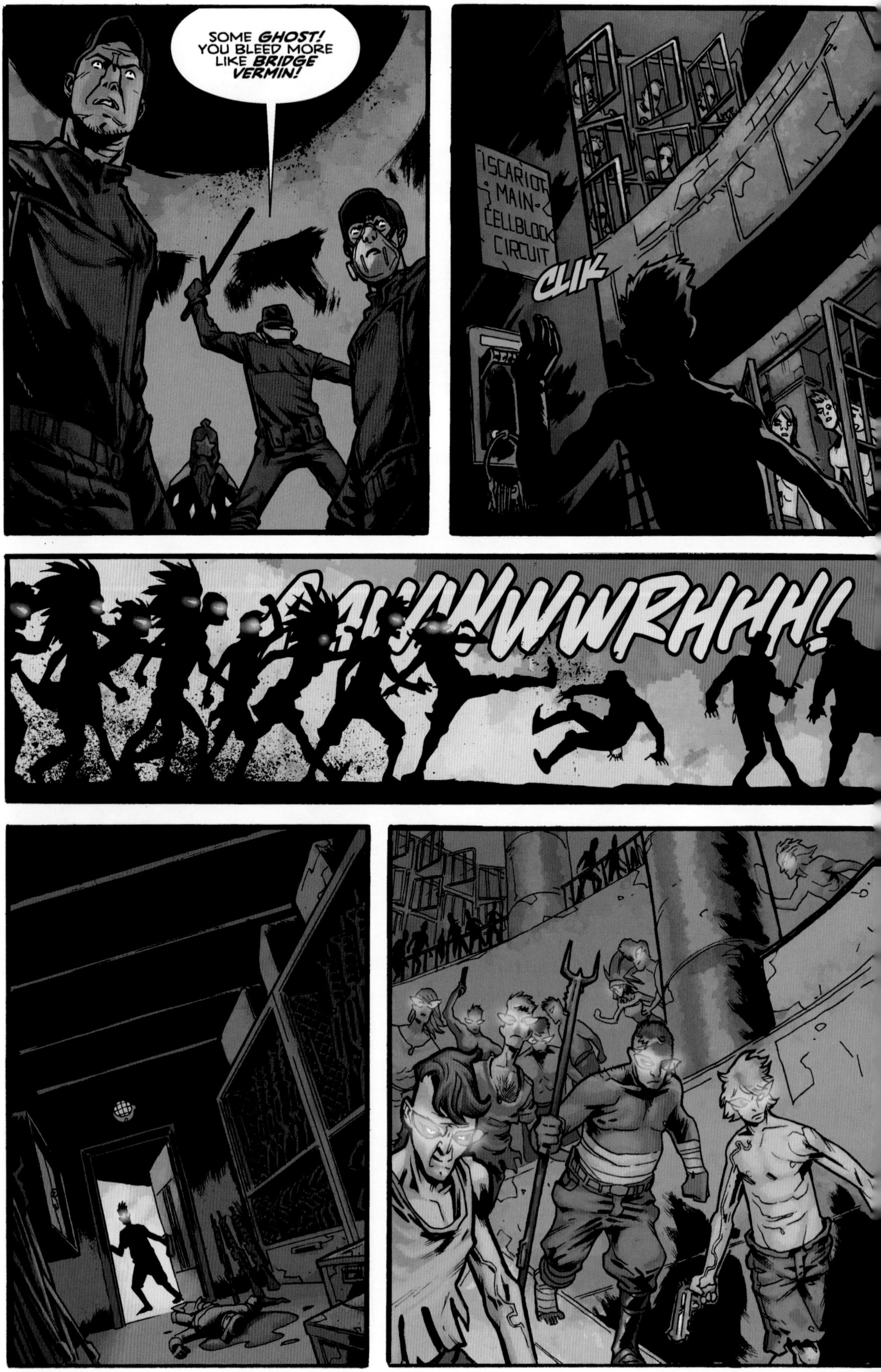
SOME GHOST! YOU BLEED MORE LIKE BRIDGE VERMIN!
ISCARIOT MAIN CELLBLOCK CIRCUIT
CLIK
WWRHHH!

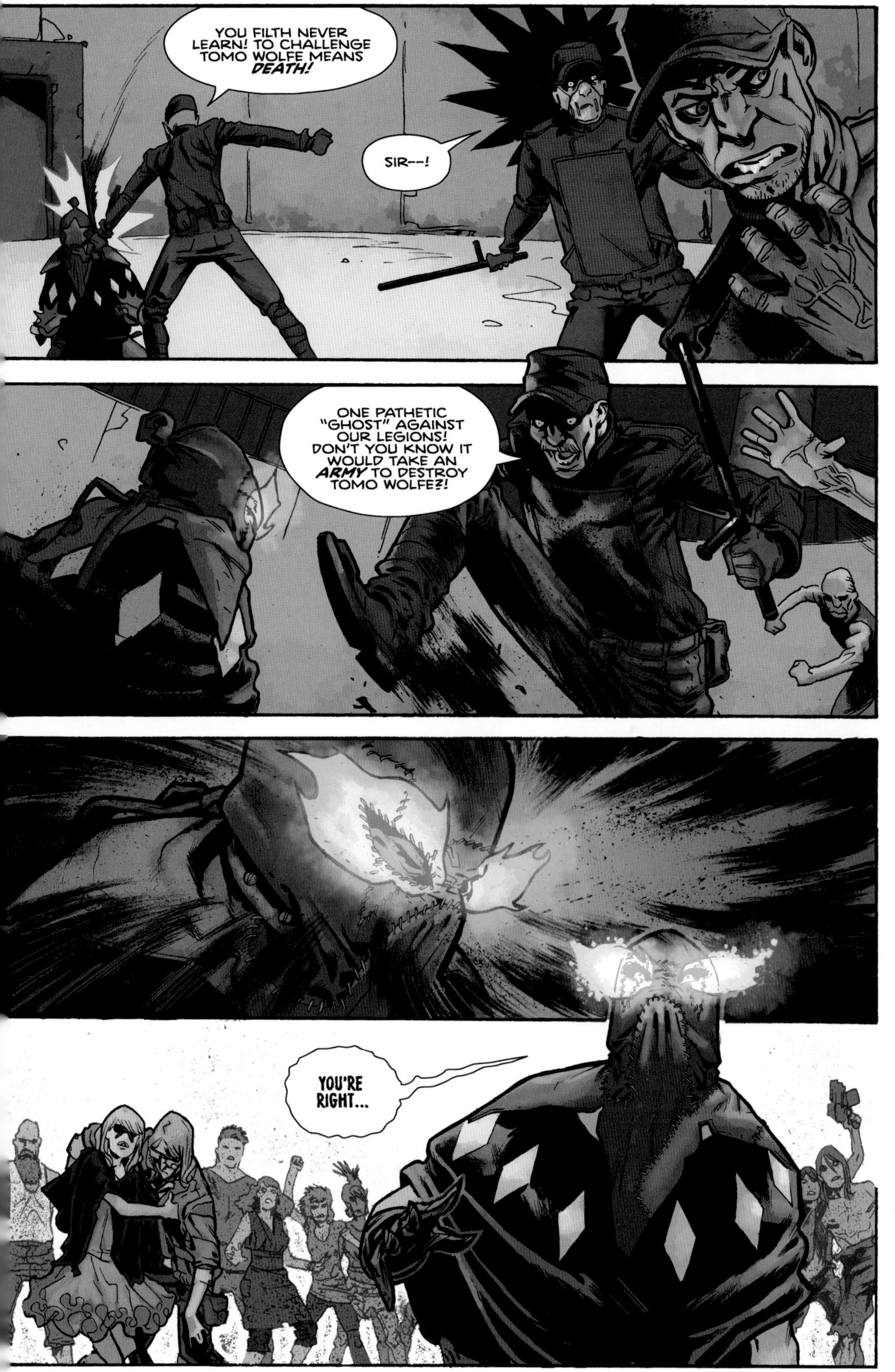

YOU FILTH NEVER LEARN! TO CHALLENGE TOMO WOLFE MEANS DEATH!
SIR--!
ONE PATHETIC "GHOST" AGAINST OUR LEGIONS! DON'T YOU KNOW IT WOULD TAKE AN ARMY TO DESTROY TOMO WOLFE?!
YOU'RE RIGHT...

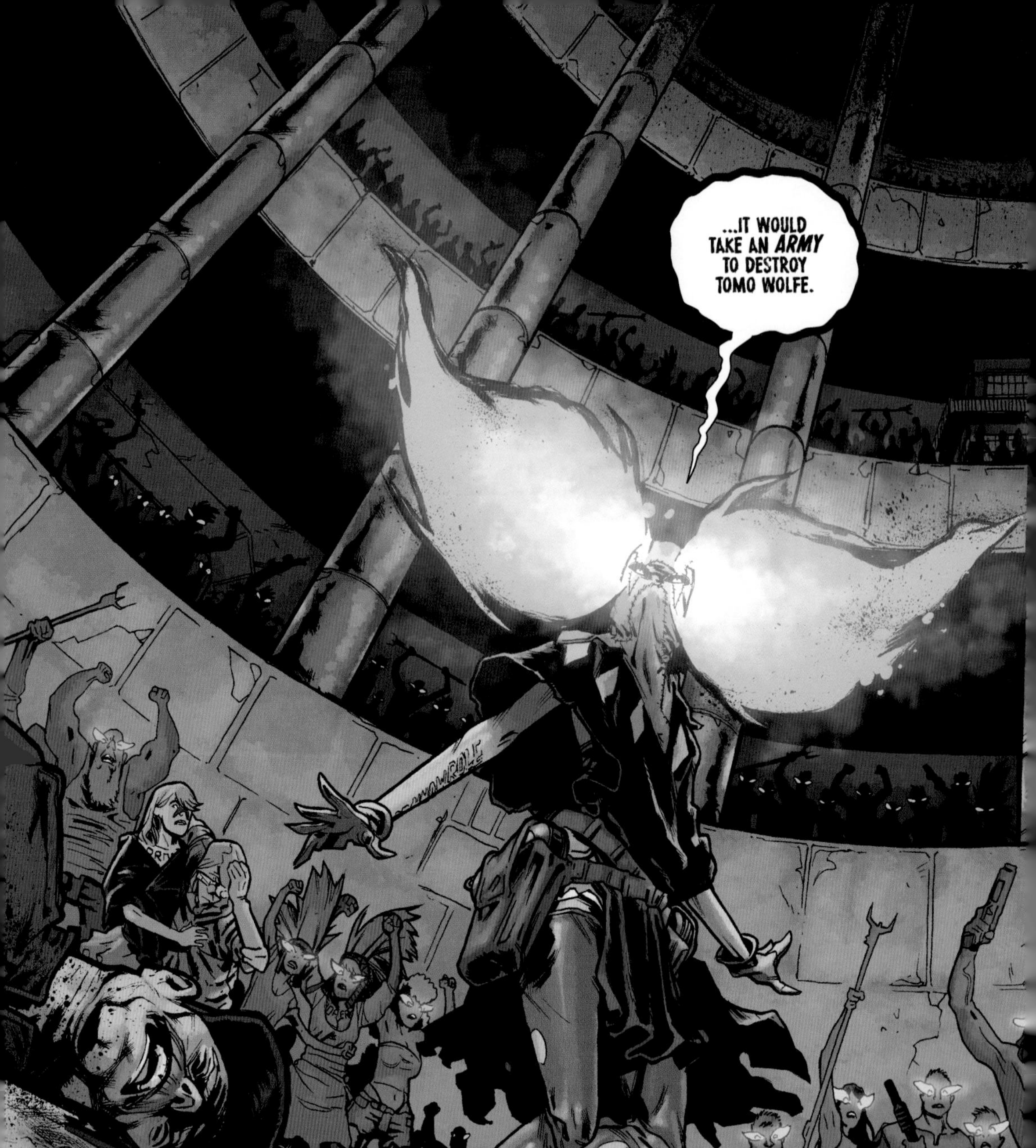
...IT WOULD TAKE AN ARMY TO DESTROY TOMO WOLFE.

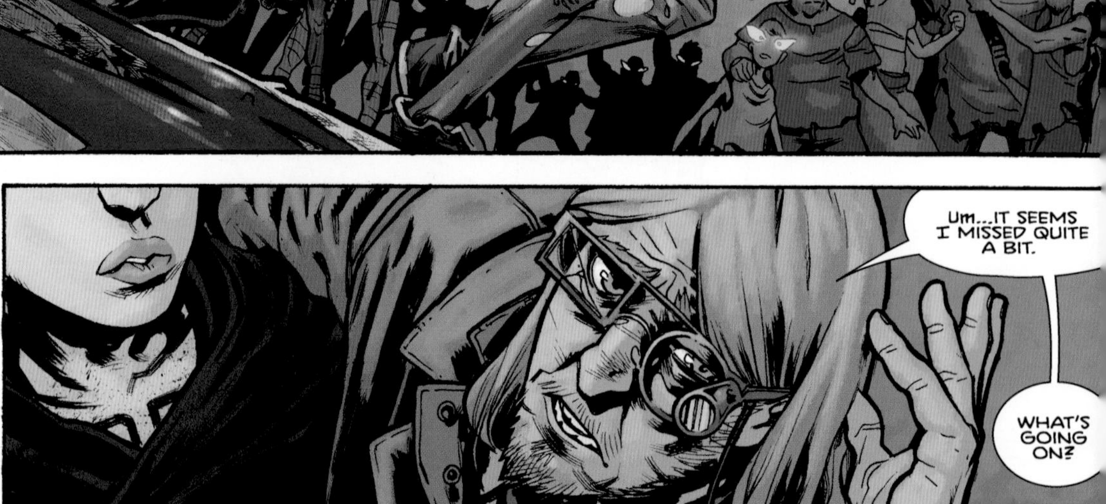
UM...IT SEEMS I MISSED QUITE A BIT.
WHAT'S GOING ON?

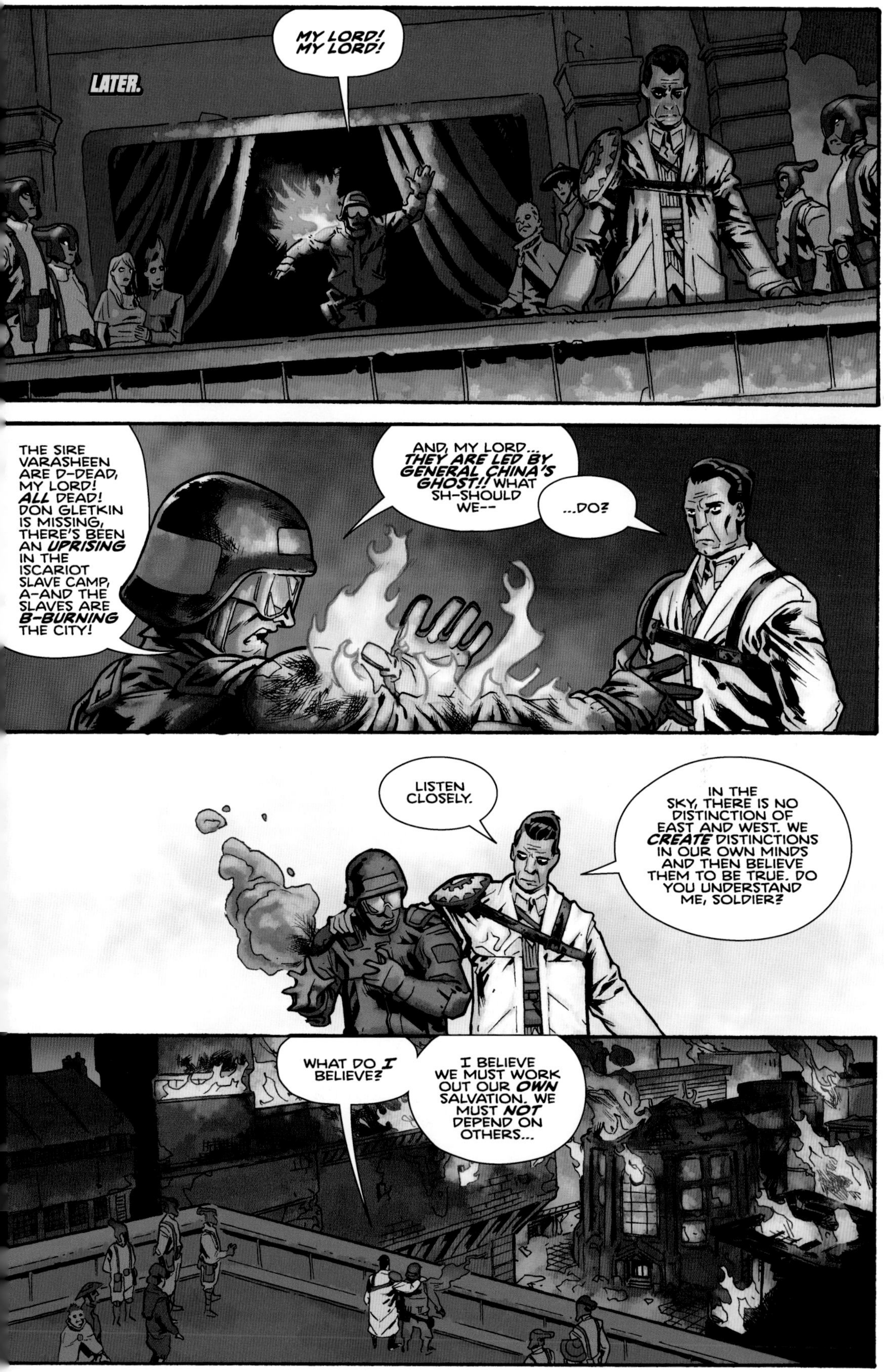

LATER.
MY LORD! MY LORD!
THE SIRE VARASHEEN ARE D-DEAD, MY LORD! ALL DEAD! DON GLETKIN IS MISSING, THERE'S BEEN AN UPRISING IN THE ISCARIOT SLAVE CAMP, A-AND THE SLAVES ARE B-BURNING THE CITY!
AND, MY LORD... THEY ARE LED BY GENERAL CHINA'S GHOST!! WHAT SH-SHOULD WE--
...DO?
LISTEN CLOSELY.
IN THE SKY, THERE IS NO DISTINCTION OF EAST AND WEST. WE CREATE DISTINCTIONS IN OUR OWN MINDS AND THEN BELIEVE THEM TO BE TRUE. DO YOU UNDERSTAND ME, SOLDIER?
WHAT DO I BELIEVE?
I BELIEVE WE MUST WORK OUT OUR OWN SALVATION. WE MUST NOT DEPEND ON OTHERS...

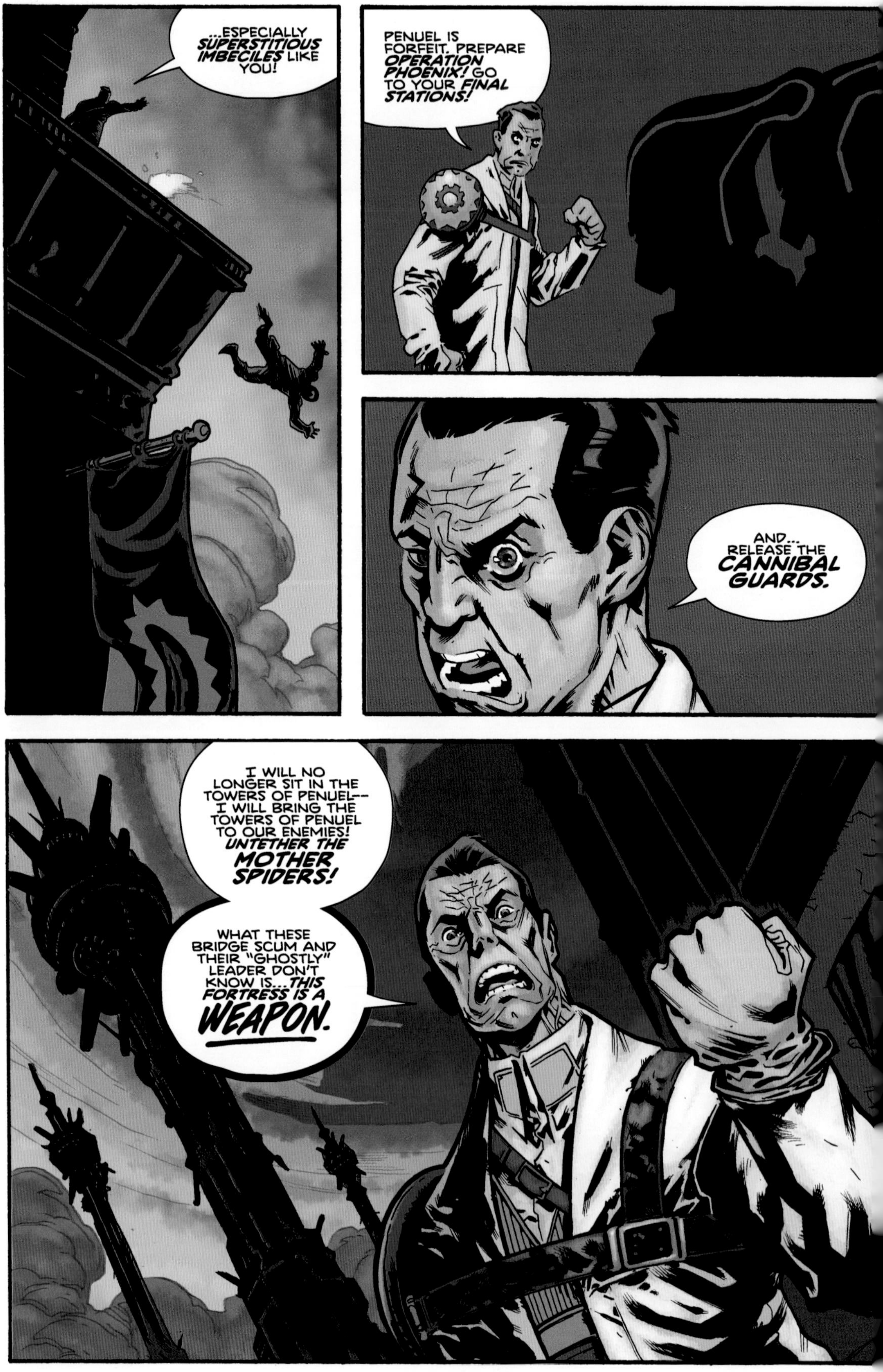
...ESPECIALLY SUPERSTITIOUS IMBECILES LIKE YOU!
PENUEL IS FORFEIT. PREPARE OPERATION PHOENIX! GO TO YOUR FINAL STATIONS!
AND... RELEASE THE CANNIBAL GUARDS.
I WILL NO LONGER SIT IN THE TOWERS OF PENUEL-- I WILL BRING THE TOWERS OF PENUEL TO OUR ENEMIES! UNTETHER THE MOTHER SPIDERS!
WHAT THESE BRIDGE SCUM AND THEIR "GHOSTLY" LEADER DON'T KNOW IS... THIS FORTRESS IS A WEAPON.

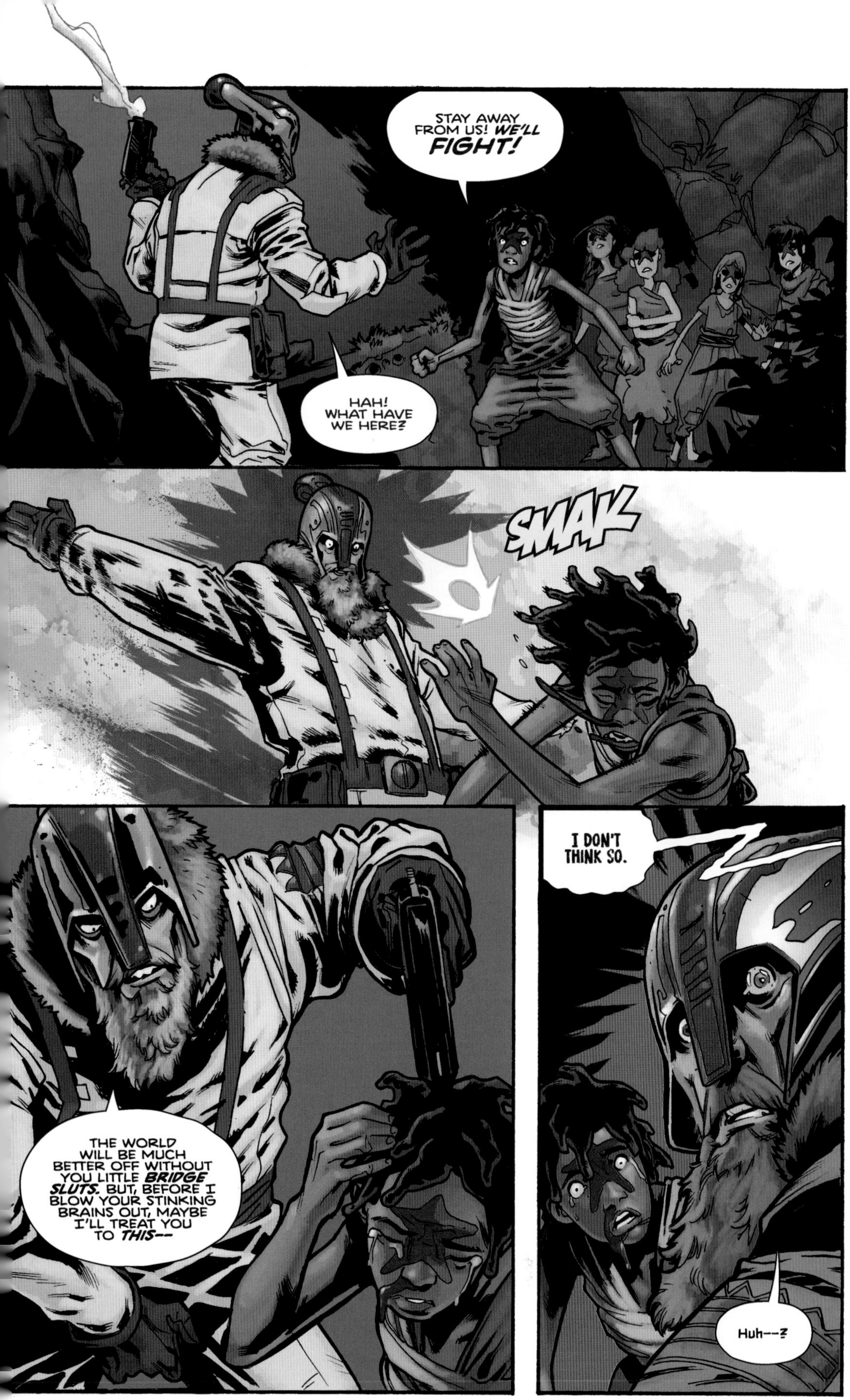
STAY AWAY FROM US! WE'LL FIGHT!
HAH! WHAT HAVE WE HERE?
SMAK
THE WORLD WILL BE MUCH BETTER OFF WITHOUT YOU LITTLE BRIDGE SLUTS. BUT, BEFORE I BLOW YOUR STINKING BRAINS OUT, MAYBE I'LL TREAT YOU TO THIS--
I DON'T THINK SO.
Huh--?

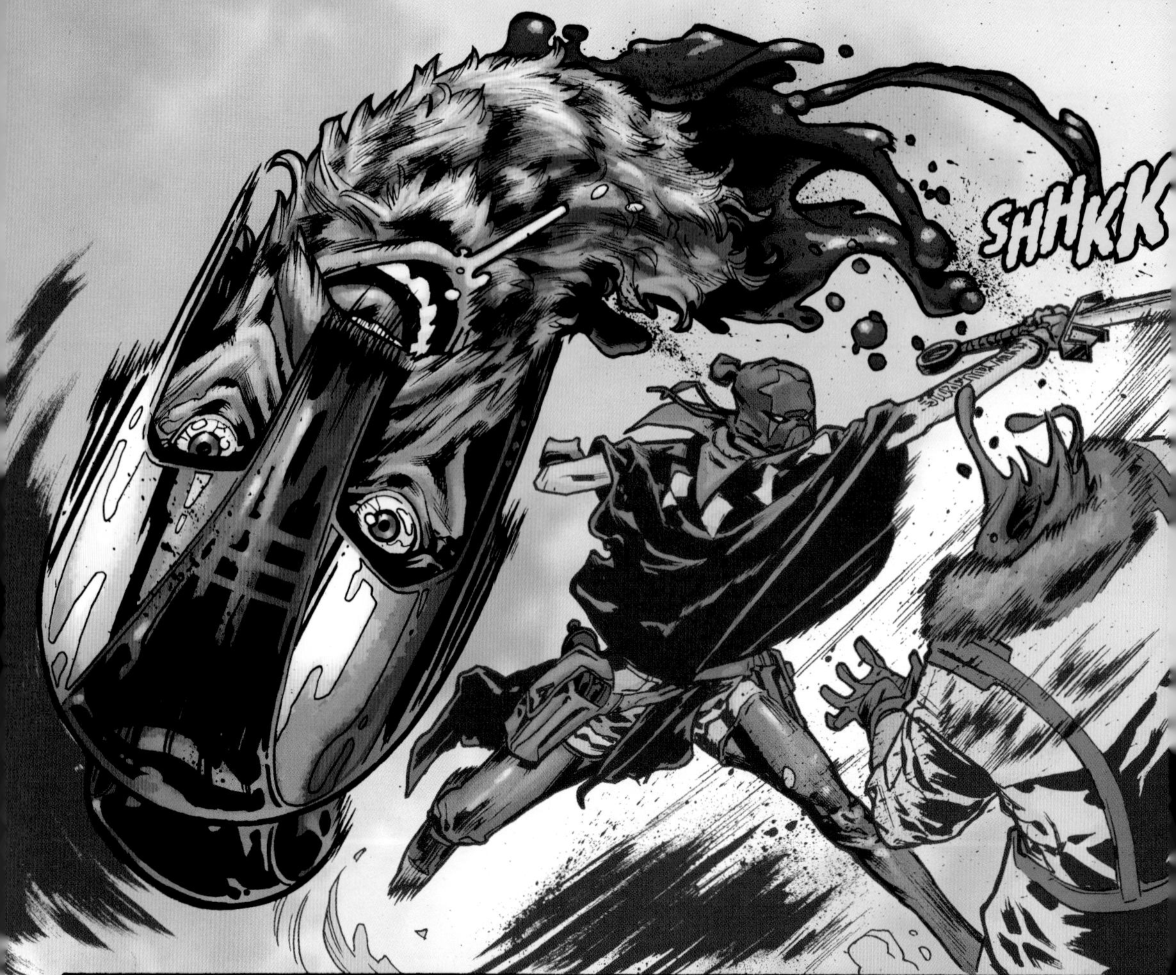
SHHKK

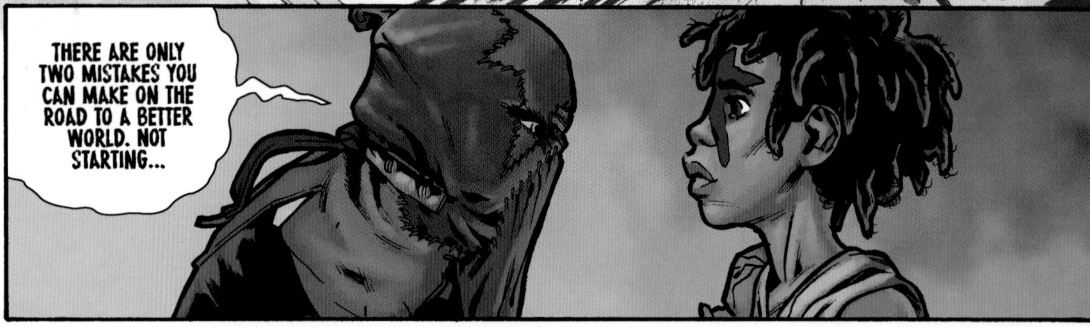
THERE ARE ONLY TWO MISTAKES YOU CAN MAKE ON THE ROAD TO A BETTER WORLD. NOT STARTING...

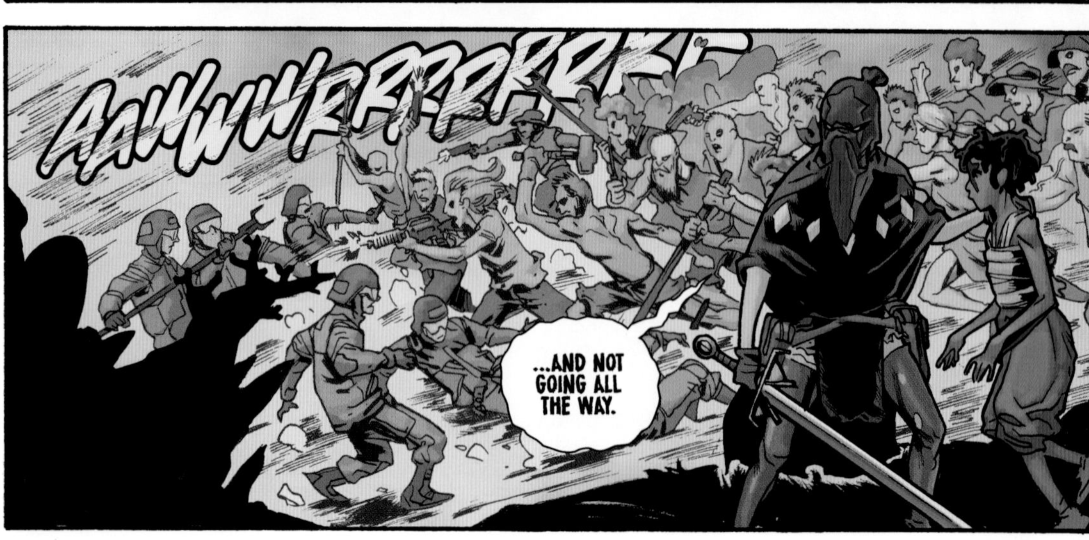
...AND NOT GOING ALL THE WAY.

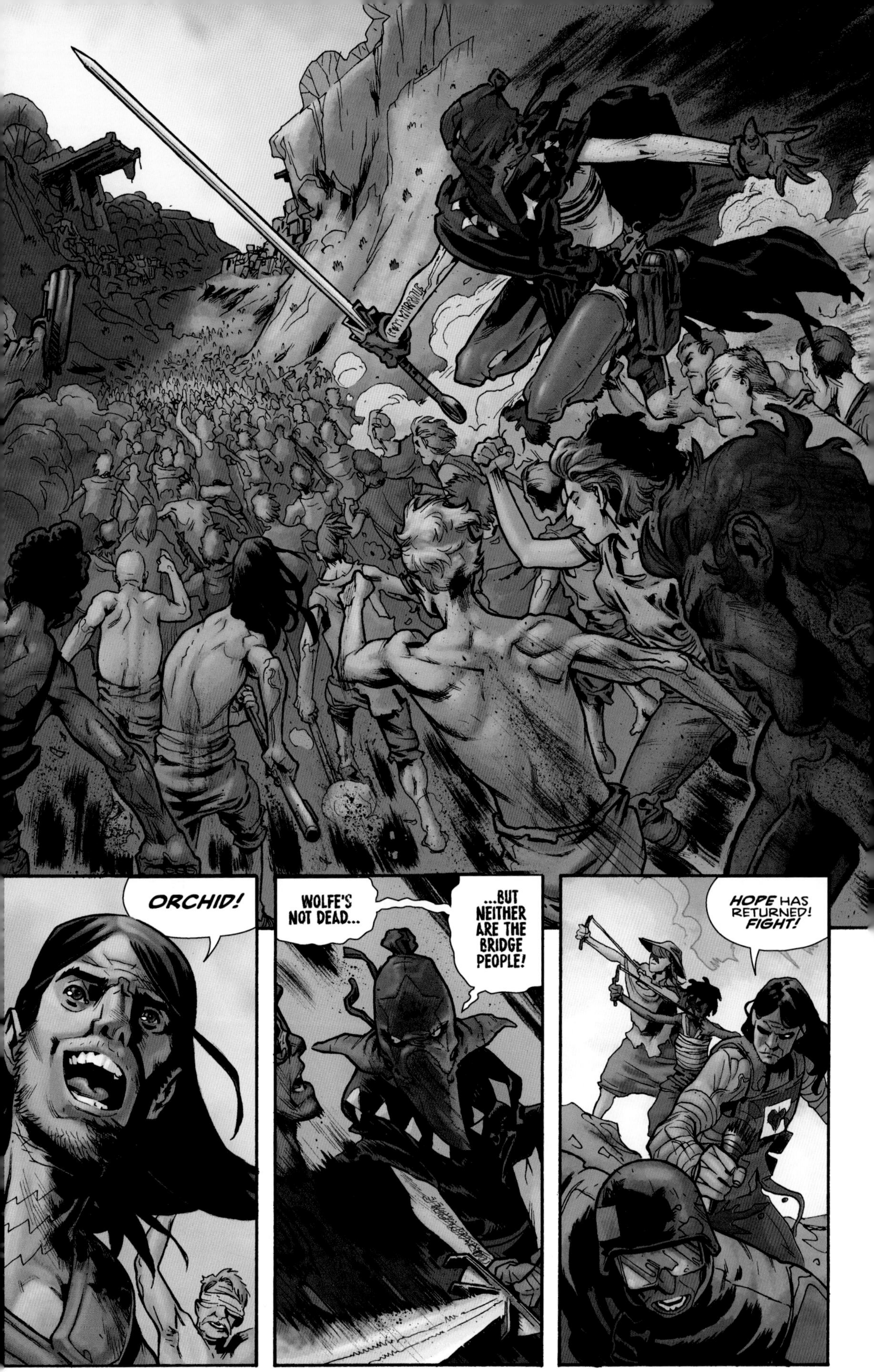
ORCHID!
WOLFE'S NOT DEAD...
...BUT NEITHER ARE THE BRIDGE PEOPLE!
HOPE HAS RETURNED! FIGHT!

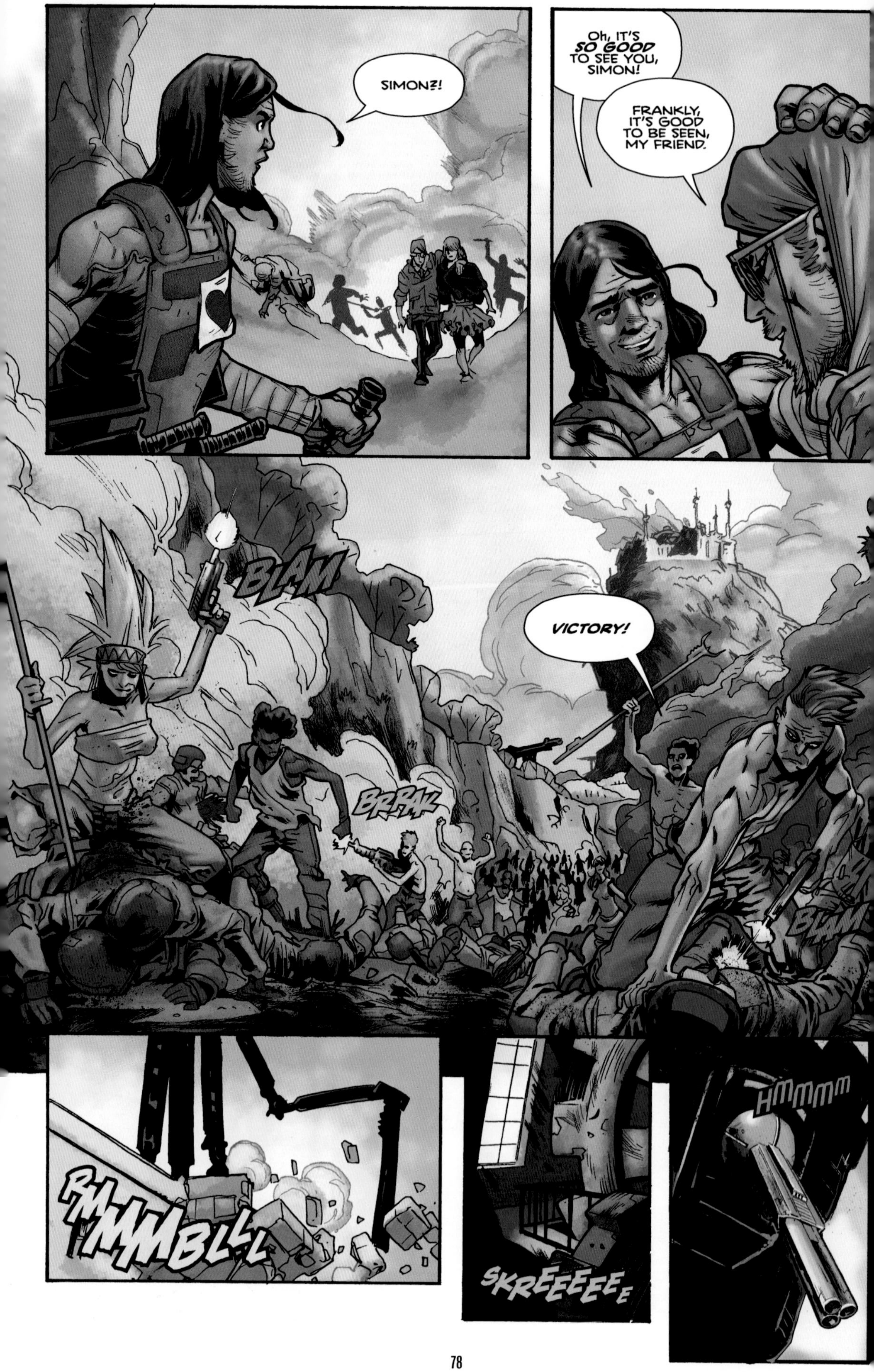
SIMON?!
Oh, IT'S SO GOOD TO SEE YOU, SIMON!
FRANKLY, IT'S GOOD TO BE SEEN, MY FRIEND.
BLAM
VICTORY!
BRRAK
RMMMBLLL
SKREEEEEE
HMMMM

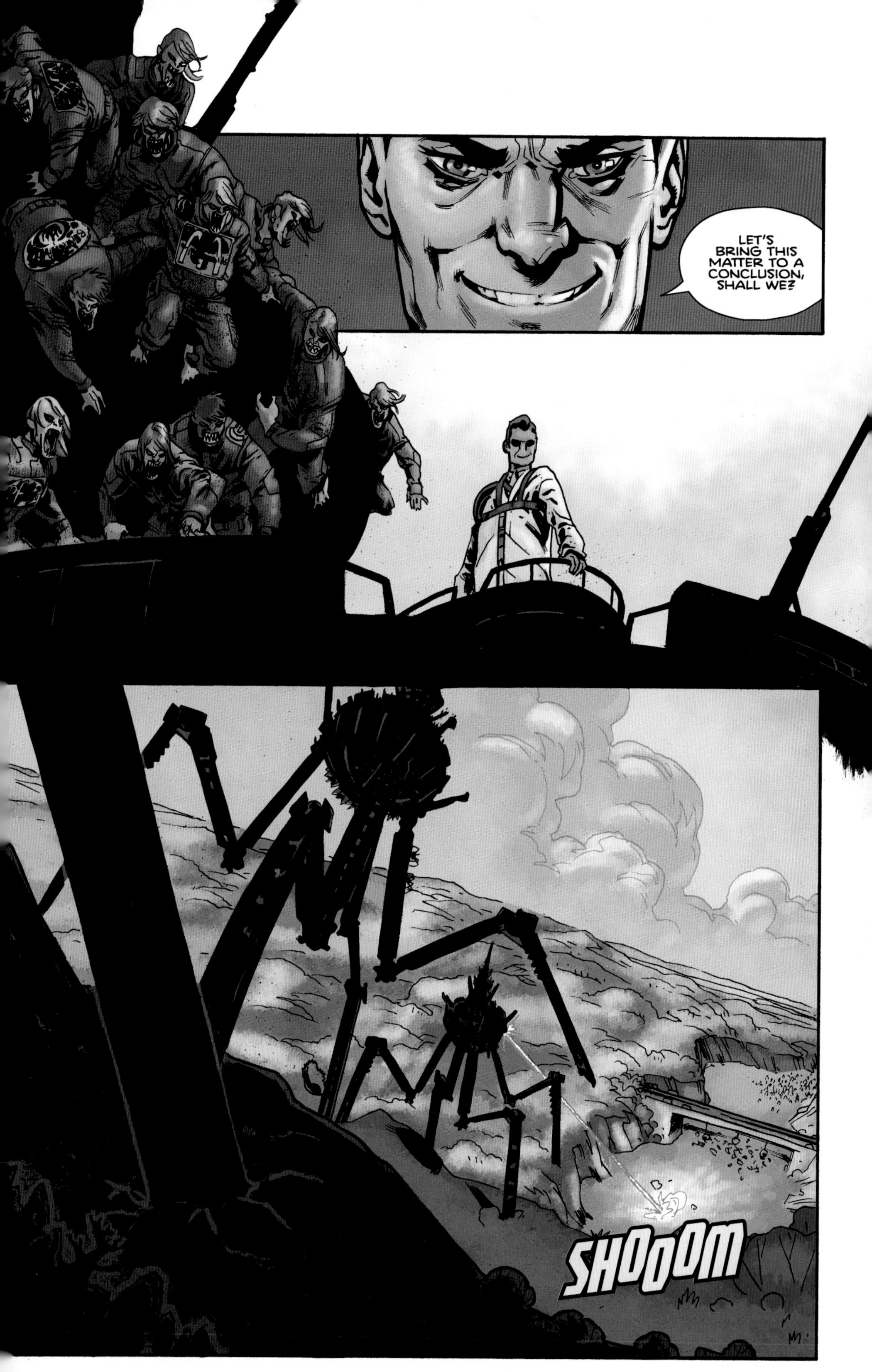
LET'S BRING THIS MATTER TO A CONCLUSION, SHALL WE?
SHOOOM

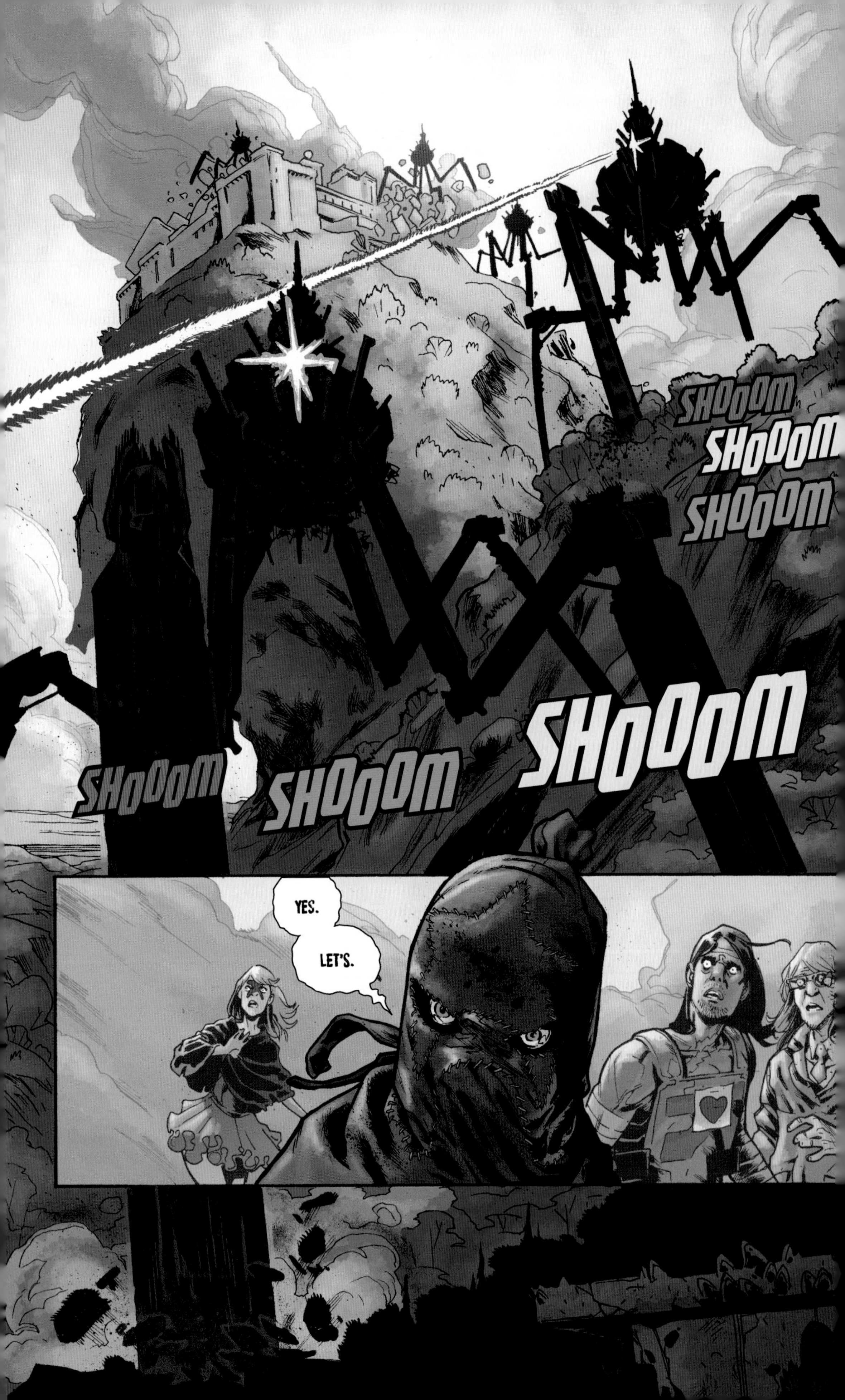
SHOOOM
SHOOOM
SHOOOM
SHOOOM
SHOOOM
SHOOOM
YES.
LET'S.

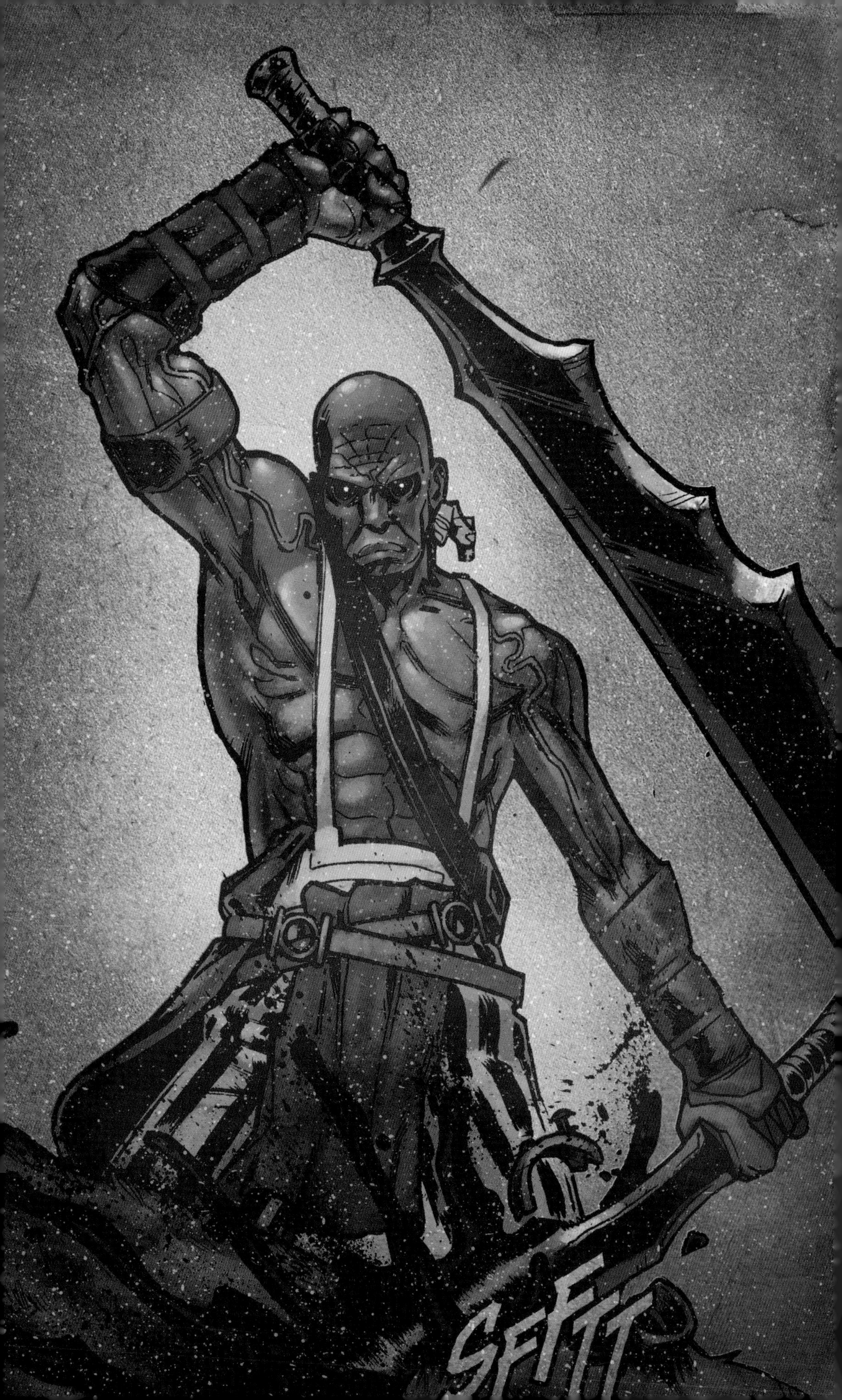
SFFT

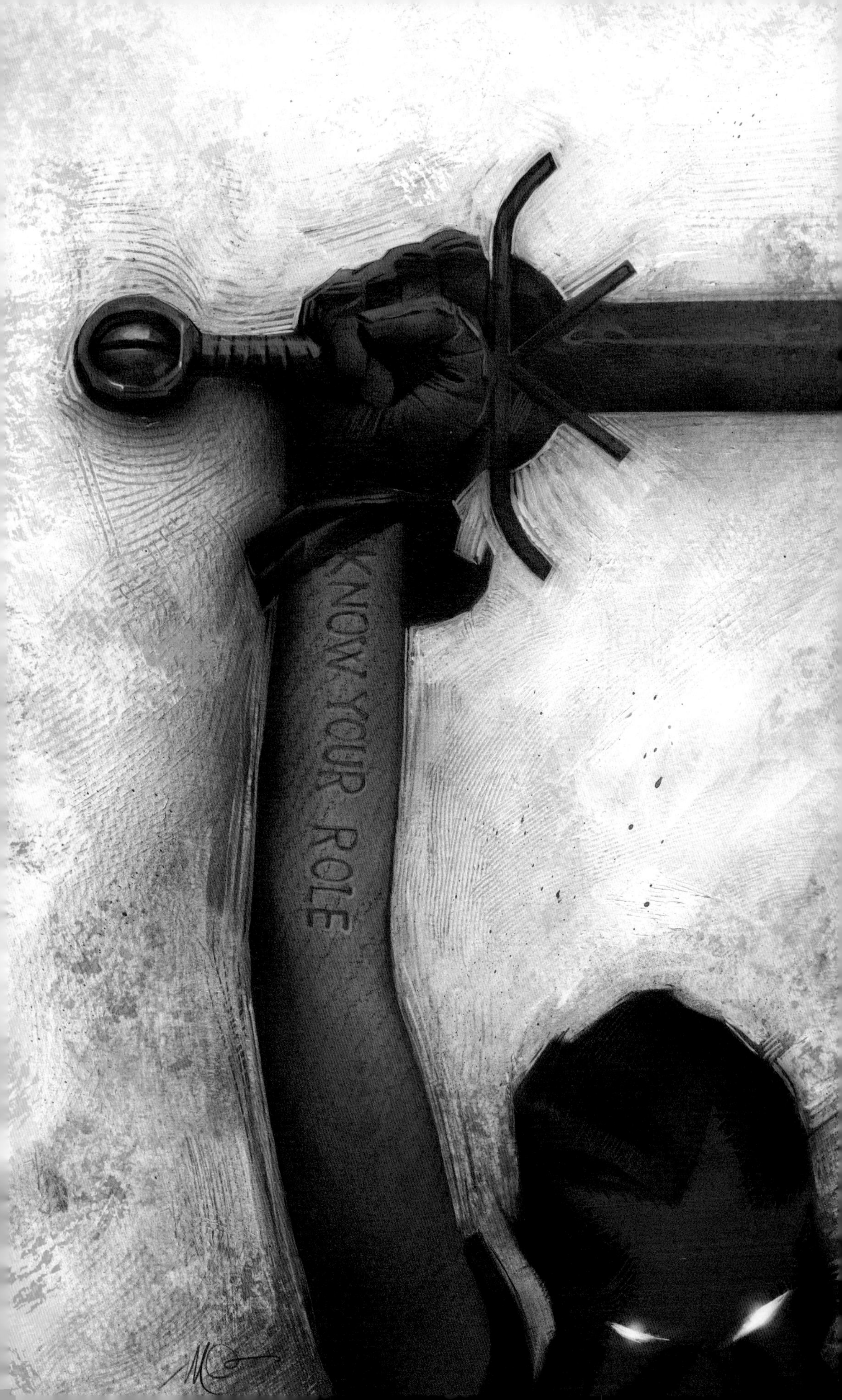
KNOW YOUR ROLE

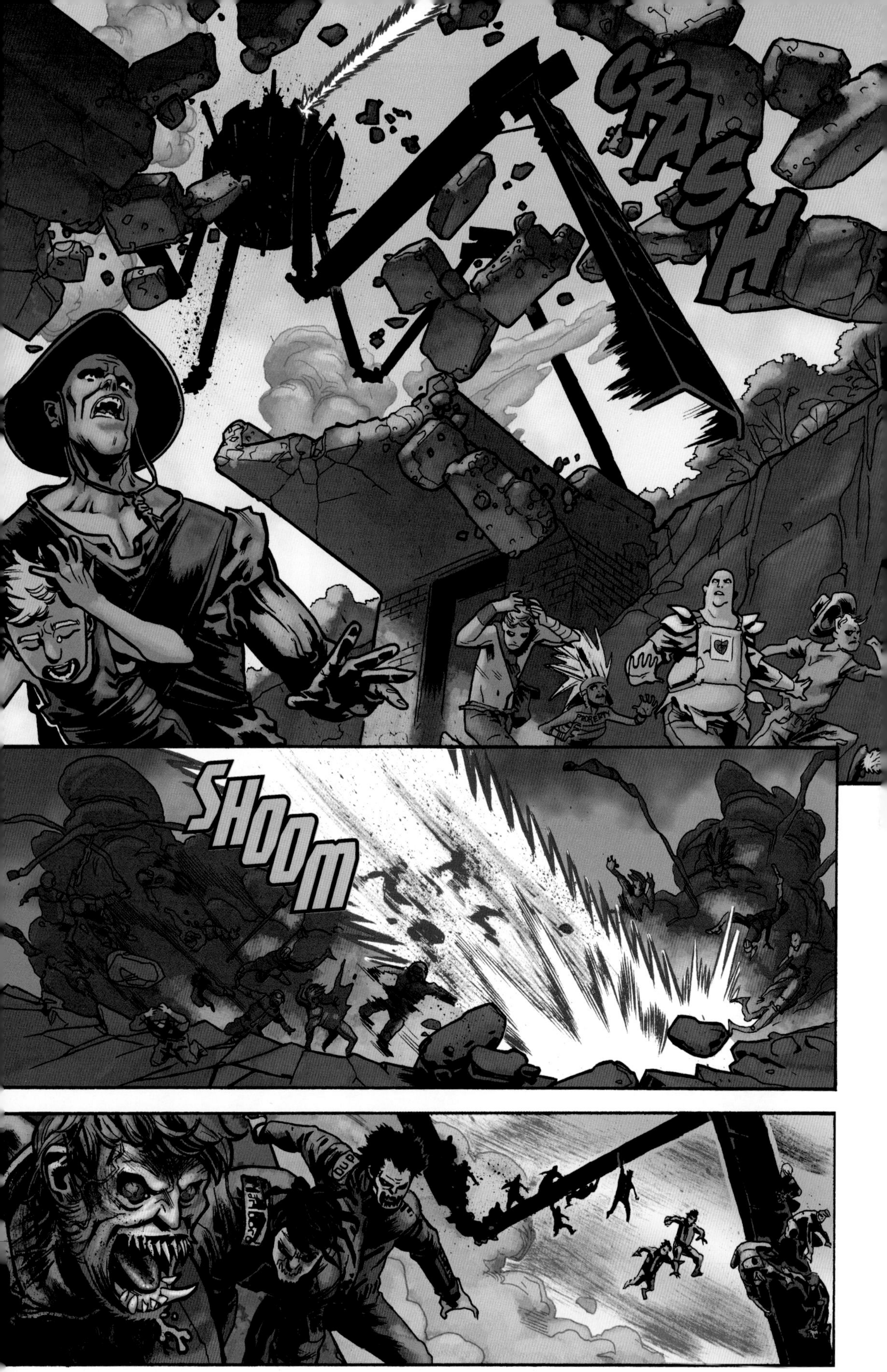
CRASH
SHOOM

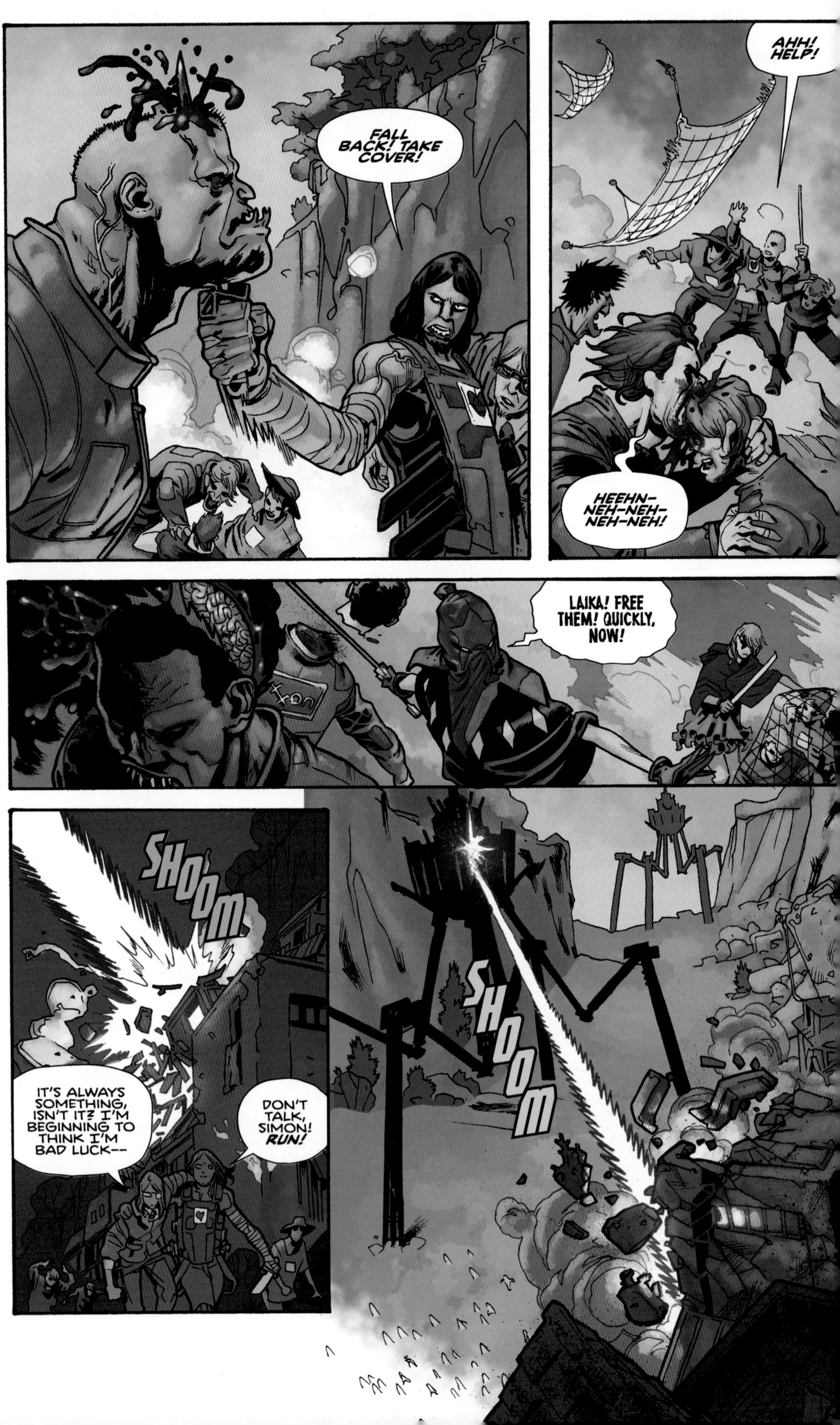
FALL BACK! TAKE COVER!
AHH! HELP!
HEEHN-NEH-NEH-NEH-NEH!
LAIKA! FREE THEM! QUICKLY, NOW!
SHOOM
IT'S ALWAYS SOMETHING, ISN'T IT? I'M BEGINNING TO THINK I'M BAD LUCK--
DON'T TALK, SIMON! RUN!
SHOOM

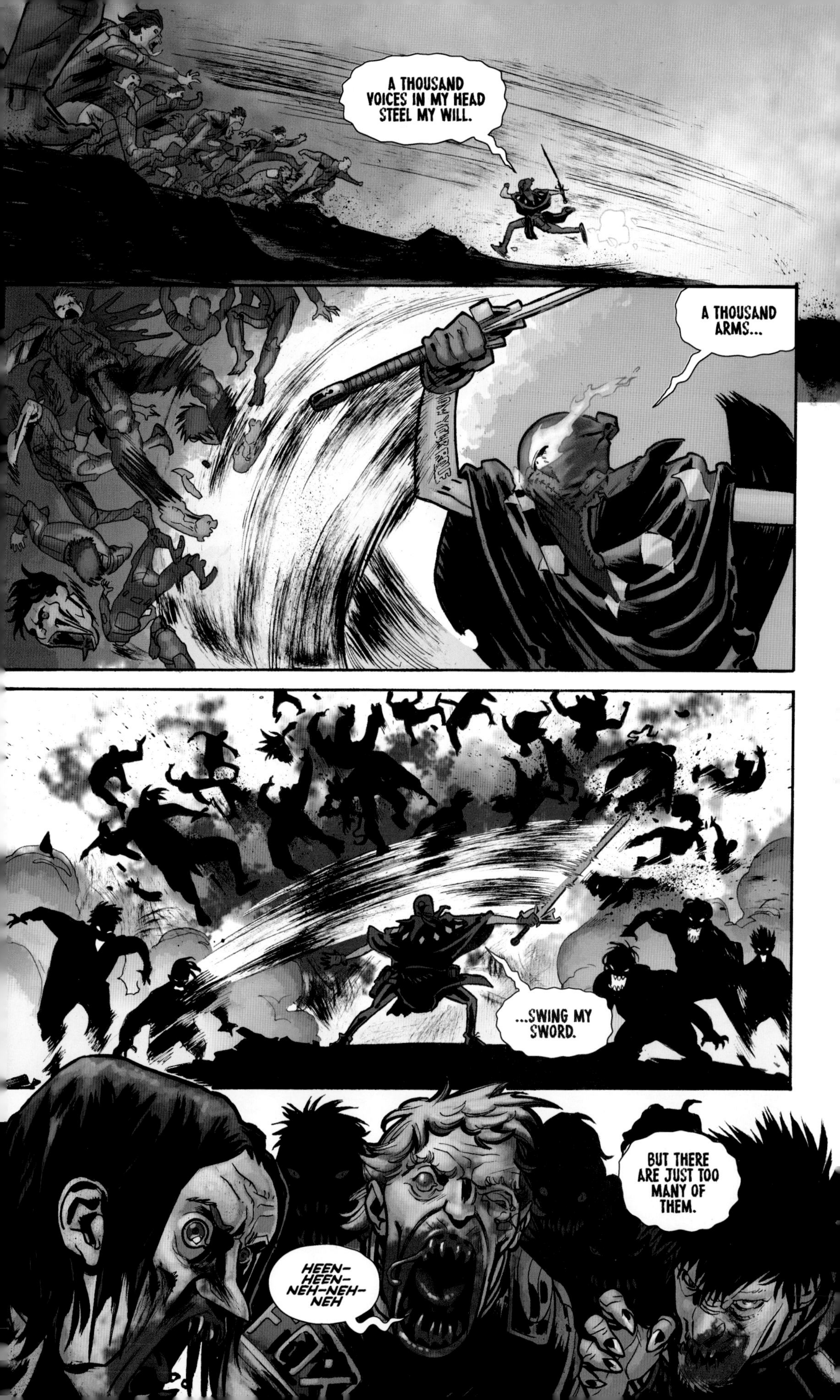
A THOUSAND VOICES IN MY HEAD STEEL MY WILL.
A THOUSAND ARMS...
...SWING MY SWORD.
BUT THERE ARE JUST TOO MANY OF THEM.
HEEN- HEEN- NEH-NEH- NEH

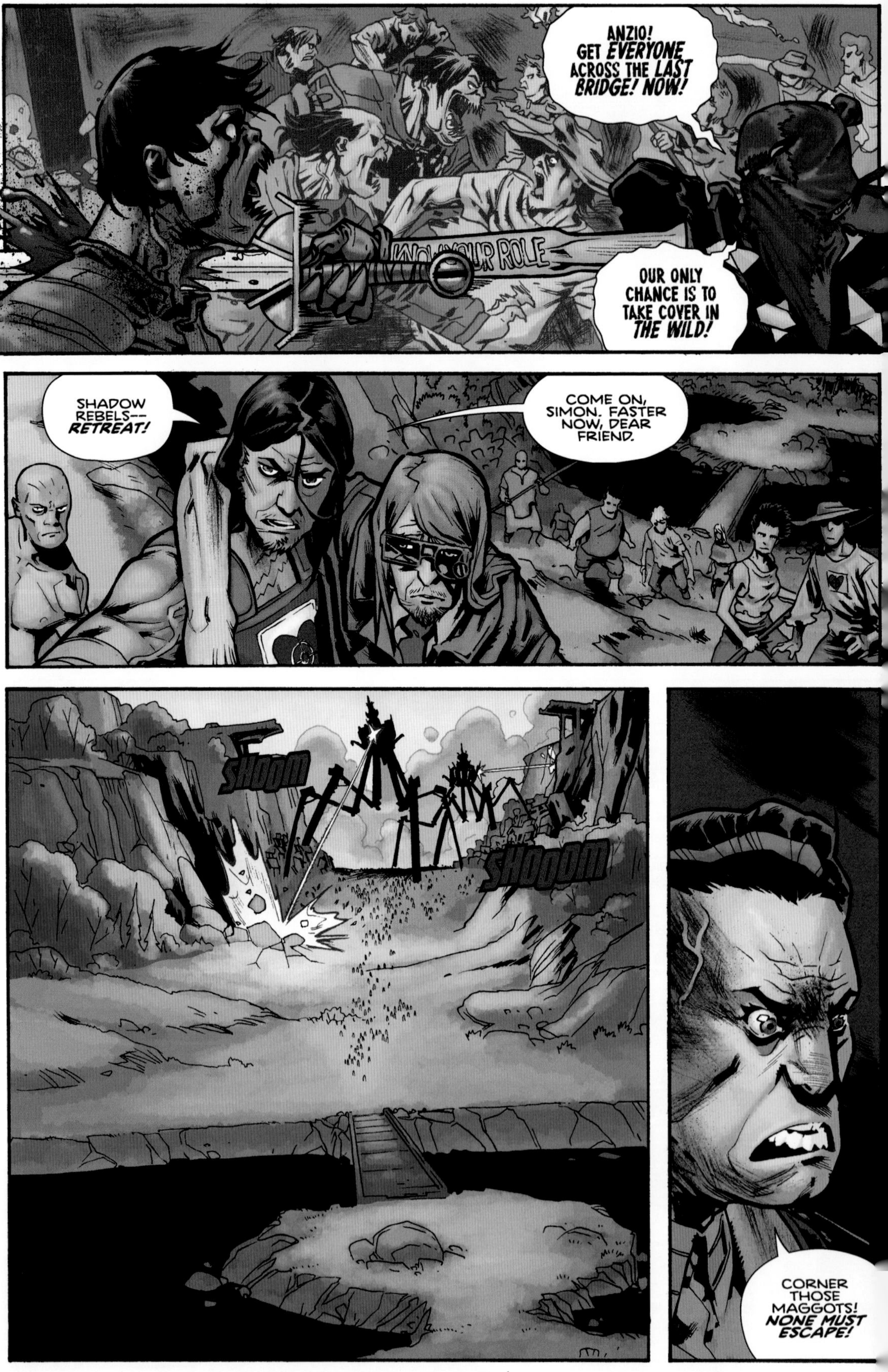
ANZIO! GET EVERYONE ACROSS THE LAST BRIDGE! NOW!
KNOW YOUR ROLE
OUR ONLY CHANCE IS TO TAKE COVER IN THE WILD!
SHADOW REBELS-- RETREAT!
COME ON, SIMON. FASTER NOW, DEAR FRIEND.
SHOOM
SHOOOM
CORNER THOSE MAGGOTS! NONE MUST ESCAPE!

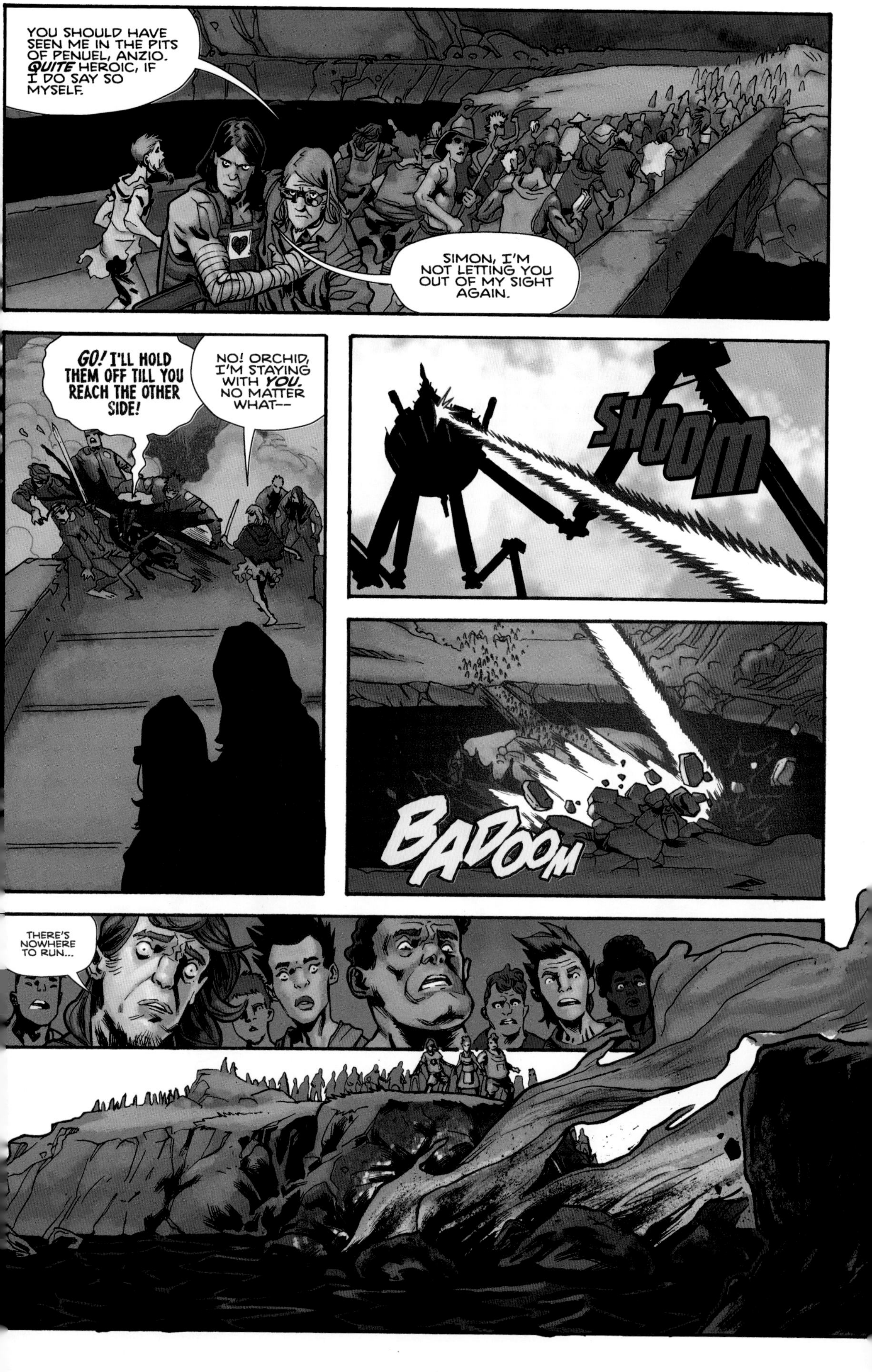
YOU SHOULD HAVE SEEN ME IN THE PITS OF PENUEL, ANZIO. QUITE HEROIC, IF I DO SAY SO MYSELF.
SIMON, I'M NOT LETTING YOU OUT OF MY SIGHT AGAIN.
GO! I'LL HOLD THEM OFF TILL YOU REACH THE OTHER SIDE!
NO! ORCHID, I'M STAYING WITH YOU. NO MATTER WHAT--
SHOOM
BADOOM
THERE'S NOWHERE TO RUN...

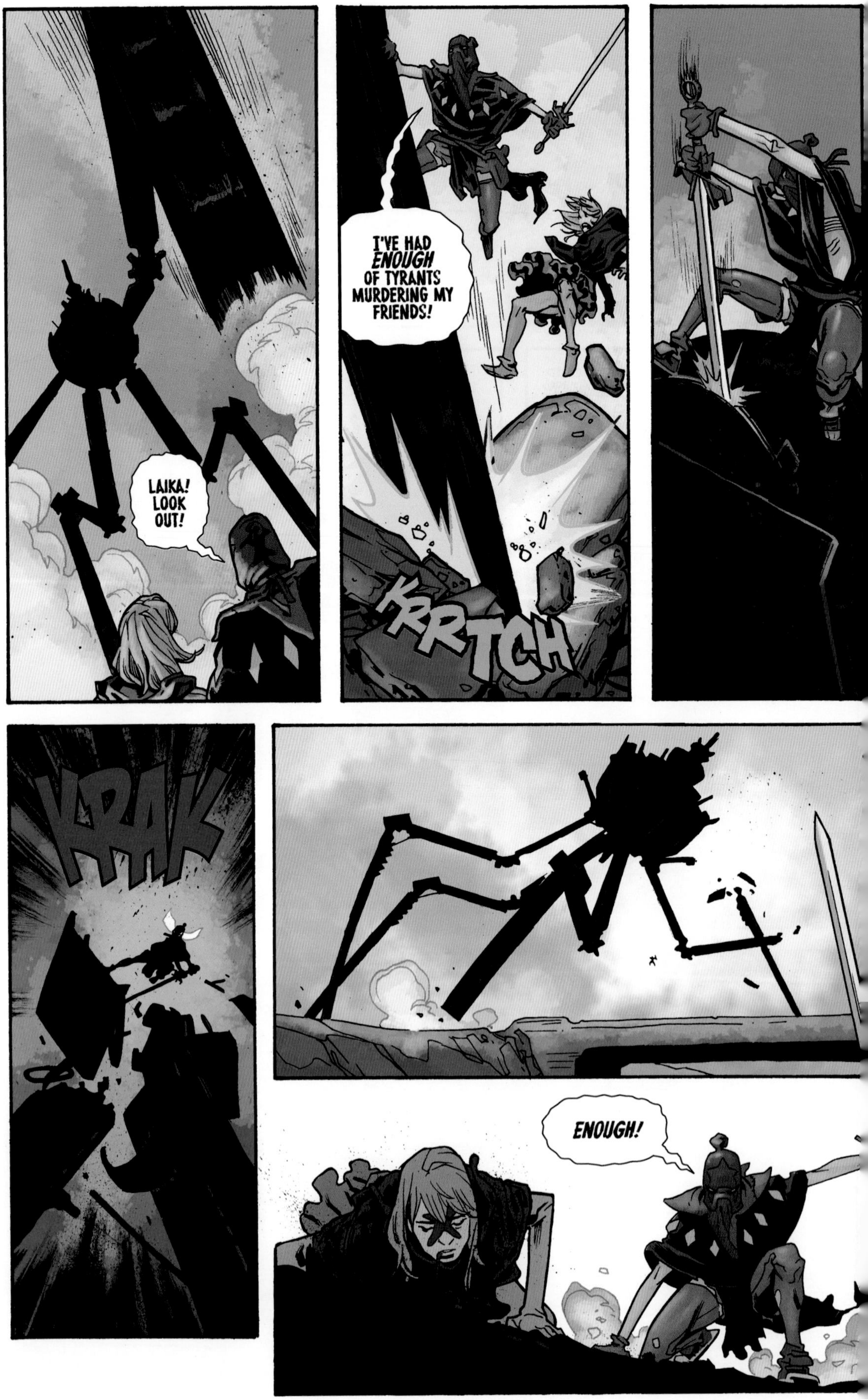
LAIKA! LOOK OUT!
I'VE HAD ENOUGH OF TYRANTS MURDERING MY FRIENDS!
KRRTCH
KRAK
ENOUGH!

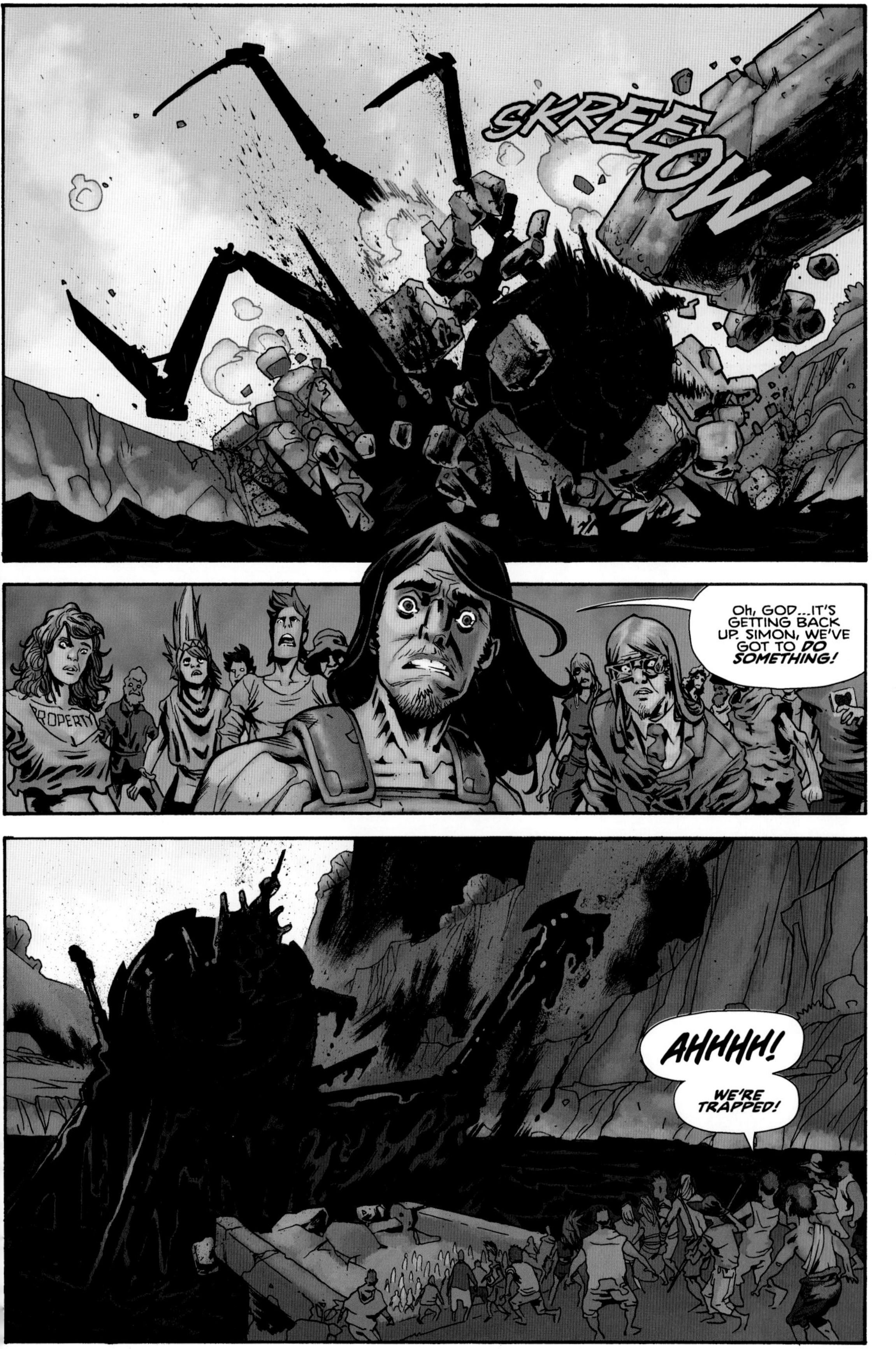
SKREEOW
Oh, GOD...IT'S GETTING BACK UP. SIMON, WE'VE GOT TO DO SOMETHING!
AHHHH!
WE'RE TRAPPED!

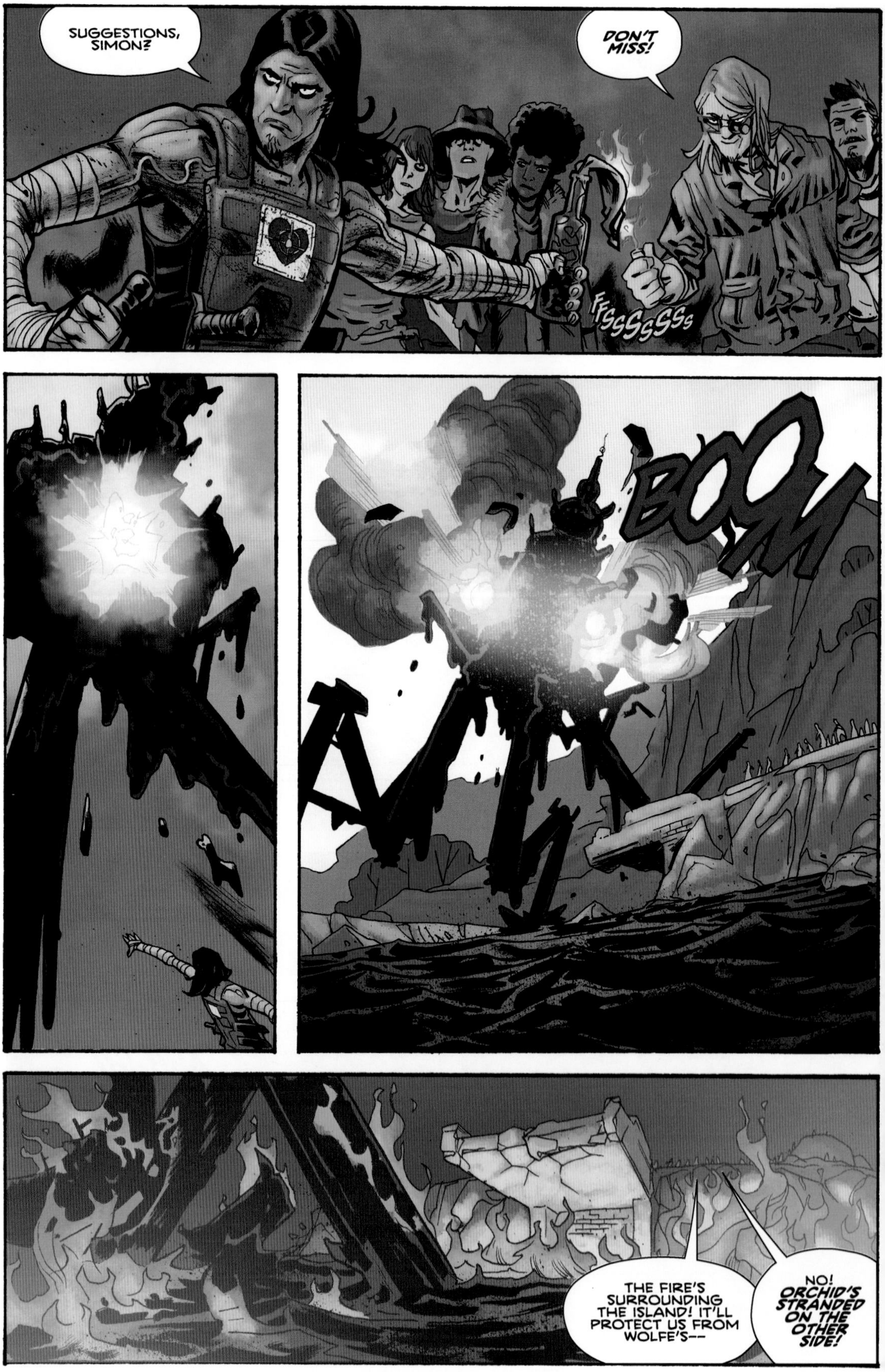
SUGGESTIONS, SIMON?
DON'T MISS!
FFSSSSSSS
BOOM
THE FIRE'S SURROUNDING THE ISLAND! IT'LL PROTECT US FROM WOLFE'S--
NO! ORCHID'S STRANDED ON THE OTHER SIDE!

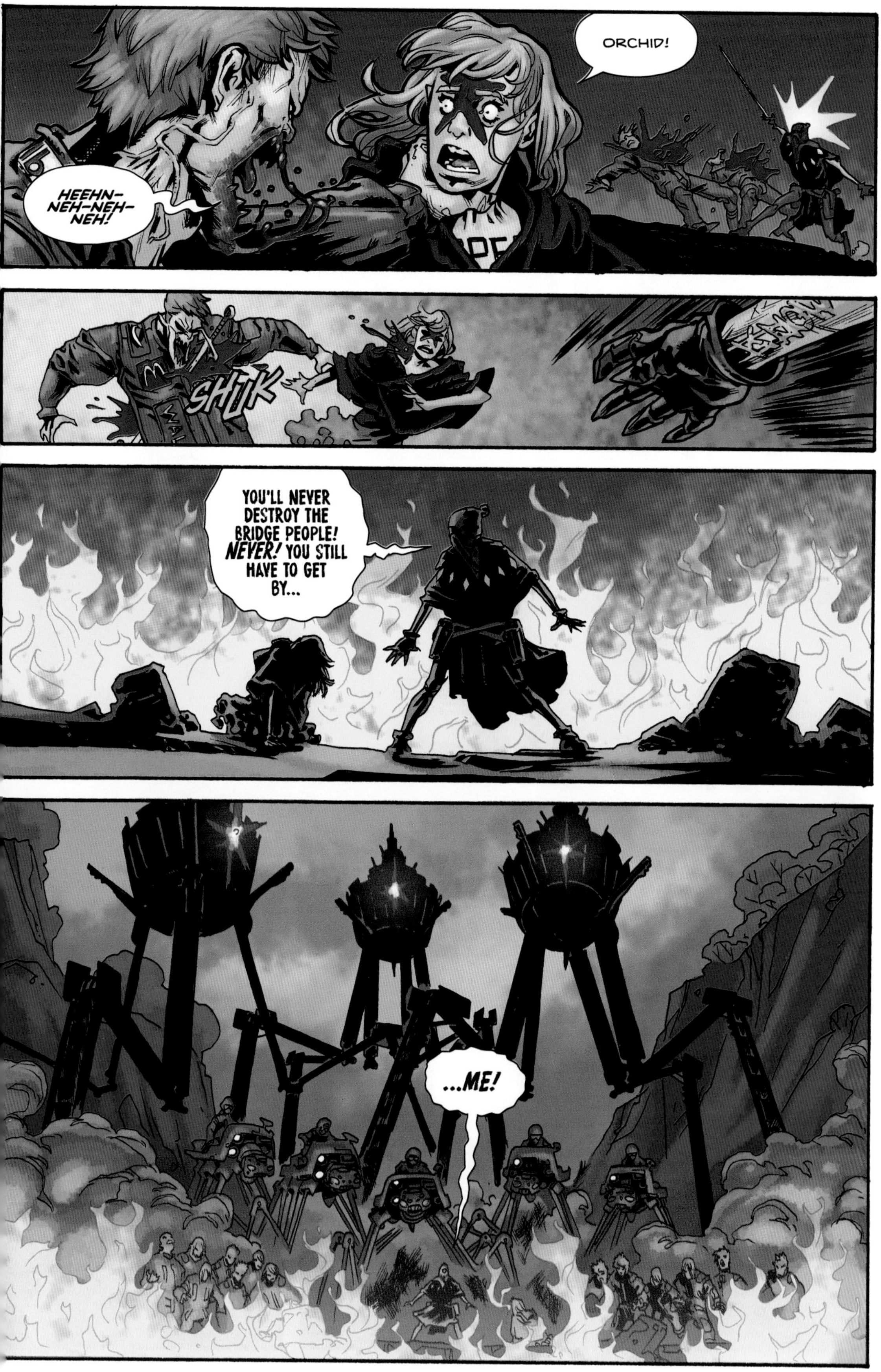

ORCHID!
HEEHN-NEH-NEH-NEH!
SHUK
YOU'LL NEVER DESTROY THE BRIDGE PEOPLE! NEVER! YOU STILL HAVE TO GET BY...
...ME!

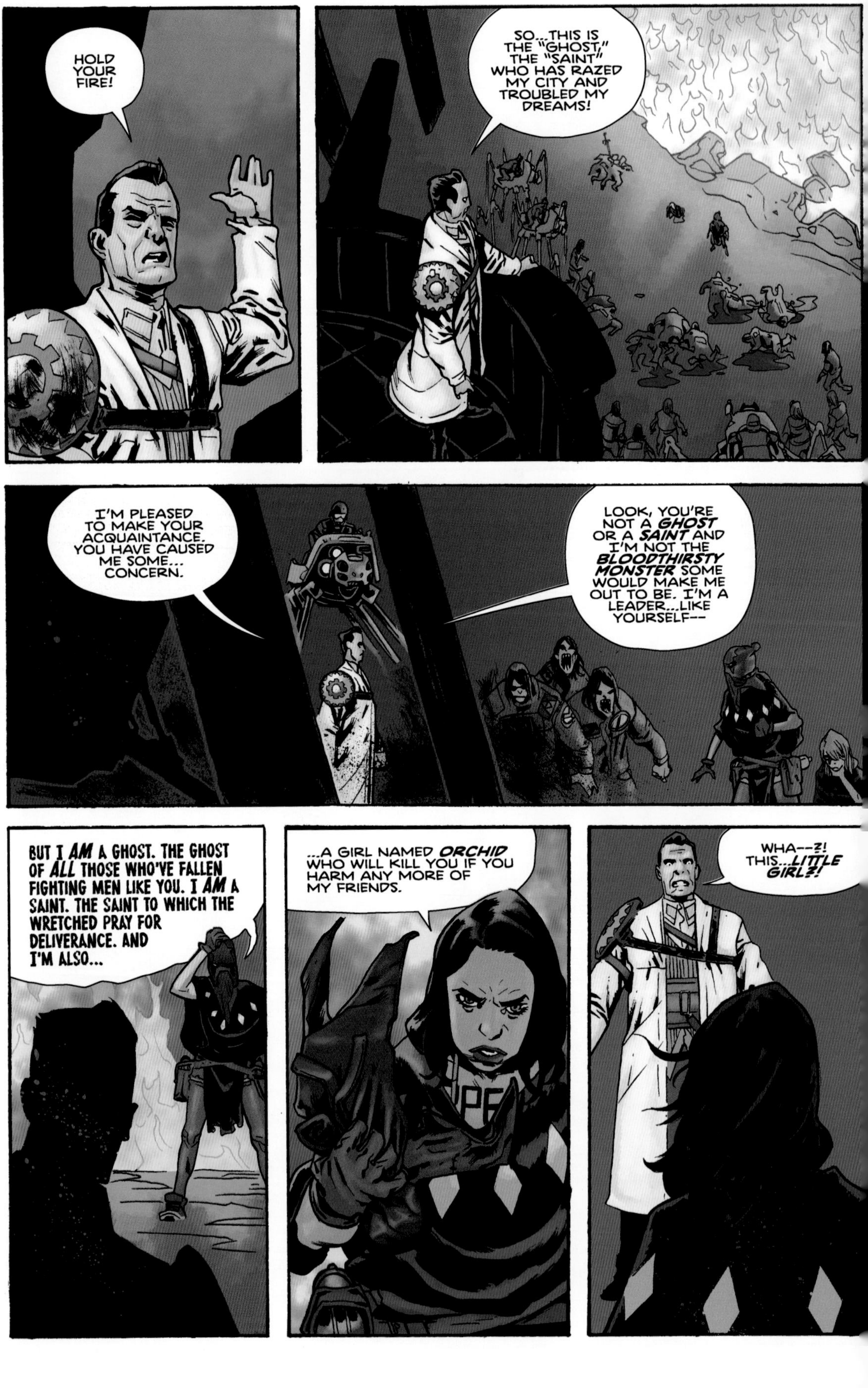
HOLD YOUR FIRE!
SO...THIS IS THE "GHOST," THE "SAINT" WHO HAS RAZED MY CITY AND TROUBLED MY DREAMS!
I'M PLEASED TO MAKE YOUR ACQUAINTANCE. YOU HAVE CAUSED ME SOME... CONCERN.
LOOK, YOU'RE NOT A GHOST OR A SAINT AND I'M NOT THE BLOODTHIRSTY MONSTER SOME WOULD MAKE ME OUT TO BE. I'M A LEADER...LIKE YOURSELF--
BUT I AM A GHOST. THE GHOST OF ALL THOSE WHO'VE FALLEN FIGHTING MEN LIKE YOU. I AM A SAINT. THE SAINT TO WHICH THE WRETCHED PRAY FOR DELIVERANCE. AND I'M ALSO...
...A GIRL NAMED ORCHID WHO WILL KILL YOU IF YOU HARM ANY MORE OF MY FRIENDS.
WHA--?! THIS...LITTLE GIRL?!

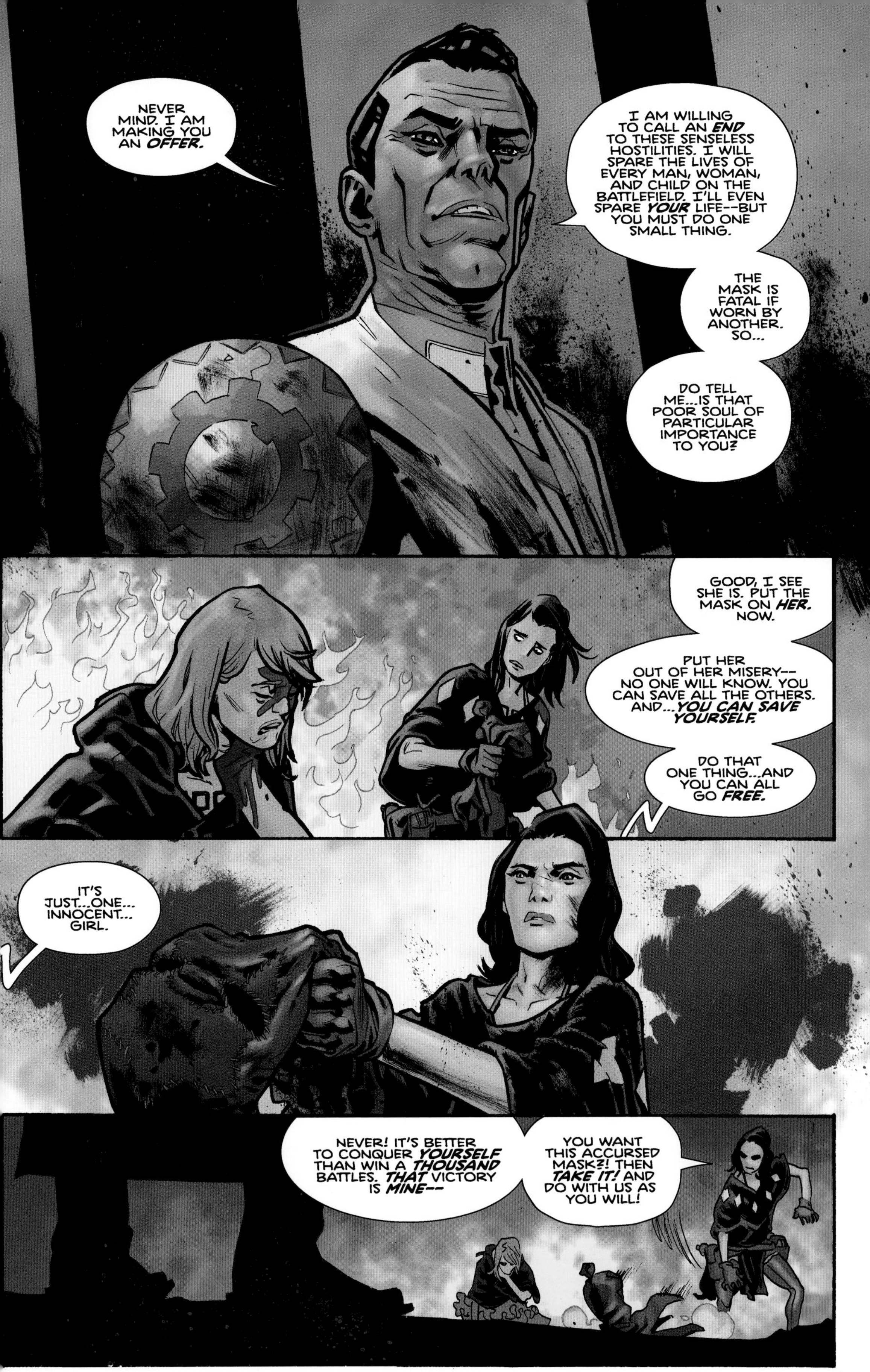

NEVER MIND. I AM MAKING YOU AN *OFFER.*
I AM WILLING TO CALL AN *END* TO THESE SENSELESS HOSTILITIES. I WILL SPARE THE LIVES OF EVERY MAN, WOMAN, AND CHILD ON THE BATTLEFIELD. I'LL EVEN SPARE *YOUR* LIFE--BUT YOU MUST DO ONE SMALL THING.
THE MASK IS FATAL IF WORN BY ANOTHER. SO...
DO TELL ME...IS THAT POOR SOUL OF PARTICULAR IMPORTANCE TO YOU?
GOOD, I SEE SHE IS. PUT THE MASK ON *HER.* NOW.
PUT HER OUT OF HER MISERY--NO ONE WILL KNOW. YOU CAN SAVE ALL THE OTHERS. AND...*YOU CAN SAVE YOURSELF.*
DO THAT ONE THING...AND YOU CAN ALL GO *FREE.*
IT'S JUST...ONE... INNOCENT... GIRL.
NEVER! IT'S BETTER TO CONQUER *YOURSELF* THAN WIN A *THOUSAND* BATTLES. *THAT* VICTORY IS *MINE--*
YOU WANT THIS ACCURSED MASK?! THEN *TAKE IT!* AND DO WITH US AS YOU WILL!

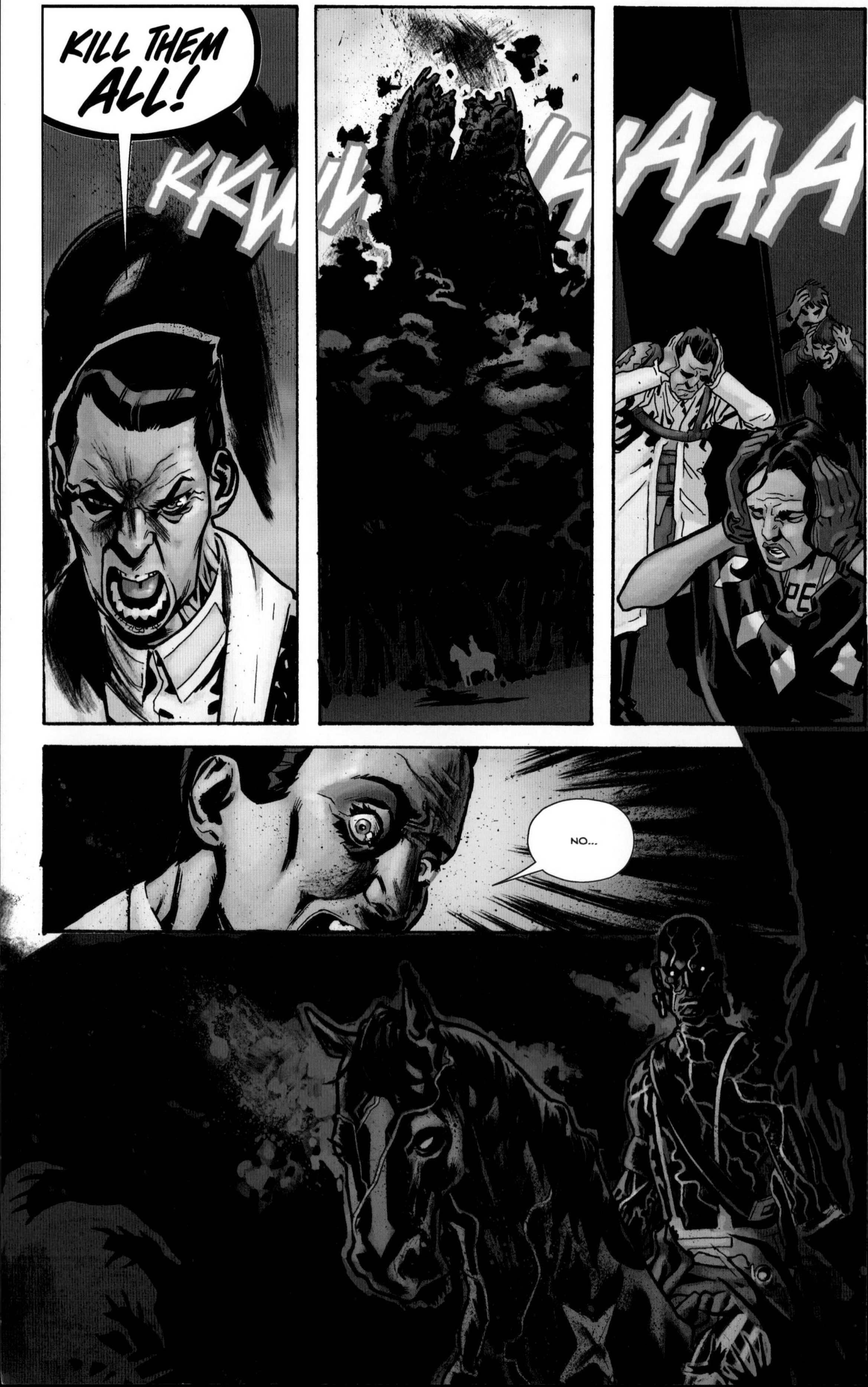

KILL THEM ALL!
KKWWAAAA
NO...

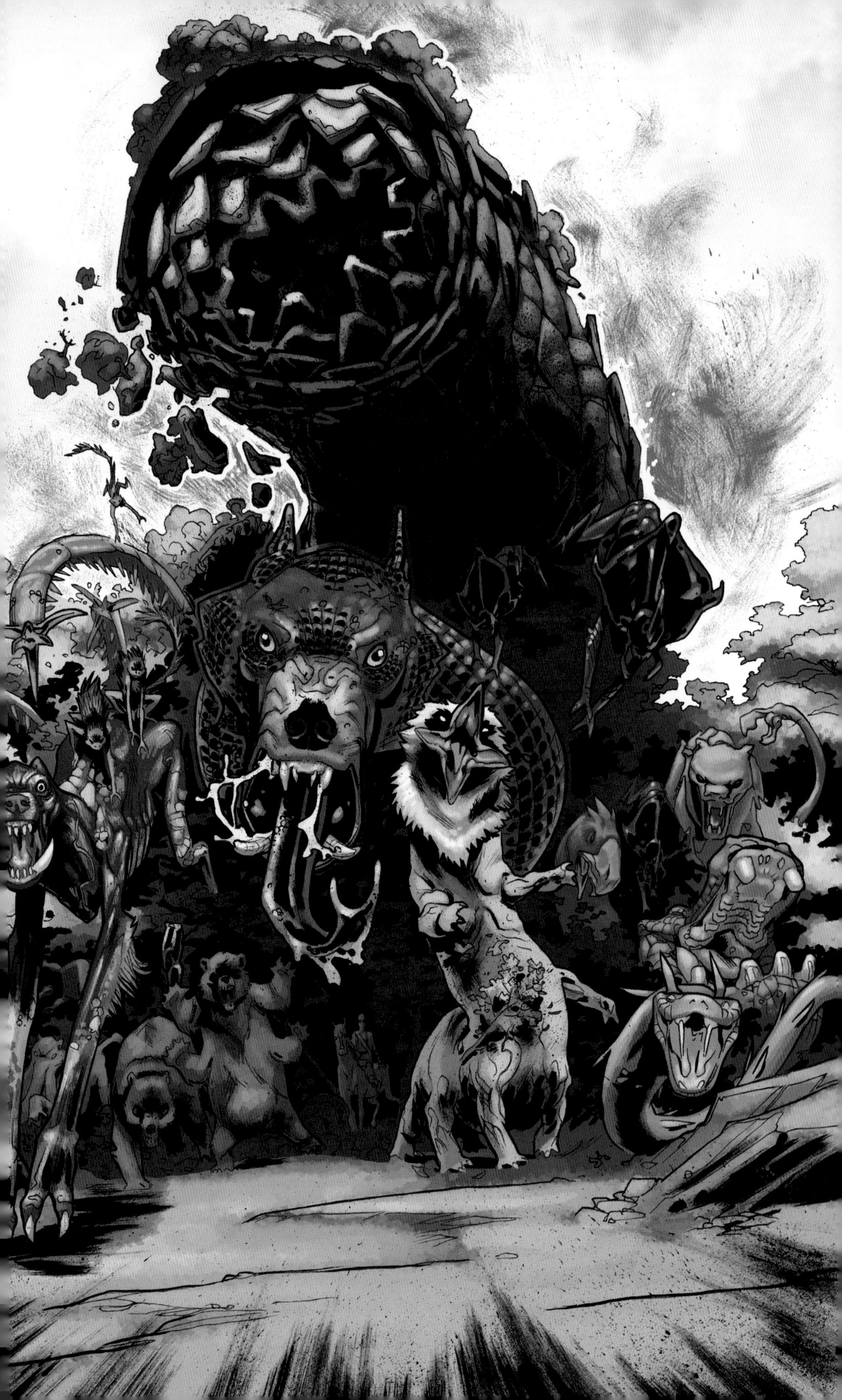

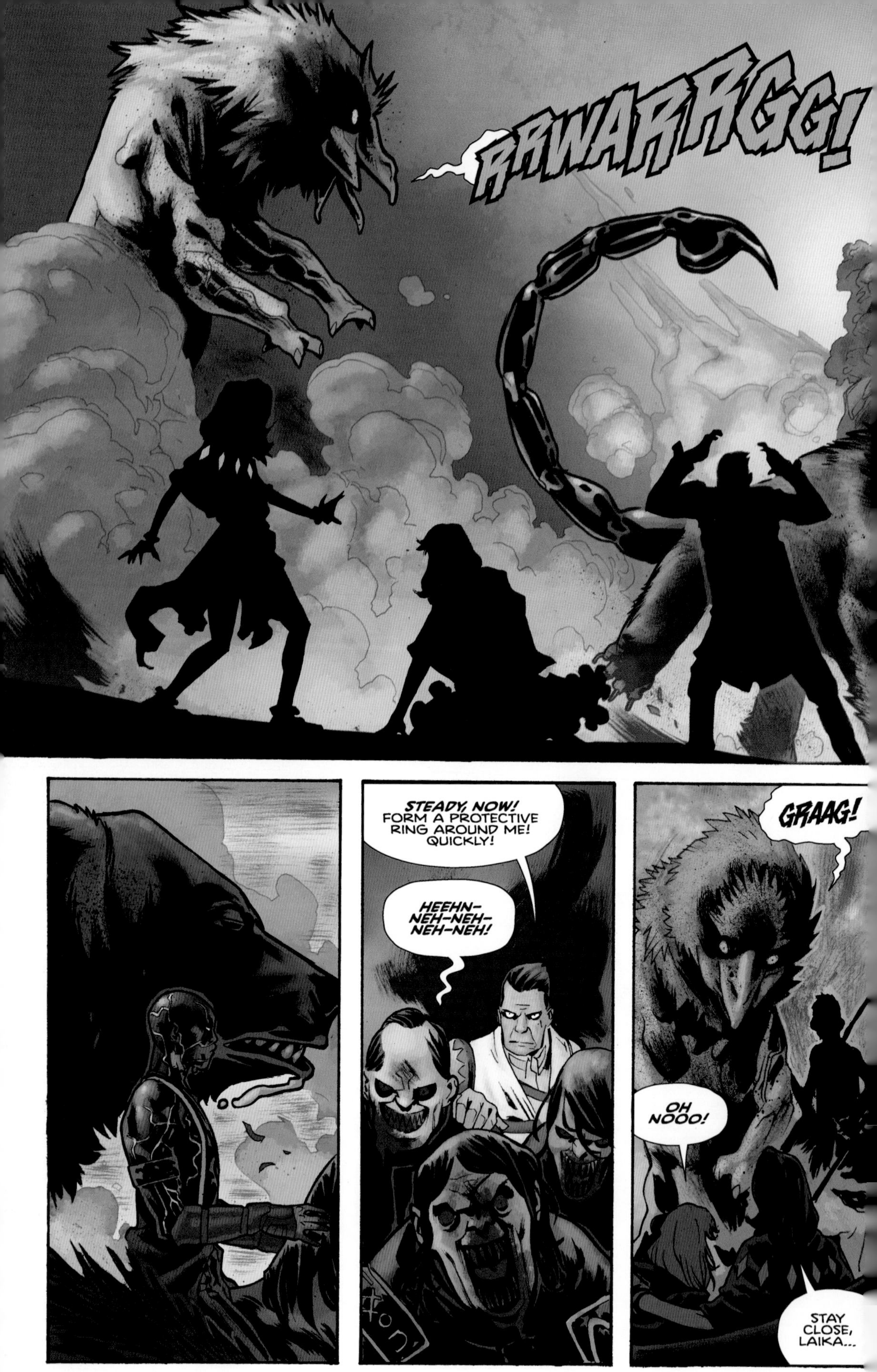
RRWARRGG!
STEADY, NOW! FORM A PROTECTIVE RING AROUND ME! QUICKLY!
HEEHN-NEH-NEH-NEH-NEH!
GRAAG!
OH NOOO!
STAY CLOSE, LAIKA...

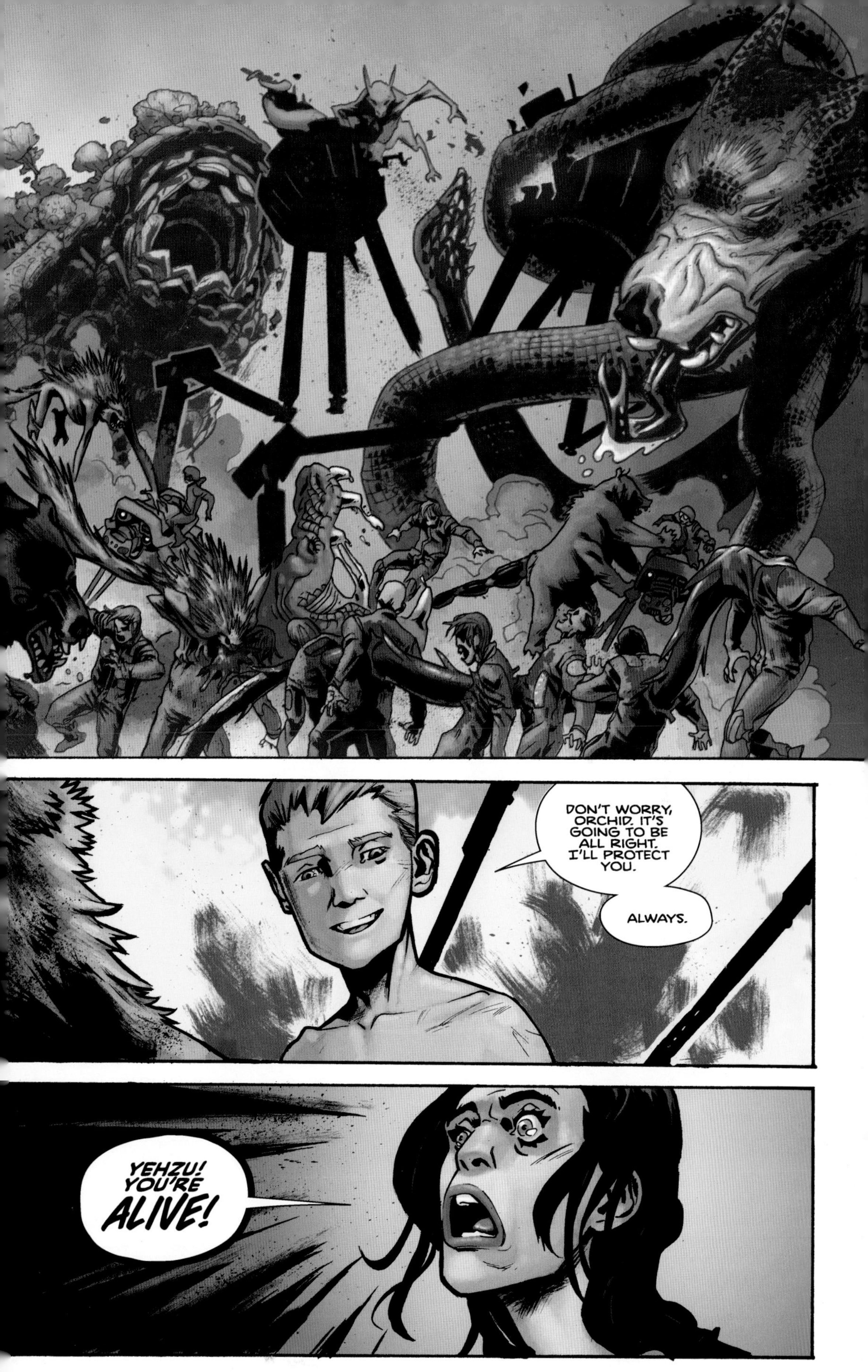
DON'T WORRY, ORCHID. IT'S GOING TO BE ALL RIGHT. I'LL PROTECT YOU.
ALWAYS.
YEHZU! YOU'RE ALIVE!

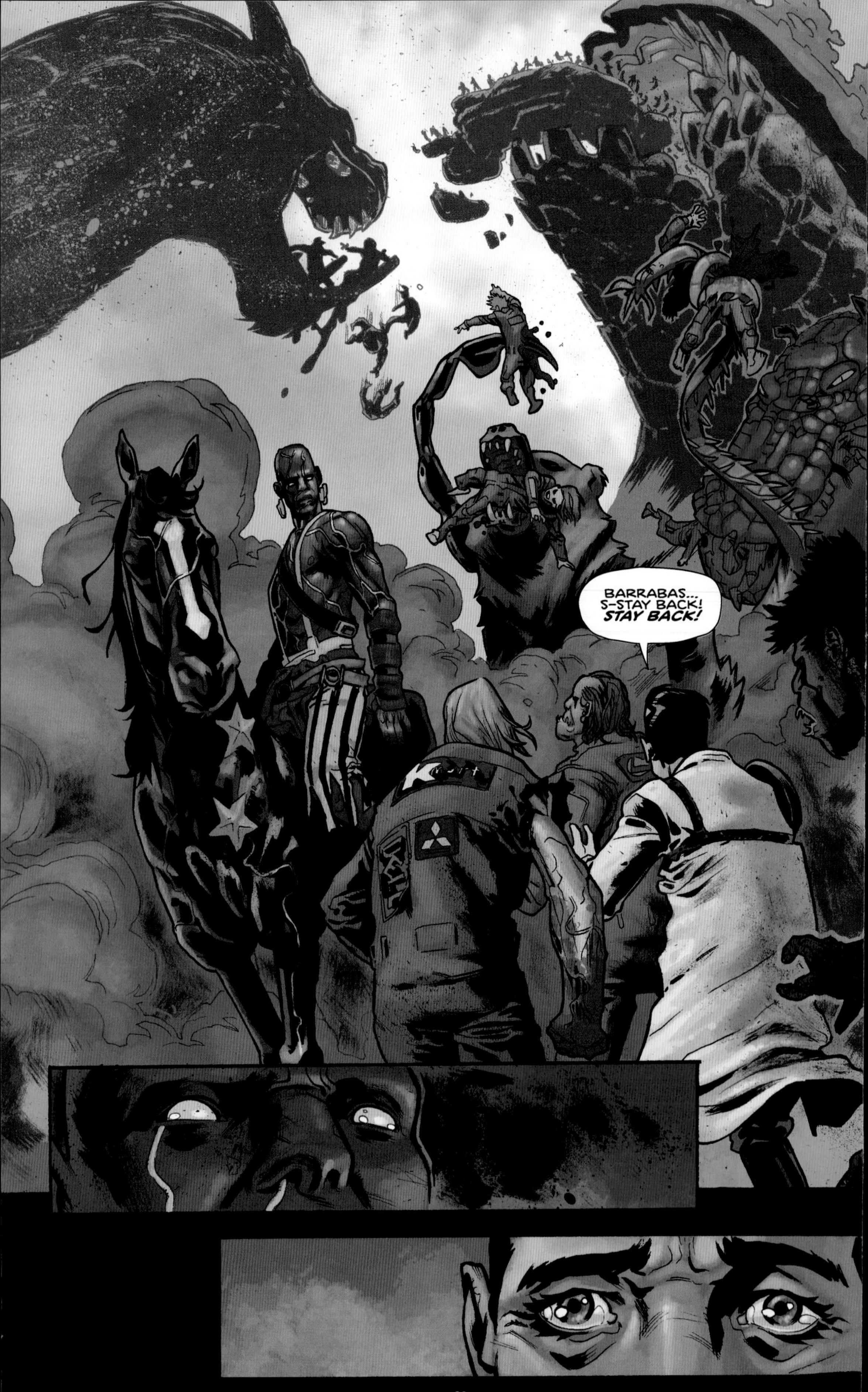
BARRABAS... S-STAY BACK! STAY BACK!

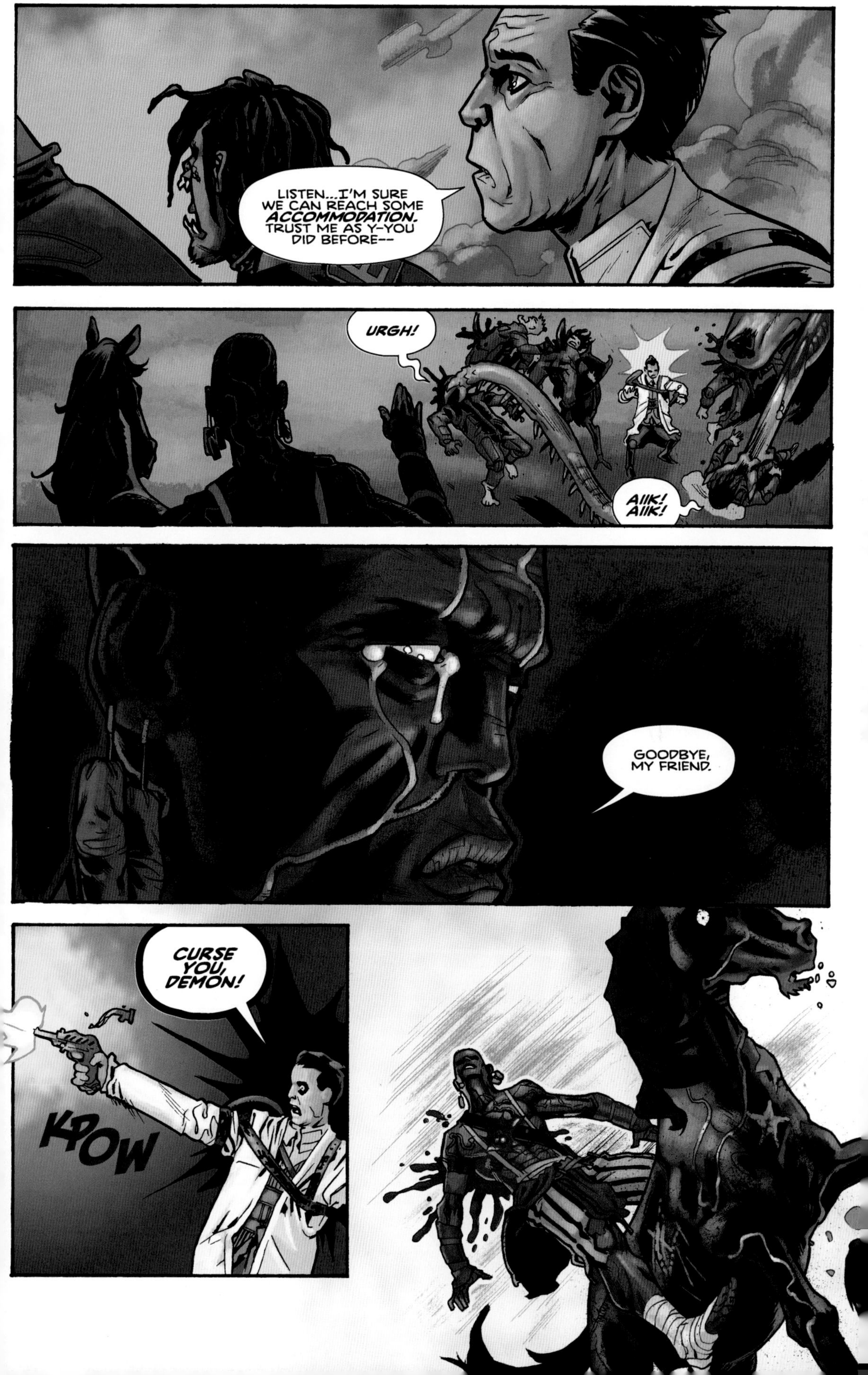
LISTEN...I'M SURE WE CAN REACH SOME ACCOMMODATION. TRUST ME AS Y-YOU DID BEFORE--
URGH!
AIIK! AIIK!
GOODBYE, MY FRIEND.
CURSE YOU, DEMON!
KPOW

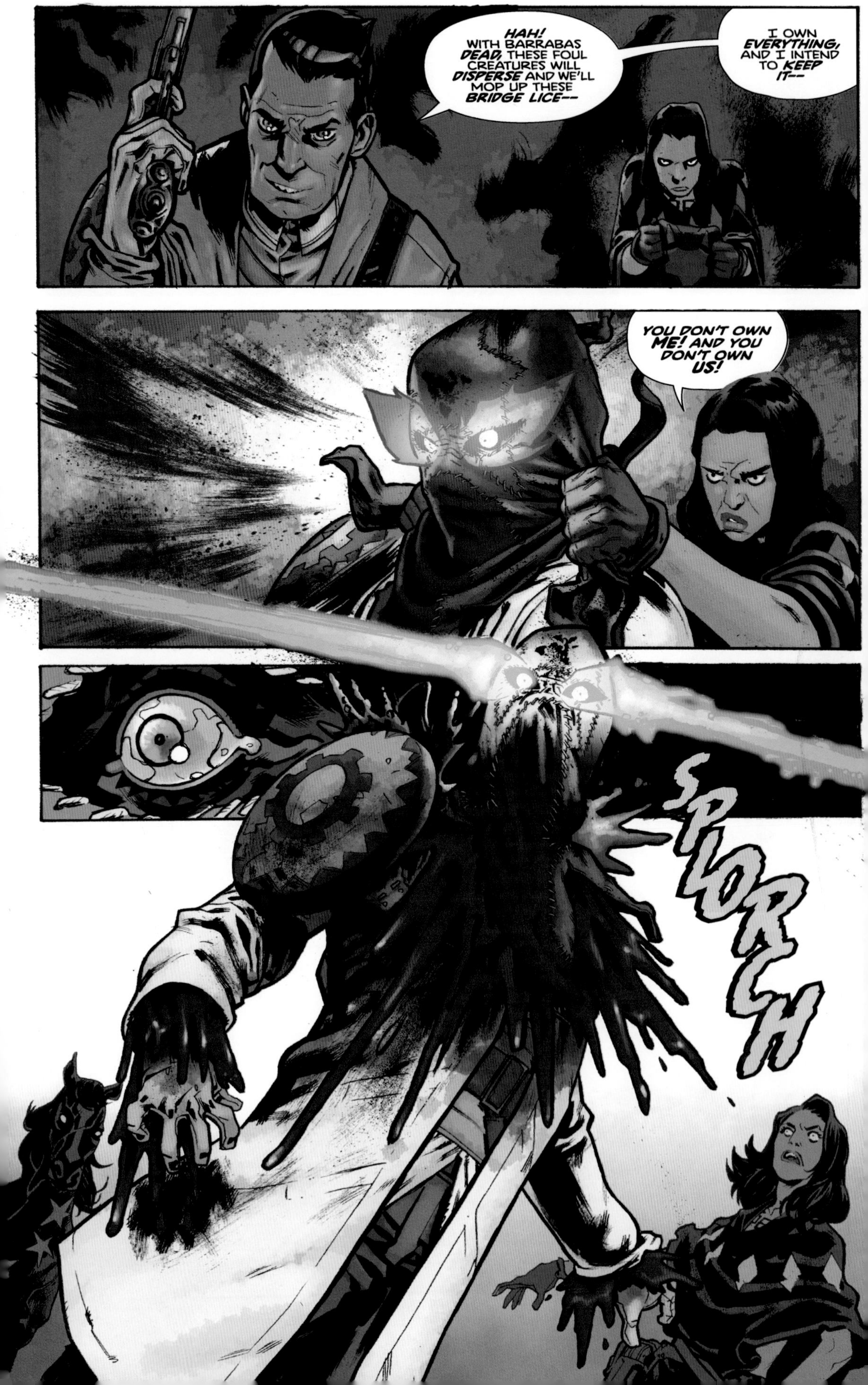
HAH! WITH BARRABAS DEAD, THESE FOUL CREATURES WILL DISPERSE AND WE'LL MOP UP THESE BRIDGE LICE--
I OWN EVERYTHING, AND I INTEND TO KEEP IT--
YOU DON'T OWN ME! AND YOU DON'T OWN US!
SPLORCH

K-SPAk

YAAAAAAAAHHHHHH!

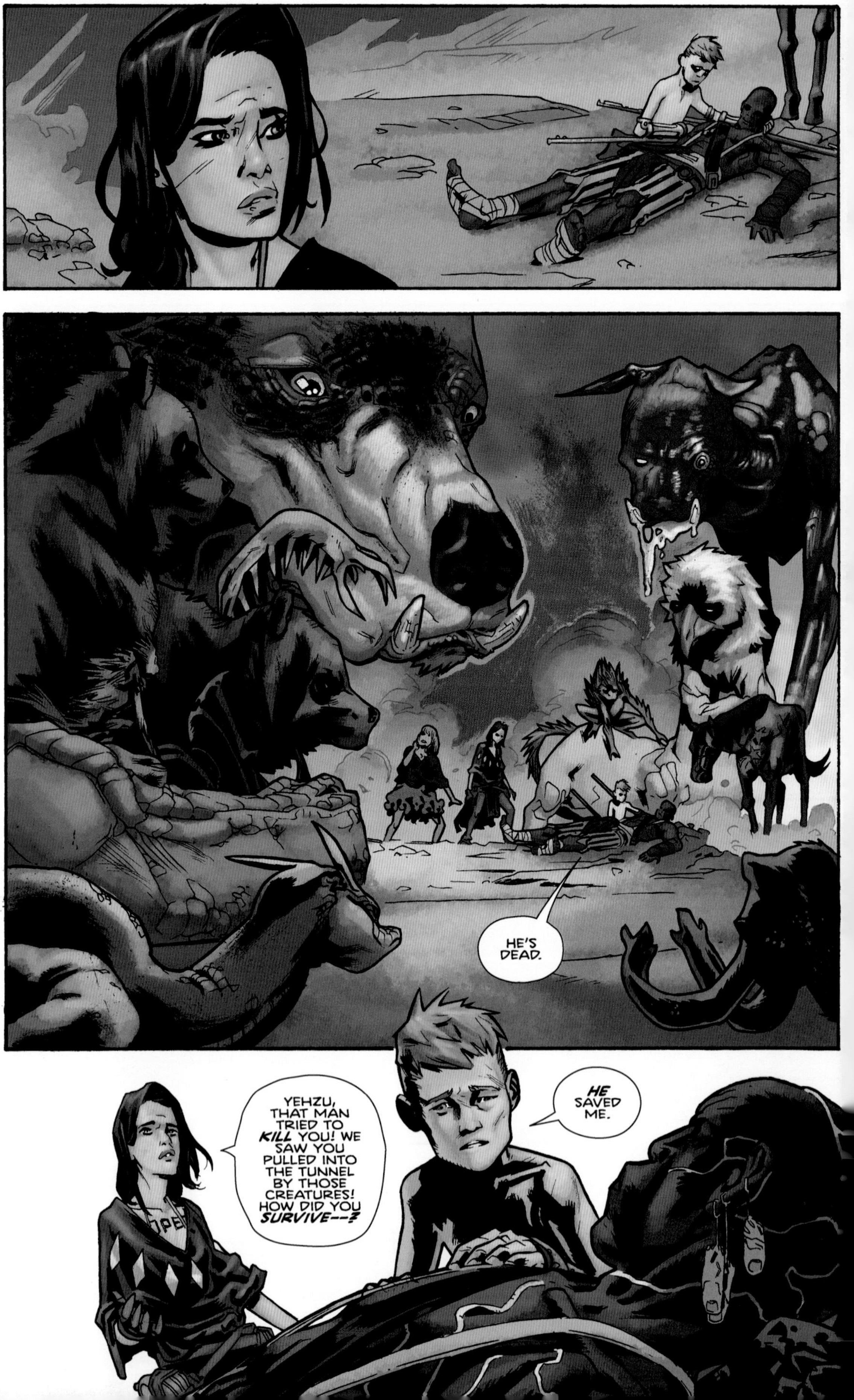
HE'S DEAD.
YEHZU, THAT MAN TRIED TO ***KILL*** YOU! WE SAW YOU PULLED INTO THE TUNNEL BY THOSE CREATURES! HOW DID YOU ***SURVIVE--?***
***HE*** SAVED ME.

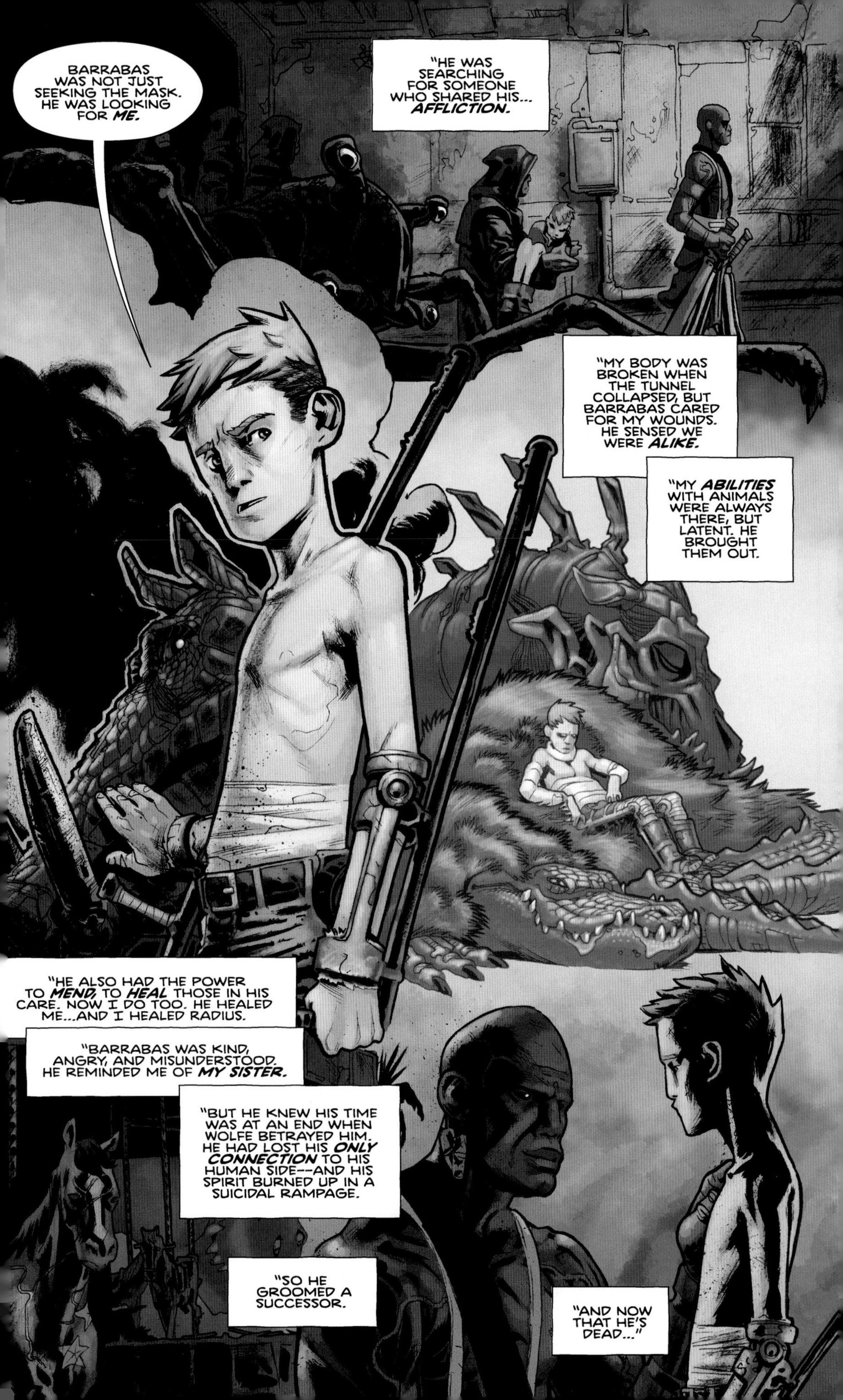

BARRABAS WAS NOT JUST SEEKING THE MASK. HE WAS LOOKING FOR *ME.*
"HE WAS SEARCHING FOR SOMEONE WHO SHARED HIS... *AFFLICTION.*
"MY BODY WAS BROKEN WHEN THE TUNNEL COLLAPSED, BUT BARRABAS CARED FOR MY WOUNDS. HE SENSED WE WERE *ALIKE.*
"MY *ABILITIES* WITH ANIMALS WERE ALWAYS THERE, BUT LATENT. HE BROUGHT THEM OUT.
"HE ALSO HAD THE POWER TO *MEND,* TO *HEAL* THOSE IN HIS CARE. NOW I DO TOO. HE HEALED ME...AND I HEALED RADIUS.
"BARRABAS WAS KIND, ANGRY, AND MISUNDERSTOOD. HE REMINDED ME OF *MY SISTER.*
"BUT HE KNEW HIS TIME WAS AT AN END WHEN WOLFE BETRAYED HIM. HE HAD LOST HIS *ONLY CONNECTION* TO HIS HUMAN SIDE--AND HIS SPIRIT BURNED UP IN A SUICIDAL RAMPAGE.
"SO HE GROOMED A SUCCESSOR.
"AND NOW THAT HE'S DEAD..."

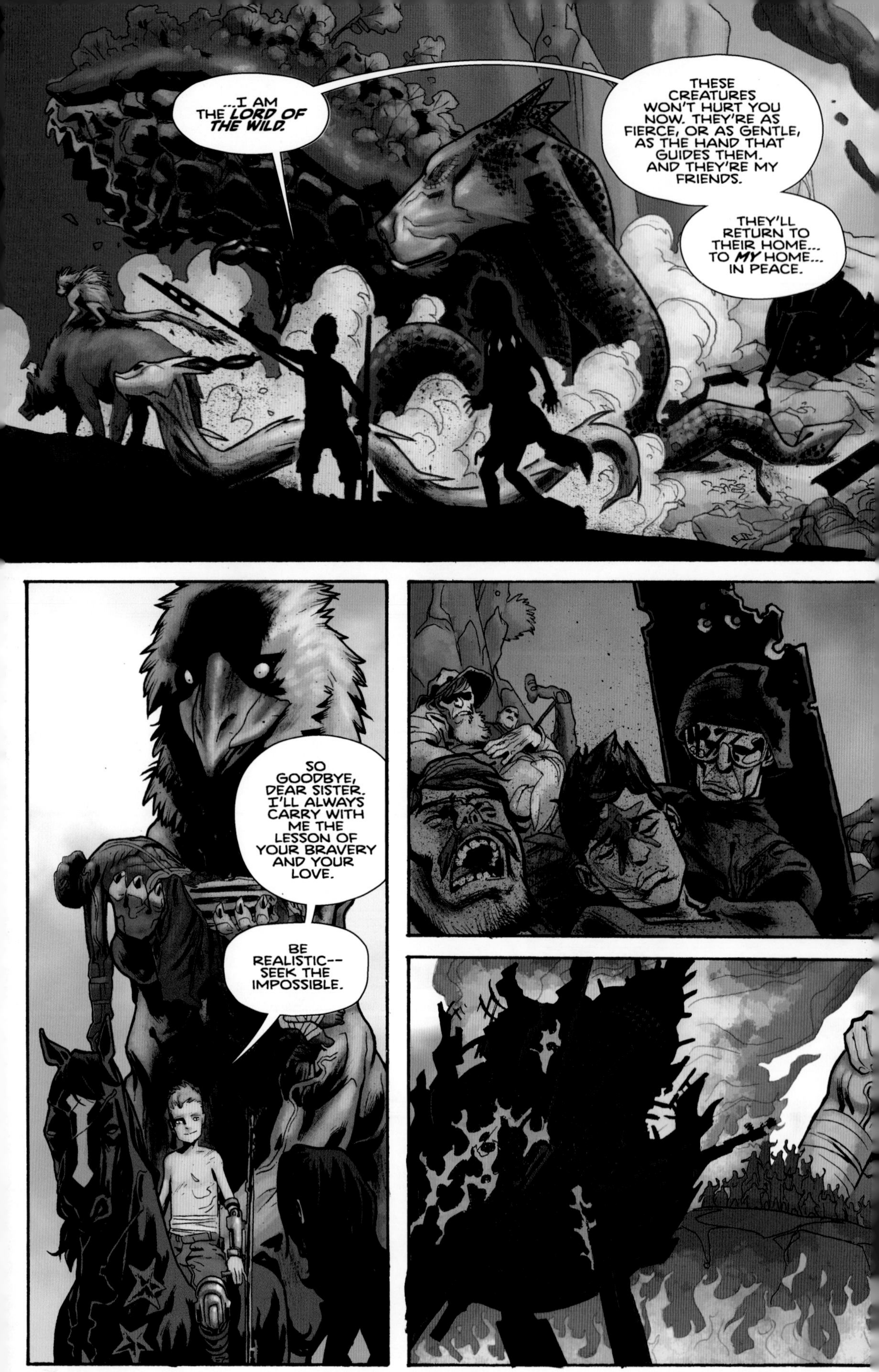

...I AM THE *LORD OF THE WILD.*
THESE CREATURES WON'T HURT YOU NOW. THEY'RE AS FIERCE, OR AS GENTLE, AS THE HAND THAT GUIDES THEM. AND THEY'RE MY FRIENDS.
THEY'LL RETURN TO THEIR HOME... TO *MY* HOME... IN PEACE.
SO GOODBYE, DEAR SISTER. I'LL ALWAYS CARRY WITH ME THE LESSON OF YOUR BRAVERY AND YOUR LOVE.
BE REALISTIC-- SEEK THE IMPOSSIBLE.

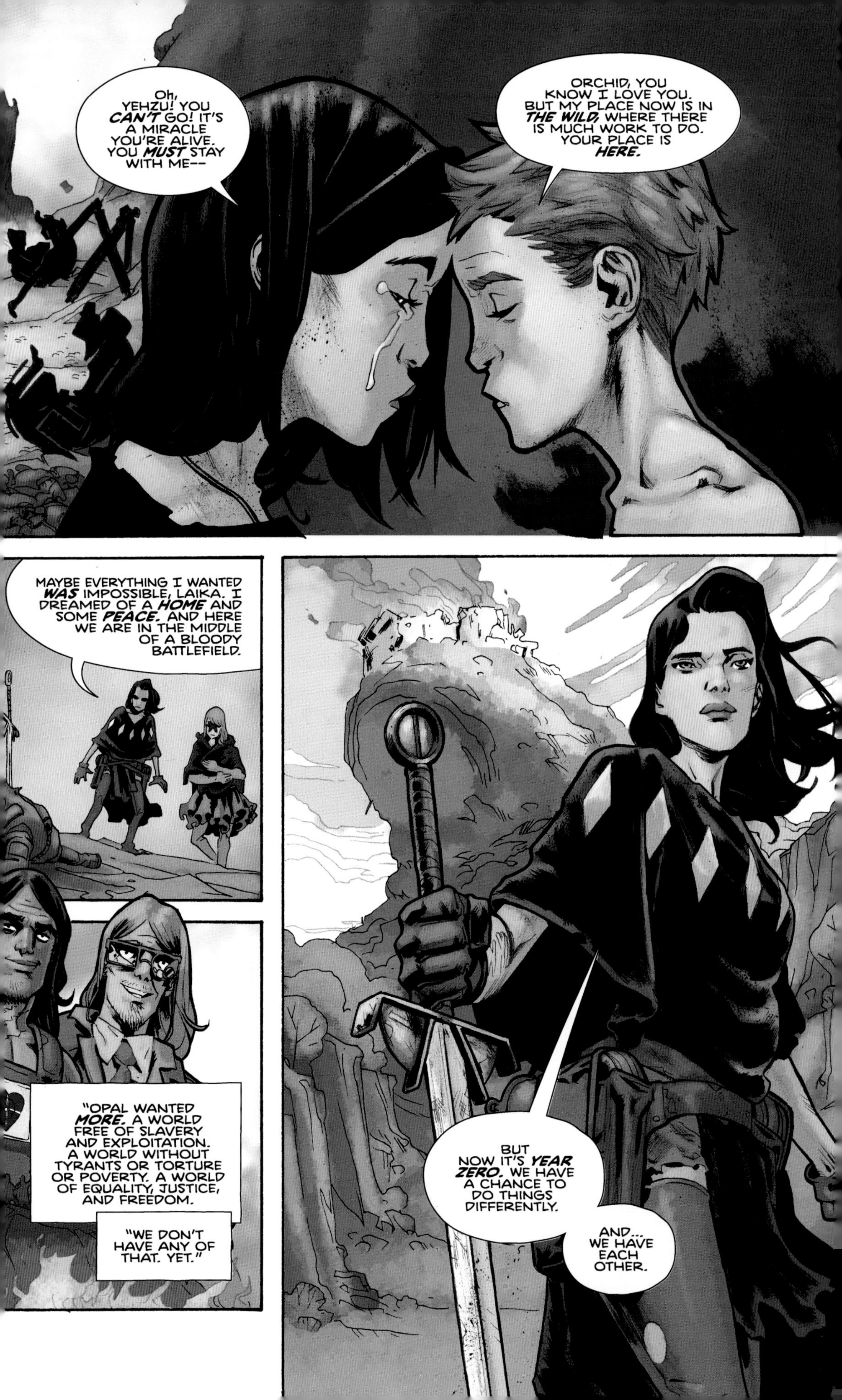
Oh, YEHZU! YOU CAN'T GO! IT'S A MIRACLE YOU'RE ALIVE. YOU MUST STAY WITH ME--
ORCHID, YOU KNOW I LOVE YOU. BUT MY PLACE NOW IS IN THE WILD, WHERE THERE IS MUCH WORK TO DO. YOUR PLACE IS HERE.
MAYBE EVERYTHING I WANTED WAS IMPOSSIBLE, LAIKA. I DREAMED OF A HOME AND SOME PEACE. AND HERE WE ARE IN THE MIDDLE OF A BLOODY BATTLEFIELD.
"OPAL WANTED MORE. A WORLD FREE OF SLAVERY AND EXPLOITATION. A WORLD WITHOUT TYRANTS OR TORTURE OR POVERTY. A WORLD OF EQUALITY, JUSTICE, AND FREEDOM.
"WE DON'T HAVE ANY OF THAT. YET."
BUT NOW IT'S YEAR ZERO. WE HAVE A CHANCE TO DO THINGS DIFFERENTLY.
AND... WE HAVE EACH OTHER.

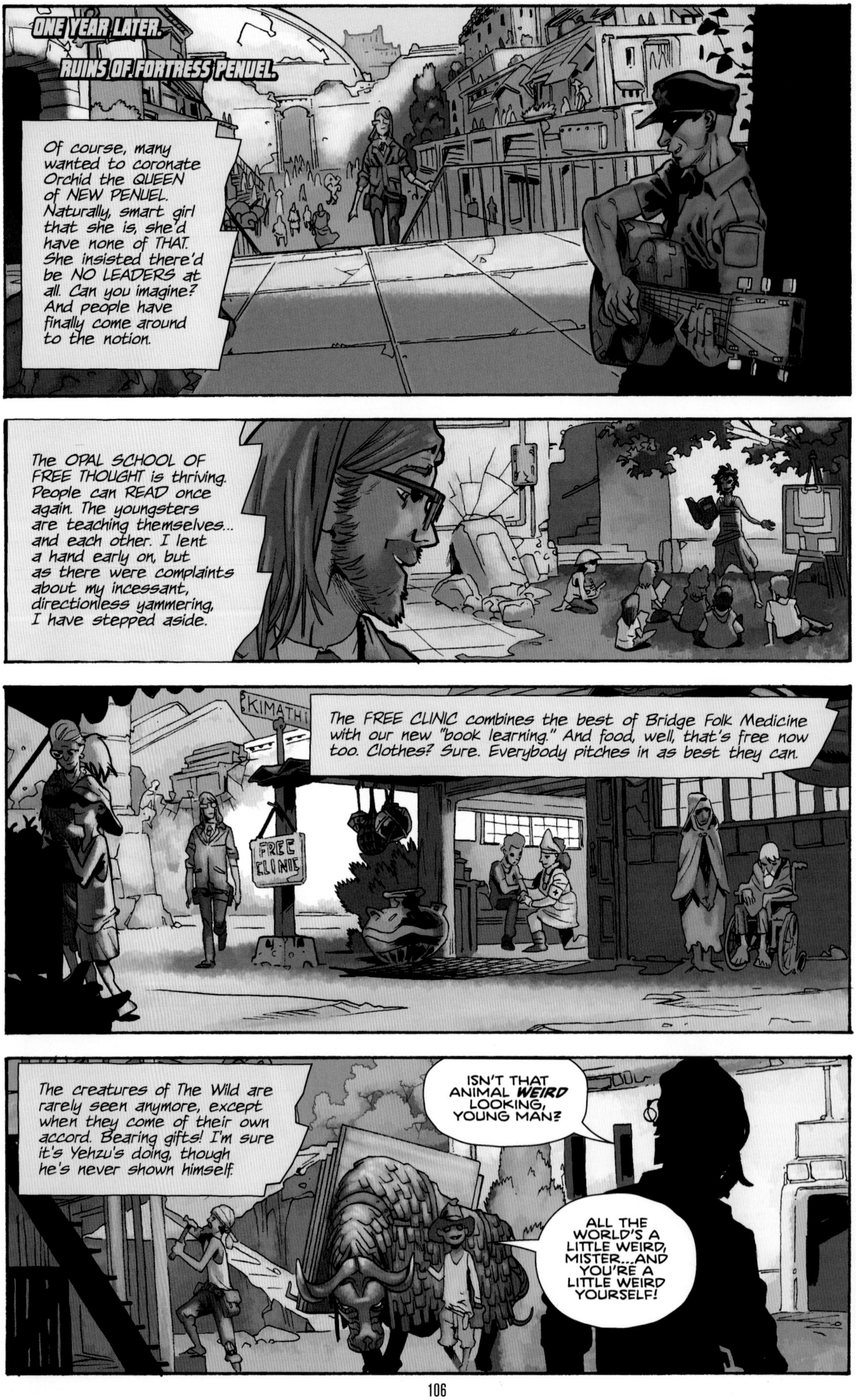
ONE YEAR LATER.
RUINS OF FORTRESS PENUEL.
Of course, many wanted to coronate Orchid the QUEEN of NEW PENUEL. Naturally, smart girl that she is, she'd have none of THAT. She insisted there'd be NO LEADERS at all. Can you imagine? And people have finally come around to the notion.
The OPAL SCHOOL OF FREE THOUGHT is thriving. People can READ once again. The youngsters are teaching themselves... and each other. I lent a hand early on, but as there were complaints about my incessant, directionless yammering, I have stepped aside.
KIMATHI
The FREE CLINIC combines the best of Bridge Folk Medicine with our new "book learning." And food, well, that's free now too. Clothes? Sure. Everybody pitches in as best they can.
FREE CLINIC
The creatures of The Wild are rarely seen anymore, except when they come of their own accord. Bearing gifts! I'm sure it's Yehzu's doing, though he's never shown himself.
ISN'T THAT ANIMAL WEIRD LOOKING, YOUNG MAN?
ALL THE WORLD'S A LITTLE WEIRD, MISTER...AND YOU'RE A LITTLE WEIRD YOURSELF!

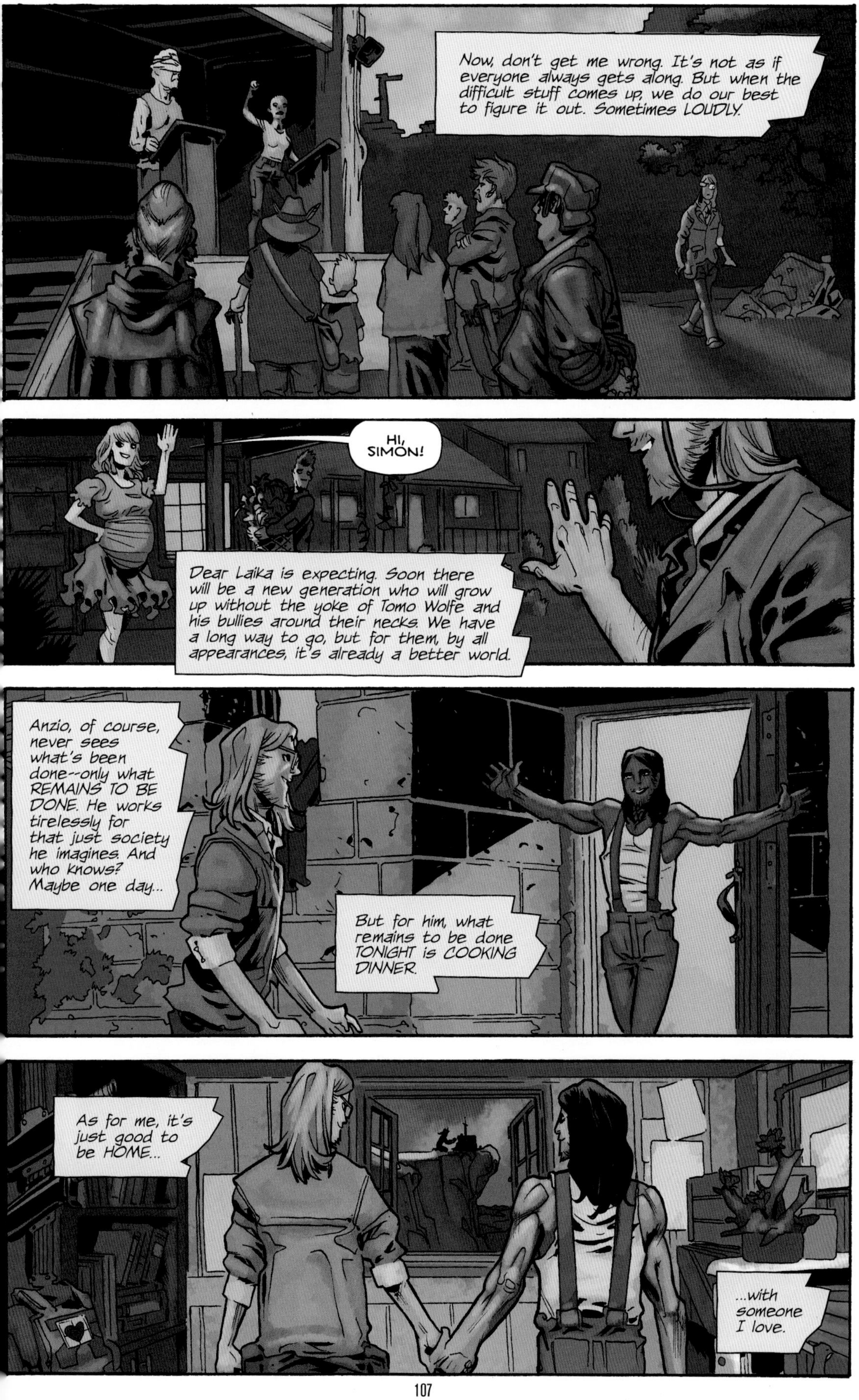
Now, don't get me wrong. It's not as if everyone always gets along. But when the difficult stuff comes up, we do our best to figure it out. Sometimes LOUDLY.
HI, SIMON!
Dear Laika is expecting. Soon there will be a new generation who will grow up without the yoke of Tomo Wolfe and his bullies around their necks. We have a long way to go, but for them, by all appearances, it's already a better world.
Anzio, of course, never sees what's been done--only what REMAINS TO BE DONE. He works tirelessly for that just society he imagines. And who knows? Maybe one day...
But for him, what remains to be done TONIGHT is COOKING DINNER.
As for me, it's just good to be HOME...
...with someone I love.

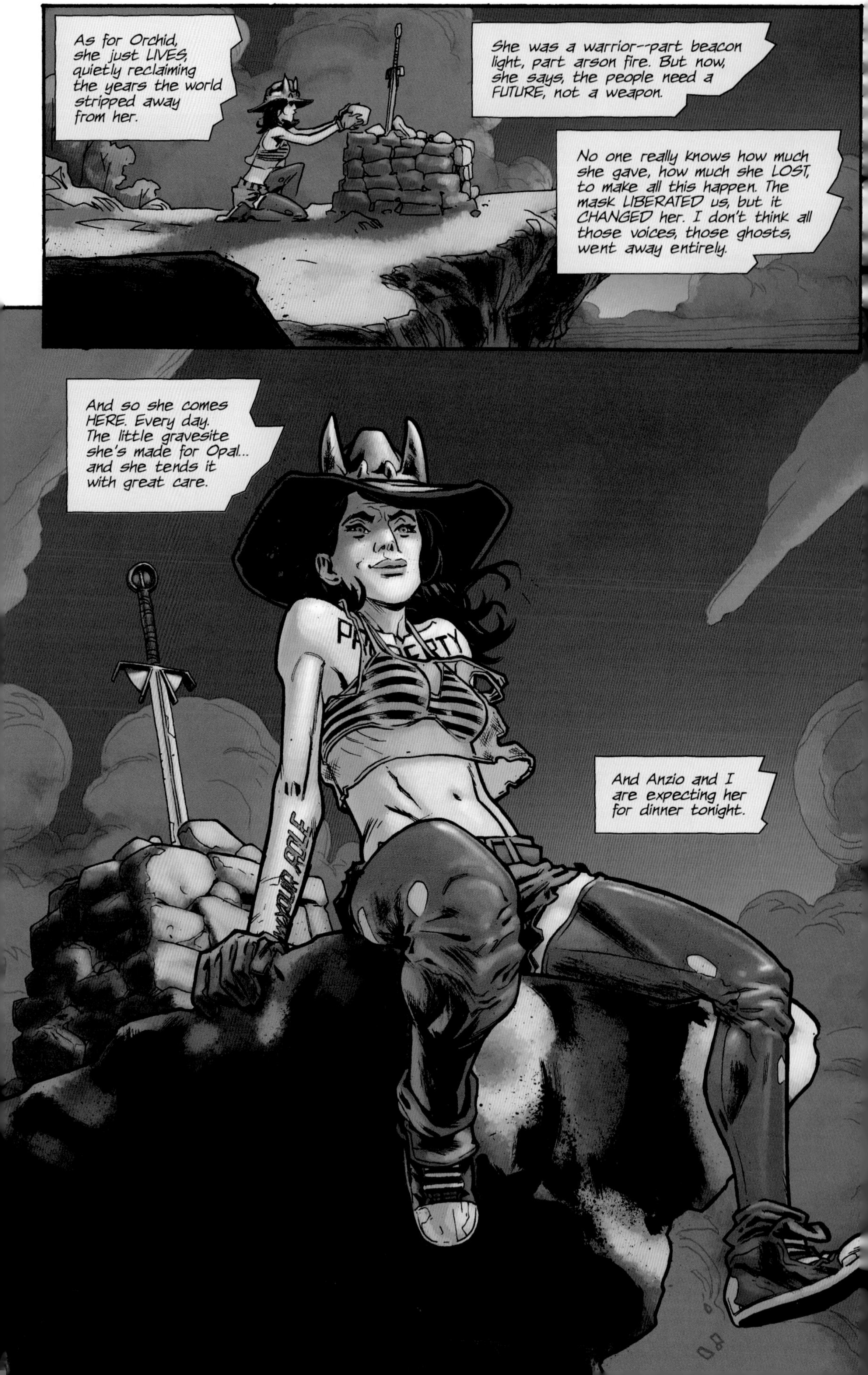
As for Orchid, she just LIVES, quietly reclaiming the years the world stripped away from her.
She was a warrior--part beacon light, part arson fire. But now, she says, the people need a FUTURE, not a weapon.
No one really knows how much she gave, how much she LOST, to make all this happen. The mask LIBERATED us, but it CHANGED her. I don't think all those voices, those ghosts, went away entirely.
And so she comes HERE. Every day. The little gravesite she's made for Opal... and she tends it with great care.
And Anzio and I are expecting her for dinner tonight.

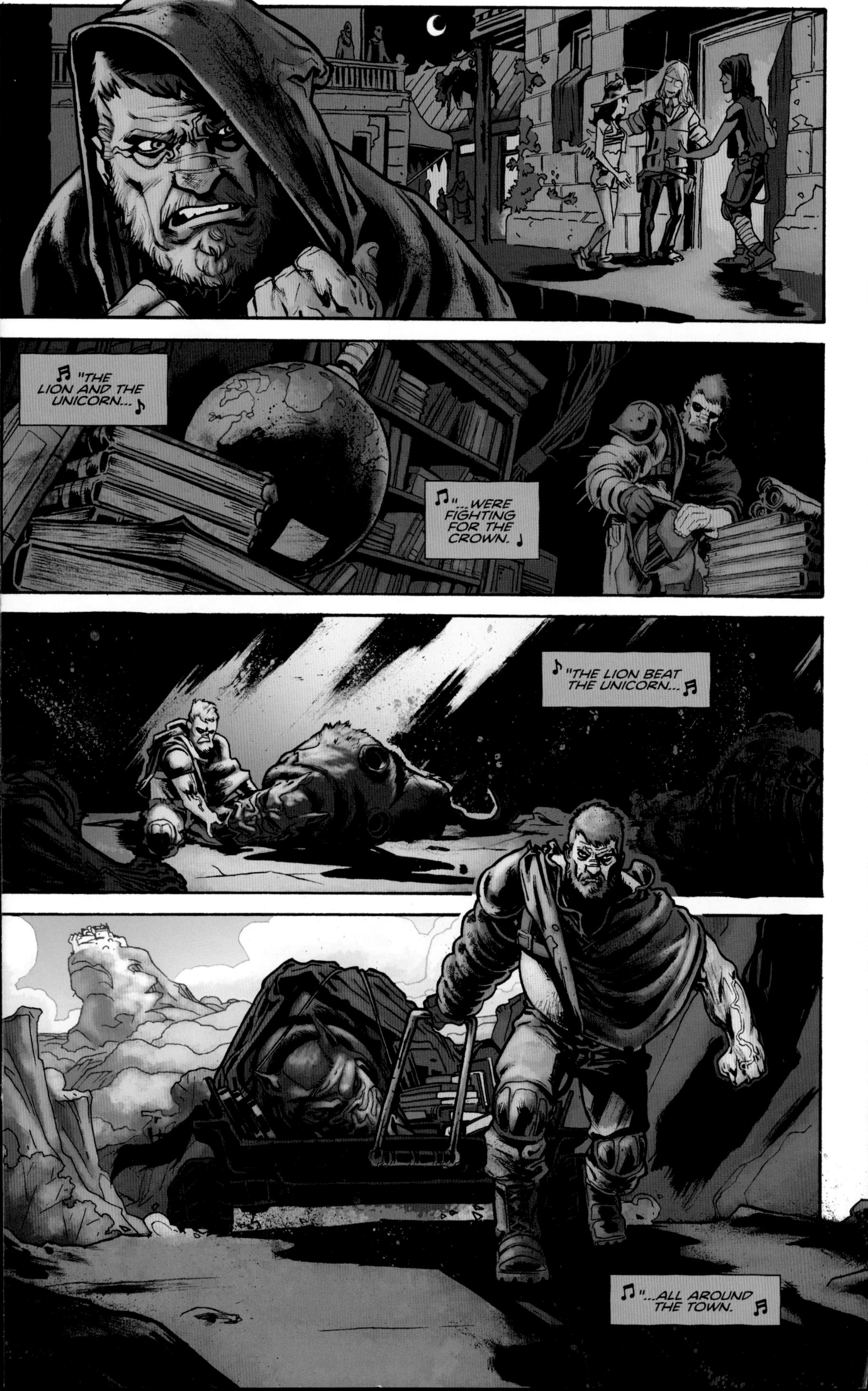
"THE LION AND THE UNICORN...
"...WERE FIGHTING FOR THE CROWN.
"THE LION BEAT THE UNICORN...
"...ALL AROUND THE TOWN.

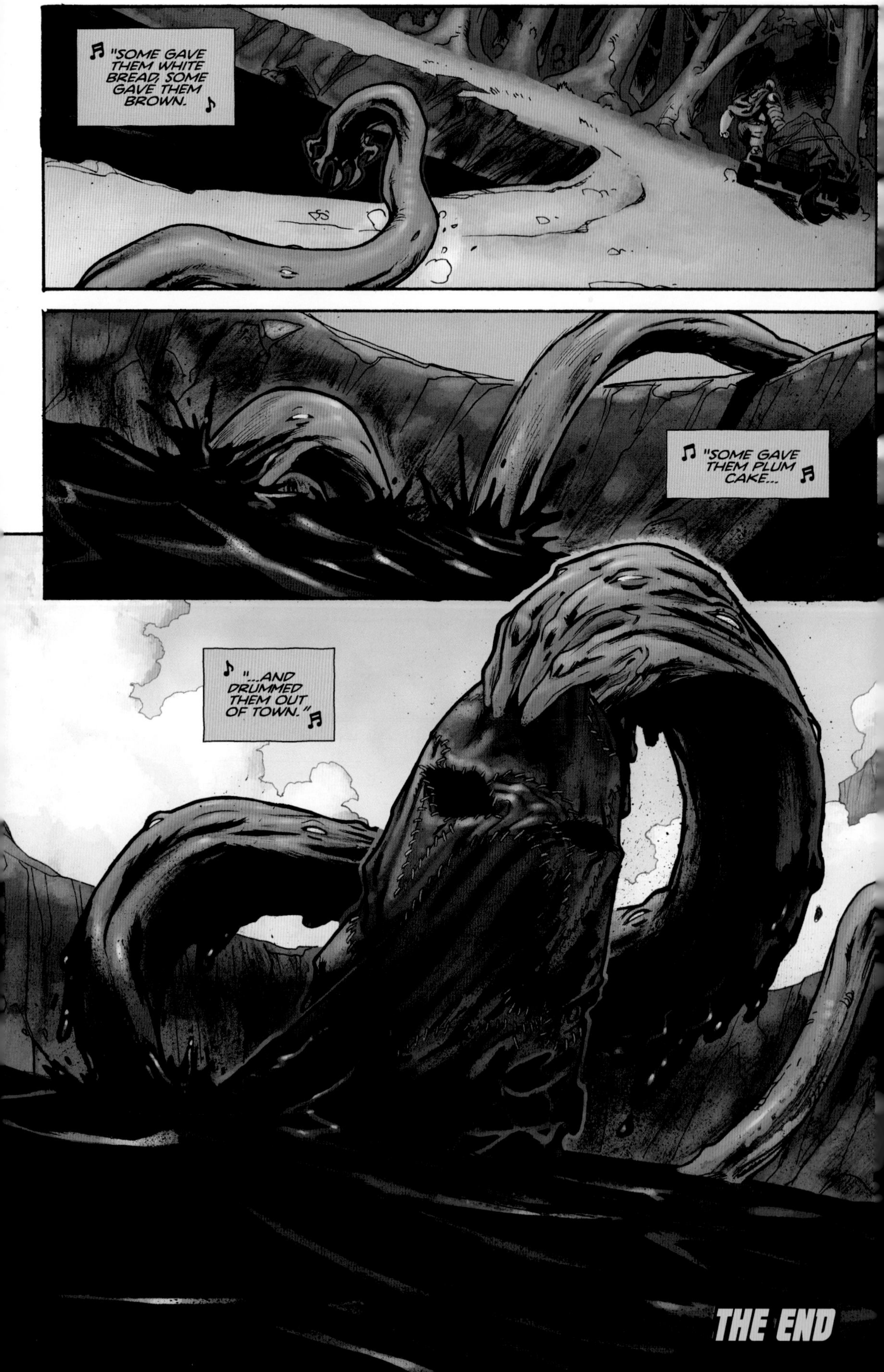
"SOME GAVE THEM WHITE BREAD, SOME GAVE THEM BROWN.
"SOME GAVE THEM PLUM CAKE...
"...AND DRUMMED THEM OUT OF TOWN."
THE END

# AFTERWORD

I DIDN'T CHOOSE TO BE A GUITAR PLAYER. Guitar playing chose me.

As a teen, I dabbled in art and acting. I even thought about being a forest ranger. Something about being a mailman appealed to me as well. Then, I started playing guitar and it felt like a *calling*. Political activism, same deal. I felt a *compulsion* to swing back at the injustice I saw in my hometown—and the world at large. Comic writing too. I had this story, *Orchid*, that just *demanded* to get out. And here it is.

I feel very fortunate. I think I was *meant* to be a musician, an activist, a writer. And here I am. Why? Well, my mom, a single, public high school teacher, was able to scrape together fifty bucks for my first guitar to unlock that dream. There were books around that stoked the fires of my political determination. And, by the time I wrote *Orchid*, I was a fairly well-known musician and the nice people at Dark Horse took my call.

I think everyone, without exception, deserves to be the person they were meant to be. But, literally, billions of people aren't so lucky. Why? Poverty. Crushing poverty. The next Mozart is likely right now slaving away in an Indonesian sweatshop. The doctor who was meant to cure cancer is instead sweeping the floors of a maquiladora along the Mexican border. Manmade circumstances that deny the essence of who we might be, who we should be, who we were meant to be.

Wrestling with personal demons and societal shackles, Orchid and her friends are simply trying to figure out who *they* were meant to be and how the hell they can be it, given the circumstances into which they were born.

The tilted playing field of our world is not so different from Orchid's. Maybe that's why you picked up this volume. Or maybe it was for the cool monsters. Either way, I'd like to thank you all for coming along on this journey. Fans of the series from all over the globe have been so supportive, and I deeply appreciate it. Thanks to the entire Dark Horse family, especially Dave Land (for the encouragement and confidence), Sierra Hahn (for always being right), Jim Gibbons (my Libertyville brother, who brought it home), and Scott Allie and Mike Richardson, who have helped me realize this story in an uncompromised and uncompromising way. Thanks to Jack Olsen and Anthony Arnove, who gave me invaluable feedback early on. Thanks to Gerard Way for passing my manuscript on to Dark Horse and getting the ball rolling. Thanks to Kevin Mills, Carl Restivo, and the Freedom Fighter Orchestra for assistance in recording *Orchid*'s musical score. And a huge thanks to the creative team: Massimo Carnevale for his dramatic covers, Nate Piekos of Blambot for his care and patience with the lettering, Dan Jackson for the incredible colors that really brought *Orchid*'s world to life, and the unquestionable MVP of the project, Scott Hepburn, whose illustrations have rocketed him to the upper echelon of his craft. Scott has been one of the most talented and pleasant collaborators I've ever had the pleasure of working with in any medium.

And finally, thanks to all the rebels and radicals who—with clear intent and purpose—have stood up in their place and time, against whatever odds, and fought for a better, more just world. Because, I suppose, it was what they were meant to do.

**TOM MORELLO**

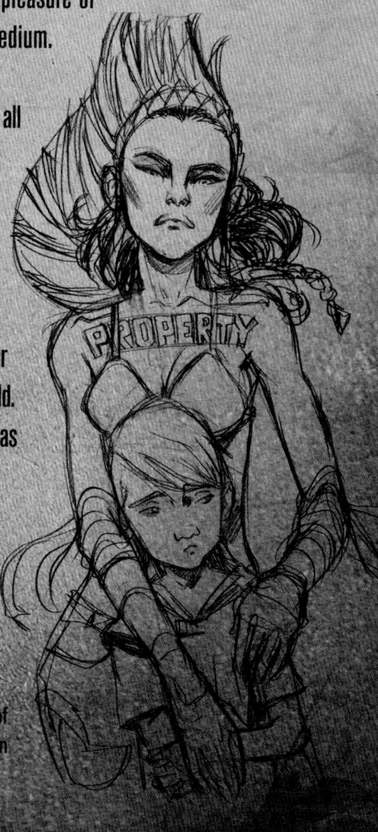
PROPERTY

An early character sketch of Orchid and Yehzu by Scott Hepburn

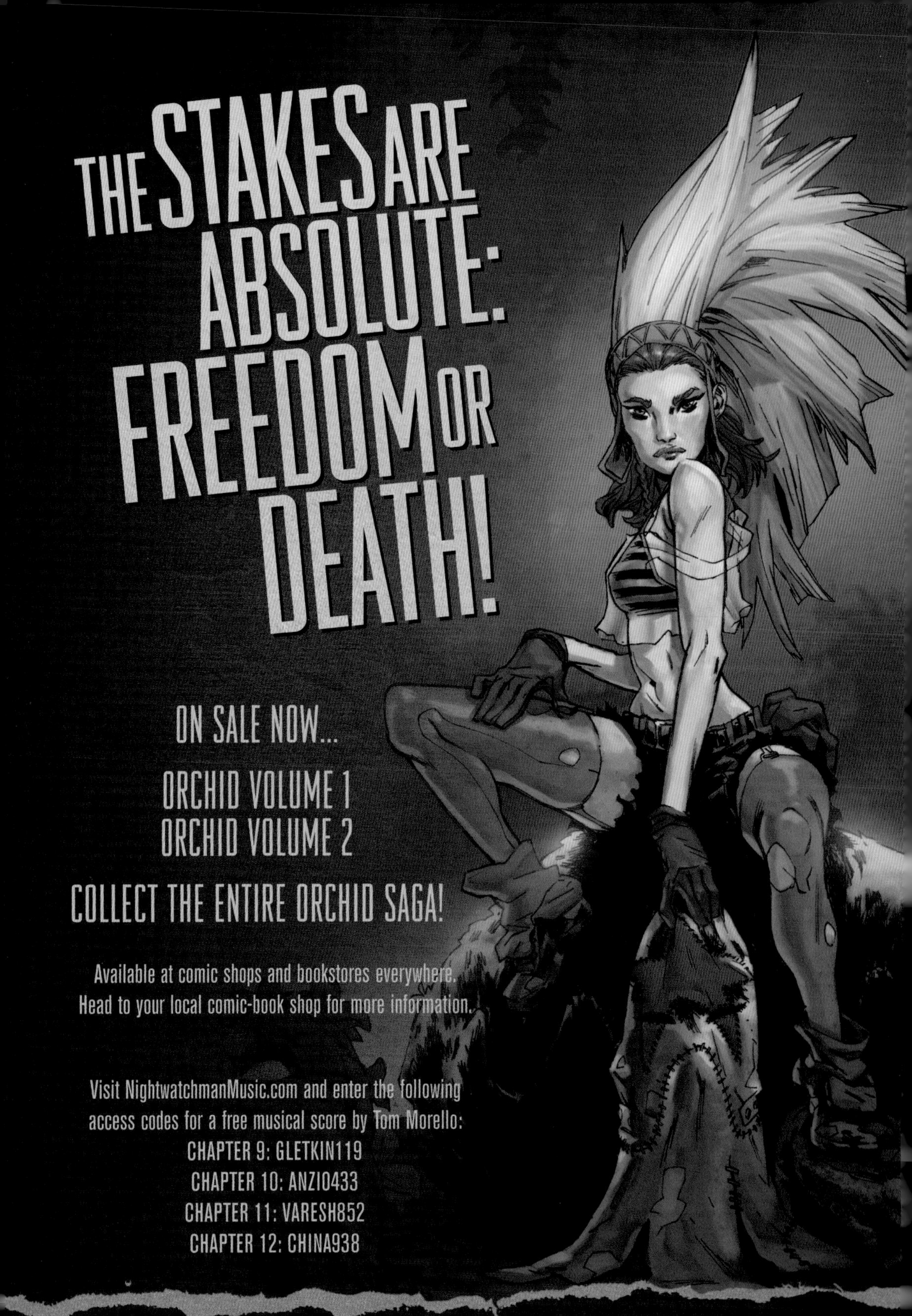

# THE STAKES ARE ABSOLUTE: FREEDOM OR DEATH!

ON SALE NOW...

ORCHID VOLUME 1
ORCHID VOLUME 2

## COLLECT THE ENTIRE ORCHID SAGA!

Available at comic shops and bookstores everywhere.
Head to your local comic-book shop for more information.

Visit NightwatchmanMusic.com and enter the following
access codes for a free musical score by Tom Morello:
CHAPTER 9: GLETKIN119
CHAPTER 10: ANZIO433
CHAPTER 11: VARESH852
CHAPTER 12: CHINA938

DARK HORSE BOOKS

DARKHORSE.COM

AVAILABLE AT YOUR LOCAL COMICS SHOP OR BOOKSTORE
To find a comics shop in your area, call 1-888-266-4226 or visit ComicShopLocator.com.
For more information or to order direct, visit DarkHorse.com or call 1-800-862-0052 Mon.–Fri. 9 a.m. to 5 p.m. Pacific Time.
Prices and availability subject to change without notice.

Text and illustrations of Orchid™ © 2013 Tom Morello.